# FIGHTING NAPOLEON AT HOME

# FIGHTING NAPOLEON AT HOME

## THE REAL STORY OF A NATION AT WAR WITH ITSELF

PAUL L. DAWSON

FRONTLINE
BOOKS

First published in Great Britain in 2023 by
Frontline Books
An imprint of
Pen & Sword Books Ltd
Yorkshire – Philadelphia

ISBN 978-1-39909-635-5

Typeset by Lapiz Digital
Printed and bound by CPI UK

Pen & Sword Books Limited incorporates the imprints of Atlas,
Archaeology, Aviation, Discovery, Family History, Fiction, History,
Maritime, Military, Military Classics, Politics, Select, Transport,
True Crime, Air World, Frontline Books, Leo Cooper, Remember
When, Seaforth Publishing, The Praetorian Press, Wharncliffe Local History,
Wharncliffe Transport, Wharncliffe True Crime, White Owl
and After the Battle.

For a complete list of Pen & Sword titles please contact

PEN & SWORD BOOKS LIMITED
47 Church Street, Barnsley, South Yorkshire, S70 2AS, England
E-mail: enquiries@pen-and-sword.co.uk
Website: www.pen-and-sword.co.uk

or

PEN AND SWORD BOOKS
1950 Lawrence Rd, Havertown, PA 19083, USA
E-mail: Uspen-and-sword@casematepublishers.com
Website: www.penandswordbooks.com

# CONTENTS

# LIST OF PLATES

1. The Rev. Dr Richard Price FRS.
2. Charles Watson Wentworth, 2nd Marquis of Rockingham.
3. The Rev Christopher Wyvill.
4.  John Cartwright.
5. The Rev. Dr Joseph Priestley.
6. Thomas Paine.
7. Edmund Burke.
8. William Pitt.
9. Charles James Fox.
10. William Wentworth-Fitzwilliam, 4th Earl Fitzwilliam.
11. Henry Redhead Yorke.
12. The Rev. Thomas Johnstone.
13. Edward Marcus Despard.
14. Thomas Walker.
15. The Rev. William Robert Hay.
16. Robert Athorpe.

# ACKNOWLEDGEMENTS

The 'home front' is an increasingly important sphere of interest for the Great War and the Second World War, but what of the age of Napoleon?

The story of the home front during the Napoleonic Wars is one of a clash between the interests of the ruling elite and those of disaffected elements of the middle and working classes. These disaffected elements had become politicised in various ways – by the press, clandestine pamphlets, radical preachers and new forms of political organisation eager to claim a place in the political realm. They sought to ensure the implementation of reforms they believed to be necessary to fulfil and protect their rights and liberties, improve their political representation and to gain access to economic and social prosperity. This book is one half of a story that is intimately linked to the French Revolution: we present here the English side of the story, with the Franco-Irish dimension being published separately, also by Frontline.

In writing this story, firstly I must thank Sally Fairweather for accompanying me to archives across England and France, and her help in taking countless photographs of archive papers. I must thank James Tozer for his editorial feedback and that of my editor Charles Esdaile. I need to thank Sarah Hollingsdale, the Methodist Church Heritage Officer, for her efforts in unearthing 'fact from rumour' about the Rev. Dr Thomas Coke. Nicholas Dunne Lynch must be thanked for his friendship, provision of research material and enjoyable discussion about the United Irishmen and their activities.

My twin, Anthony, and our mutual and much missed friends and colleagues, Kate Taylor MBE and John Goodchild M. Univ, need to be thanked for their support and encouraging me to embark on this scheme of research over a decade ago. John, in particular, needs to be singled out for our Thursday 'coffee and chats' in his rooms at Newstead Road archive office, and allowing me access to his collection of archive material so as to hunt down obscure references about long-dead Unitarians. Staff at North Yorkshire Record Office, The National

Archives Kew and the National Records of Scotland all need to be thanked for allowing me access to their holdings and permission to quote their material. Before we start, as a Unitarian, I am like my ancestors in faith, left wing, an avowed socialist and naturally opposed to the ideology of Edmund Burke. I worship where Dr Priestley was minister; I have preached from the very pulpit where Rev. William Turner denounced government corruption and from which Rev. Thomas Johnstone was dragged to prison for preaching the rights of man. I have endeavoured to be objective and even-handed in my treatment of the narrative, but I do freely admit and acknowledge my own bias, and readers are free to make and draw their own conclusions and even disagree with me on my interpretation of the sources and the rights and wrongs of the argument. The nature of the archive sources that exist primarily concern the North of England: the Fitzwilliam Papers and reports of Crown spies from Lancashire result in a bias towards Yorkshire and Lancashire. The famine periods of 1795 and 1800 were a nationwide and not just a northern phenomenon and are ably served by Roger Wells' excellent book, *Wretched Faces*, for those wanting to know more about this episode in British history.

As I researched this book, the similarities between my own upbringing in the 1980s with industrial unrest with the miners' strikes, and at the steel works in Sheffield, as well as the threat from the IRA and Loyalist paramilitary organisations, with bomb attacks in Ireland and the mainland became very obvious. History tends to repeat itself. Mrs Thatcher used the Falklands War, like William Pitt had done with the Revolutionary Wars, to rally the nation behind the Union Flag and the Queen. Society was fractured between the working class whose very way of life was under threat with the closure of shipyards, steelworks and coal mines, and those who were making 'loadsamoney' in the City of London. Coupled with virtual civil war in Ireland which spilled over onto the streets, the parallels with the 1790s are all too clear. As a member of the Royal Navy Volunteer Reserve, I remember being ordered not to wear uniform on the streets, as it made me a target. This book I hope shows the reality behind 'the gloss and glamour' of the era of Jane Austen. For the working class, life was short, brutal and hellish. For the middle class who wanted a say in society, their voice was unheeded. For non-Anglicans who demanded the same rights as Anglicans, their call for equality went unheeded. For the Irish who wanted Home Rule, their voice went unheeded. With a government deaf to the will of the people, is it little wonder men and women took matters into their own hands?

Paul L. Dawson, Wakefield, 5 December 2022

# A WAR OF IDEAS

The period before the American Revolution was an important formative period in the development of British radical politics. Ideas of democracy and political reform were shaped by John Wilkes, Lord Mayor of London, whose slogan of 'no taxation without representation' inspired what has been described as the first era of English radicalism. It was in this period that the radical movement really began to find its voice, as if changing from puberty to at least young adulthood. The messages of enfranchisement and participation became clearer, the organisational techniques sounder, and the critical mass of discourse in the public sphere, particularly amongst the working classes, slowly but surely grew, as did the perceived threat the increasingly disaffected working classes posed to the established political order. The issue of who British political rights belonged to and how they might be exercised was at the core of not only the grievances English radicals had with the British state, but also the fundamental differences between a succession of British governments and the American colonists over what rights the colonists had as British subjects and how they were to be governed. From the 1770s the country was beginning to polarise between loyalists and radicals.

## Loyalism

Loyalism grew from ideas of 'Britishness', as in fact did radicalism. It drew together aristocrats – both Tories and those who would become known as the Old Whigs – merchant princes and a cross section of the middling sort who were on the road to prosperity. Loyalists saw citizenship in terms of 'traditional' British values – property, social order, church and monarchy. They believed that the British political system established by the restoration of the monarchy in 1660 and the 1689 Bill of Rights was the wisest and most reliable form of

1

government. Loyalists believed that politics and governance were best handled by the social elites – those with the largest stake in the country – and in consequence were opposed to an expansion of the electoral franchise to include the middle classes, let alone women or the working classes.

Loyalists were also opposed to religious freedom and toleration, linking the idea of Dissent – non-attendance at the national church – to anti-establishment activities and even treason. The Anglican Church became the intimate mouthpiece of the Tory party.

Loyalist elites, in general terms, were pro-slavery and the slave trade, and they were educated at grammar schools as well as public schools like Eton and Harrow. They belonged either to the landowning classes, who believed in their natural superiority and right to rule, or were rich 'merchant princes' and industrialists who had made their fortunes from slavery and had transitioned to become members of the elite, like the Lascelles family. By and large, loyalism was centred on the parish church, but from 1790 onwards the Wesleyan chapel – indeed the growth of Wesleyan Methodism – drew working-class communities into the loyalist sphere. It is undeniable that the bedrock of loyalist support came from middle and working-class communities, which – then as now – included those who supported the state and were opposed to religious toleration. The Gordon Riots of 1780 showed how deep the hatred of Catholics ran. The attacks on Unitarian meeting houses and chapels in the 1790s that we shall see in Chapter 2 also demonstrated the depth of feeling against non-Anglicans.

## Radicalism

The radicals, by contrast, thought that citizenship came from universal 'natural rights'. This was not new thinking, as these ideas had emerged from the political milieu of the Civil War. It drew together aristocrats like Lord Lansdowne, merchant princes and well-to-do members of the middle classes and became assimilated with the Whig ideology that was the conflict's other main legacy in respect of political progress. The 'Foxite' Whigs' key policy positions were the supremacy of Parliament (as opposed to that of the King) and religious tolerance. In the middle years of the eighteenth century, Whiggism, though split into two distinct factions, had evolved into a belief system that emphasised innovation and liberty and was strongly held by about half of the leading families in England and Scotland, as well as most merchants, Dissenters and the middle classes. The great Whiggish achievement was the Bill of Rights of 1689 which made Parliament, not the Crown, supreme. In many regards, Whig ideas were little different to the Tory position: political participation was to be restricted to those with a stake in society, the primary difference being the desire to place restrictions on the ability of the Crown to interfere in the political process. In both cases removal of obstacles to free trade was the goal.

Desire for economic change soon became linked with a more political agenda. From the 1770s an increasing number of Whigs – the faction known as the 'New Whigs' – came to desire a recasting of the state and constitution in a fairer and more democratic form, and this in turn led to an upsurge in participation in politics and, more particularly, the formation of public associations such the Society for Constitutional Information founded in 1780 by John Cartwright, a prominent campaigner for parliamentary reform. From these associations emerged mass public meetings, and the publication of a staggering array of pamphlets, tracts, journals, newspapers, books and other works, outlining grievances with the current state of British society and putting forward ideas for parliamentary, political, economic and social reform, including an end to religious tests for participation in public life, the abolition of slavery and even, thanks largely to the efforts of such figures as Mary Wollstonecraft, Ann Jebb and Hannah Lindsey, the inclusion of women in the political process. This new ideology attempted to marry the Rousseauist civic humanist focus on public virtue and political liberty with the rational empiricism of the Enlightenment.[1]

In all this, there was a strong religious dimension. Thus, many of the men and women who participated in reformist circles were united by Unitarianism: a belief that stated Jesus was not God. Since 1697 Unitarianism, and the denial of the Trinity which it implied, was illegal by reason of the Blasphemy Act. Unitarians, quite rightly, wanted the freedom to practise their faith, but, if they were uniquely penalised in this respect, the entire Dissenting community suffered in one way or another. Thus, according to the Test and Corporation Acts, anyone who wished to go to university, become an MP or a Justice of the Peace, or hold other local and national administrative offices had to take communion in the local parish church on pain of a fine of £500 against which there was no legal defence. The Acts also stated that non-Anglicans could not act as guardians or executors, or even inherit a legacy, all such monies being forfeited to the Crown.[2] In consequence, like Catholics, Dissenters found themselves 'second-class citizens'. Since 1753, meanwhile, fresh laws forced Unitarians and other non-Anglicans to be married in an Anglican church according to Anglican rites, the result having been to stir up much resistance (in one instance,

3

an entire Unitarian wedding party turned their backs on the celebrant whenever the Trinity was invoked, the bride and groom also writing complaints in the register).[3] The lack of equality with Anglicans drove Unitarians and other Dissenters to seek political equality and liberty.[4] Unitarians shared a differing world view to mainstream Christians. They denied the doctrine of original sin. They believed – then as now – that 'man' was inherently good, and that contrary to prevailing religious dogma, that man could improve their lot through education and progress towards perfection in this life. Moreover, they believed the world could only be made better by people through collective effort rather than through diving intervention. Calvinistic ideas which filtered through Anglicanism and Methodist thinking said that the poor were poor, the rich were rich and that the poor would receive their eternal reward in heaven. Unitarians did not believe such notions, and adroitly worked to improve working conditions of the poor, to make all men and women equal. In response, Churchmen believed that Christianity was under threat by 'infidels' who sought to change the establishment for the better. The alliance of Church and State, created in 1662, saw any critique of the Church as an attack on the state and vice versa. Unitarians critical of both Church and State, challenged the bedrock of the alliance between the two, and asked why am I a second class citizen? Why do I not have equality? Nothing defines a person more than their world view: Anglicans, Methodists and others believed that society was fixed by God, that equality's origin lay in 'the fall'; man was imperfect, evil, tainted by sin. Unitarians believed that very nature of society was evil and had corrupted man, and believed that Christ and his earliest followers were the radical opponents of the government of his day, and sought in emulating Christ to bring about the change in the world they believed was necessary to make all men equal. Such divergent world views triggered a war of ideas. Not for Nothing, then, has it been said that Nonconformity was the midwife of English radicalism, social identity and class.

Chapter 1

# THE AMERICAN REVOLUTION

In 1773 a little-known Frenchman, Jean-Paul Marat, who had moved to Newcastle upon Tyne published *A Philosophical Essay on Man* and followed this with a polemic on political theory, *Chains of Slavery*, in 1774. This work earned him honorary membership of the patriotic societies of Berwick-upon-Tweed, Carlisle and Newcastle. The purpose of Marat's writing was to encourage his readers to attempt by any means to destroy the chains of destitution and slavery imposed upon them by their rulers who governed not for the good of the people, he argued, but for the good of their social order, class and religion. We must 'espouse the cause of any individual oppressed', Marat declared. His ideals of the oppressed shaking off the chains of slavery and tyranny would inspire a generation of English radicals to take action against a corrupt government. Marat's thinking could be found in the writings of the Rev. Dr Richard Price and the Rev. Dr Joseph Priestley, as well as Thomas Paine in his work *The Rights of Man* and Mary Wollstonecraft's *Vindication of the Rights of Women*.

Marat's work echoed the increasing tensions over the right of the American Colonists for self-determination. The debate splintered society: on the one hand loyalists were for 'Church and King' and fighting a war to retain the American colonies; on the other, the patriots or radicals understood the Americans were jettisoning the shackles of English tyranny and foreshadowing the events that would unfold in England from 1792. It also chimed with those who were 'second-class citizens' in their own country. Unitarians, who had no legal rights, understood that in supporting freedom for America, they could free themselves from the hated Test and Corporation Acts.

For English radicals like John Cartwright and the Dissenters, the events in America led to an upsurge in opposition to the status quo: when Americans began to speak out against the injustices meted out to them by English tyranny, the Dissenters understood their rhetoric, and took up the cause as their own. The leaders of the radical cause tended to be wealthy Unitarians, who were by and large members of a new merchant-gentry elite that dominated towns such as Hull, Leeds, Nottingham, Derby, Belper, Sheffield and Wakefield. By 1800 Unitarians wielded considerable economic power in Liverpool, Bristol, and Manchester as well, and were conspicuous for civic leadership and political influence. They figured large in the making of provincial middle-class culture across the country.

The Boston Tea Party in December 1773 led to an escalation in tensions between the American Colonists and the British Crown. In retaliation, the Crown enacted a series of punitive laws which effectively rescinded the Massachusetts Bay Colony's privileges of self-government. In response the other colonies rallied behind Massachusetts, and twelve of the thirteen colonies sent delegates in late 1774 to form a Continental Congress for the coordination of their resistance to Britain. War seemed inevitable as Rev. Theophilus Lindsey opined in a letter to Rev. William Turner of Wakefield on 7 December 1774:

> Farewell to Old England's greatness, if the sword is drawn and bloodshed in America. What will three battalions or 30 battalions do? But our infatuation is astonishing. Not the least symptom of kindness or humanity towards our brethren in America from the throne, or in the speeches of the Ministerial people, but all war and vengeance. . . . Nothing but calamity seems capable to awaken us out of our unfeelingness towards justice and our true interests: And that seems to be coming.[1]

The Whigs sought to harness the increasing wave of public opinion against the war. A potent figurehead in this crusade was the 2nd Marquis of Rockingham, Charles Watson Wentworth, a former prime minister (and to be again in 1782) and de facto leader of the Whig movement. Rockingham's spokesmen to the Dissenting, and largely Whig, merchant class of Yorkshire were Pemberton Milnes of Wakefield[2] and his brother John.[3] Rockingham had no time for those he called 'luke-warm occasional Conformists to good Principles' and sought political reform when organising a Yorkshire-wide petition on behalf of 'The Society for the Supporters of the Bill of Rights' in favour of John Wilkes' reformist agenda.[4] Rockingham believed that if America was to be retained as a colony by the British Crown, then the entire continent would have to be conquered and the people would have to be kept in subjugation.[5] For Rockingham and his circle this was little more than 'enslaving' the American people. The cause of the American Colonists became a rallying point for the Whigs.

With Rockingham's blessing petitions were raised across the country opposing the war in America and demanding 'freedom' for the American colonies from the 'Tyranny' of the British Crown, stating furthermore that any war would cause severe economic hardship. Petitions came from Wakefield (led by the Milnes family), Bristol (led by Unitarians from Lewins Mead Chapel) and Nottingham (led by the Rev. George Walker MA FRS at High Pavement Unitarian Chapel) against war over America. Rockingham himself handed to Parliament the petition from Bristol. In Newcastle, Unitarians were to the fore, and no lesser persons than John Wilkes and Lord Effingham headed the Newcastle radicals' petition. The radical *Newcastle Chronicle* printed an edition of Marat's *Chains of Slavery* as a propaganda exercise on behalf of the radicals, exposing the 'Tyranny of the Crown'. In Taunton, the Unitarian Dr Thomas Amory – a member of Rev. Joshua Toumlin's chapel in Tancred Street – led the Whig Dissenting faction against the 'Church and King' faction. For the loyalists, Toumlin's petition was a 'traitorous attempt to subvert . . . legislative authority . . . it will never be submitted to'.[6] Such Tory reaction was not limited to the West Country: the Rev. Theophilus Lindsey wrote to his colleague the Unitarian Rev. William Turner on 17 January 1775, expressing his sympathy and concern for the violence shown against him and the congregation for backing the Americans. War had not yet been declared, but tensions in England were rising between increasingly polarised political positions. Benjamin Franklin and Josiah Quincy, a Harvard-educated lawyer, who came to England to argue the case for American independence in the autumn of 1774, are recorded as sending statements of solidarity to Turner. Wakefield and Leeds were hotbeds of loyalism and those who took the opposing view were the object of hostility.[7] The American war raised the spectre of a new way of government, one in which all people had a stake in the future of the nation: the simmering discontent at paying taxes yet having not say in the political direction of the country could no longer be ignored. This boiled over in summer 1775 with petitions sent to the Crown in favour of American self-determination, and 'Loyal Addresses' to the Crown in support of the war which made reference to 'seditious' and 'disloyal' people who sent the petitions: exactly the same language that would be used against the peace petitions in 1801 and 1807. By and large the petitions were driven by the Dissenting community: the Rev. George Walker MA at Nottingham, Rev. Caleb Evans in Bristol, Rev. Newcome Cappe of York and Rev. William Turner of Wakefield all played a leading role in petitioning.

The supporters of the Crown never understood that opposition to their ideas was not treason: questioning the status quo was, for many loyalists, nothing short of sedition nor could they understand that the radicals considered themselves patriots and also loyal subjects. This view that opposition was wrong was later 'cemented' into national life by William Pitt as he created a sense of 'Britishness' to win over public opinion.

However, despite public opposition to the war, as a skilled politician Rockingham was astute enough to admit to Pemberton Milnes that however laudable the petition's aim was, that the government 'seem determined not to hear or consider any petition which they may receive from the body of merchants or manufacturers in any part of Great Britain. I believe that they dare not look at the infinite distress and inconvenience which the measures they pursue will too probably bring on.'[8]

Legitimate expression of grievances through petitions and protest had been ignored by the Crown. The divisions in society that the American conflict generated would be 'set in stone' in a decade's time. War it was to be. War meant an end to free trade and an increase in taxation which was met with abject horror by the Whigs. The Continental Congress proclaimed the American Colonies free and independent states on 4 July 1776. The Declaration of Independence proclaimed that all men were created equal, and in the new republic no tests were placed on participation on public life based on religion.[9]

Rejoicing at the events in America, Rev. Dr Richard Price penned and quickly published a defence of the American colonists, *Observations on the Nature of Civil Liberty*. In many ways it echoed Marat's sentiments and defended the Americans' resistance to the coercive policies of the British government on the grounds that they violated their natural rights. Foreshadowing Thomas Paine, Price approved of rebellion against the state when undertaken on behalf of liberty against authoritarian power and furthermore stated that he believed that armed resistance was necessary against tyranny. His pamphlet quickly sold thousands of copies and he composed a second address on the subject, *Additional Observations*, published a year later in response to his detractors. In this Price took up the theory of the government as a trust as espoused by John Locke, who had argued in defence of the right of resistance to the

Crown, in the last chapter of the *Second Treatise of Government* (1690), in case of a 'breach of trust' by it. Taking Locke's idealism as his baseline of social theory, Price asserted that popular sovereignty should be used to 'crush the doctrine of the omnipotence of parliament', adding that parliaments '. . . possess no power beyond the limits of the trust for the execution of which they were formed'. He concluded that: 'If they contradict this trust, they betray their constituents and dissolve themselves. All delegated power must be subordinate and limited. If omnipotence can, with any sense, be ascribed to a legislature, it must be lodged where all legislative authority originates; that is, in the people.'[10]

In Yorkshire, Price's friend and colleague Rev. William Turner launched a violent polemic against the Crown and boycotted the national fast day on 13 December 1776 – as did Rev. Richard Price in London – as an act of passive disobedience. Turner denounced the corruption of the government, desired a wider electoral franchise, argued passionately for an end to slavery and espoused freedom for the American Colonies.[11] He subjected his congregation to a vehement denunciation of the corruption of the ruling class. Turner preached that power to govern was to be given by common consent for the common good and not for the particular interests of a narrow group, noting men had been 'blinded by ambition and avarice, hardened against the feelings of humanity, and having perverted or lost all principle'.[12] Turner's congregation included the great merchant families of Milnes, Naylor, Heywood and Holdsworth who dominated the West Riding cloth trade. Yet it is wrong to assume all the merchants were pro-America. Arrayed against the Whigs in Yorkshire were the Cooksons and Blaydes of Leeds, and from Wakefield the Charnocks, Zouch and Strawbenzee families, as well as the vicar of Wakefield, the Rev. Dr Bacon.[13]

Self-determination and freedom from oppression became a rallying point for English radicals like Major John Cartwright. In 1776 he published his first work on parliamentary reform, which, with the exception of Earl Stanhope's pamphlets (1774), appears to have been the earliest publication on the subject. It was entitled, *Take your Choice*, a second edition appearing under the new title of *The Legislative Rights of the Commonalty Vindicated, and advocated annual parliaments, the secret ballot and manhood suffrage*. His life's focus thereafter was to work for the attainment of universal suffrage and annual parliaments. In 1778, he conceived the project of a political association, which took shape two years later as the Society for Constitutional Information, including among its members some of the most distinguished men of the day. From this society sprang the more famous London Corresponding

Society. Major Cartwright worked unweariedly throughout his life for the promotion of reform, and was gaoled on numerous occasions for his beliefs.

## The Yorkshire Association

By 1779, the British Crown was losing the war to retain the American Colonies, and a collapse in trade through loss of export markets to Europe and of course America, and increasing taxes to fund the conflict, which even the middle class were starting to struggle to pay, had brought economic distress. This resulted in an extraordinarily widespread upsurge of discontent provoked by Lord North's inept handling of the American crisis. Rev. Christopher Wyvill, nominally an Anglican vicar, called a county meeting at York on 30 December 1779 to discuss petitioning the Crown to end the war. By this date, the national debt stood at £167 million and further taxation was needed to repay the loans the Crown had taken out to cover the cost of the war. Land, property and trade were all taxed. For those who were struggling to pay their taxes or had seen their businesses collapse, the war seemed to have no end and no purpose. It was seen as one of princes and elites fighting a war against the interests of the people. Wyvill was no stranger to public politics and, like Rockingham before him, used petitions to gauge public opinion. He championed the claim of non-Anglicans for full civil rights in 1772 with the abolition of the Test and Corporation Acts.

Wyvill sought to harness to his cause the new socially and politically underprivileged group of middle-class merchants, tradesmen and shopkeepers who were starting to feel their collective strength. The goal was twofold: 1. End the war, 2. Bring about political reform. Wyvill hoped that an increased franchise, coupled with economic reform, would reduce the power of the Crown. Peace and prosperity would follow. He drew up a circular letter enunciating his political sentiments, and took a leading part in drawing up the Yorkshire petition presented to Parliament on 8 February 1780. A number of moderate Whigs regarded Wyvill's manifesto as chimerical, Horace Walpole writing that it was full of 'obscurity, bombast, and futility'. Sir Cecil Wray wrote in a similar vein, and Rockingham wanted to know if the Association had ever considered the practicability of the annual parliaments which they recommended. Wyvill's contention was that the long American war was due primarily not to the wishes of the people but to the votes of the members of the close boroughs. The Association had the sympathy of politicians including Pitt and Charles James Fox. A committee under Wyvill was appointed to continue the pressure by correspondence, and the example of Yorkshire was followed by other counties, twenty-five in all. In the period 1779 to 1781, when there was a delegate conference, the movement gained a broad base. With Walpole's and Wray's opposition, however, Wyvill was ready to concede defeat on 5 December 1779.[14] His last hope of success lay in obtaining support from Pemberton Milnes, the erstwhile leader of the Yorkshire Whigs and the Dissenting community.[15] If he could convince the Milnes family to support the Association, he would attract all the woollen manufacturers and Dissenters in Yorkshire.[16] Furthermore, support from the merchants might bring into the Association members of the middling orders denied the vote by antiquated constituency boundaries and a restricted suffrage. Lastly, Wyvill banked on parliamentary Whigs, whose ambitions for office were blocked, supporting his cause. To gauge support, in spring 1780 Wyvill launched a mass petition in support of reform. Pemberton Milnes' nephew, John Milnes Jnr, known in his own lifetime as 'Jack Milnes the Democrat', explained to the secretary of the Yorkshire Association John Holmes that 'though we had the Insinuations of a Powerful Adverse Party, and the Prejudice of the People to surmount, yet our Success was beyond our expectations'. Taking advantage of the crowds of people attending the weekly market in Huddersfield, they had obtained signatures from many of the surrounding villages – three-quarters of those approached had agreed to sign the petition. He commented further: 'Had I more time I don't doubt getting a great majority of the freeholders in this part, but in this manufacturing county, the houses are wide from each other so makes it very tedious.'[17] Jack went on to give Holmes a detailed account of the current situation of the Association's campaign in the West Riding, pointing to those areas which had not been canvassed and detailing several individuals who should be formally approached. He himself undertook to canvass the Huddersfield area where the commercial influence of the Milnes would be decisive in getting the support of the clothiers. This would not be a surprise as Milnes believed that the family business purchased over 50 per cent of all white cloth produced in the county.[18] Jack wrote to William Grey, Chief Executive Officer of the Yorkshire Association six weeks later:

> The districts I have canvassed have almost universally signed, have several parchments out at present, I don't doubt being able to get fifteen hundred or two thousand to sign provided the York committee allow me to proceed with it when I come home. I shall write them more fully upon this & other matters as soon as I have leisure. I beg you will excuse

this scramble. I have given several parchments out to my manufacturing friends, who if they have exerted themselves, don't doubt that number already amounts to six hundred or a thousand – In many parts of the country the committee have been very remiss, I shall write the chairman more fully upon this head & I am in very great haste, your most humble servant, John Milnes.[19]

When we look at the signatures collected, we see that the same merchants and Dissenters who backed reconciliation with America lead by Rockingham also backed Wyvill. Clear battle lines had been drawn which divided the country almost a decade before the 'atomic bomb' in English politics that was the French Revolution exploded. As we shall see, it would be the self-same woollen merchants and manufacturers, led by largely the same men, who would dominate anti-establishment politics in Yorkshire. Conflicting visions of society emerged: the revolution in America released pent-up frustrations against those in authority, and pointed to deep structural fissures in the nature of English society. The development of a new force of political opposition challenged government policy. The latent radicalism of Nonconformity became explicitly so, championed by Unitarians across the country seeking the same rights as Anglicans. For the radicals, society needed to be more equal and the people needed a greater say in how the country was governed.

The Yorkshire Association flexed its new political muscle in autumn and winter 1780. The general election was a chance to end the hated war and to get reformers into power. Wyvill set his sights on returning MPs for Yorkshire. The West Riding – the largest population centre in Yorkshire – had two MPs in the Borough of Pontefract and Wyvill hoped that his reform plans would change this. Henry Duncombe, in spite of his initial hesitation, soon became a member of the Yorkshire Committee of Association, and on 28 March 1780, at a county meeting seconded Wyvill's proposals for shorter parliaments and an increase in the number of county members.[20] Writing to Wyvill a few weeks later Duncombe stated 'I wish with you that there may be spirit enough yet found in the county to express a proper resentment and sense of the insanity of the Administration and to lead the first steps to the amendment of an almost ruined constitution'.[21] In the ensuing election, Henry Duncombe was chosen as the candidate for Yorkshire, standing jointly with Sir George Savile, with the support of both the Yorkshire Association and Rockingham, who provided the funding for the campaign. James Milnes Jnr wrote to Wyvill about the election on 1 October 1780 commenting 'I have the pleasure to inform you, that

I entirely concur with the Gentlemen concerned in the subscription, for supporting the election of Sir George Saville and Mr Duncombe, in their late resolution of charring [*sic*] them free from any expense'.[22] Co-religionist and Westgate Chapel man Robert Lumb also subscribed to cover the costs of the election: 'I approve of the sense of the meeting of the 26th September to return Sir George Saville and Mr Henry Duncombe as candidates as free from expense' and added 'please do advise if needful to send the whole of my subscription; or part; if the later please do advise what proportion; if so to remit to Messrs Garforth & Co'.[23] Their opponent, Edwin Lascelles, withdrew before the poll and they were returned unopposed. However, the election was more a vote of no confidence in the government and against the war, than one for reform. Duncombe, backed by the merchant princes of the West Riding, gave a voice to the manufacturing centre for the first time and showed the inadequacy of the current electoral franchise. On 19 May 1781 Duncombe wrote again to Wyvill explaining 'I am more than ever convinced that the only hopes of security to our liberties and of redress of our grievances, are to be derived from the integrity of Parliaments and a juster representation of the people'.[24]

On 27 March 1782, the leader of the Whigs, the Marquis of Rockingham, became Prime Minister. Hopes for a speedy end to the war and reform were dashed when he died aged just 52 on 1 July. He was replaced as by Lord Shelburne who along with Charles James Fox had been Secretary of State under Rockingham. Shelburne, unlike Rockingham, was more reluctant to accept the total independence of America, and felt that Dominion status would be more acceptable to the Crown. However, by April 1783 he had succeeded in securing peace with America by the Treaty of Paris, and this remains his legacy to this day. Ironically, making peace forced him from office, hastened by his plans for reform. Charles James Fox and Lord North in a coalition of Whig and Tory took power. Fox was an advocate of reform, believing that Parliament should govern without royal interference and that government should, therefore, be managed on a 'democratic principle'. The official head of the government was William Cavendish-Bentinck, 3rd Duke of Portland, who took office on 2 April 1783. The unholy alliance of Tory and Whig simply as means for Fox to gain power was too much for many of Fox's supporters and moderate Whigs. The Treaty of Paris was signed during his government on 3 September 1783, formally ending the American Revolutionary War. The government came under further strain when from the opposition benches William Pitt introduced a proposal for electoral reform to tackle bribery and rotten boroughs. The proposal did not pass but caused further tensions within the coalition which contained both proponents and opponents of political reform.[25]

Before Shelburne's fall, given the strength of local feeling for greater parliamentary accountability and political representation, on 31 October 1782 Wyvill resolved to poll national sentiment about political reform. He declared he would abolish at least fifty rotten boroughs and bring political representation to the rapidly growing industrial towns and sought to make politicians accountable to the people and not to cliques and factions, introduce tri-annual parliaments and lastly extend the franchise to all taxpayers. Pemberton Milnes headed the lists in Yorkshire, the Rev. George Walker, the Unitarian Minister of High Pavement Chapel Nottingham, dominated the Midlands, as he had done in 1775.[26] In York, Sir William Mordaunt Milner collected 423 signatures, Unitarian ironfounder Samuel Shore in Sheffield collected 471, and Wyvill 238. In total some ninety-four parchments were gathered in: of these the Milnes family handed in twelve, bearing 1,463 signatures! Later in January 1783 Pemberton Milnes complained of the efforts he and his family had gone to collect names, reporting to Wyvill, 'I am, oblig'd to send a Person with it from House to House, not the least regard was paid to the Printed advertisement, of its laying at such and such Places for signing, I have also sent Persons with it into the villages many miles around this Neighbourhood'.[27] He added later the same month that 'both Messrs. R. S. Milnes and Mr. John Milnes have taken immense and indefatigable Pains and Labour in getting the Petition signed and are still going on with the circulation thereof'.[28] Across the county 10,500 freeholders signed the petition for reform: this was the largest mass-participation political act outside an election.[29] Henry Duncombe wrote to Wyvill on 20 October 1783 that 'the true source whence our calamities are derived is the very inadequate state of the representation of the people, by which the salutary restraints originally interposed against the errors, the weakness, and the wickedness of ministers have been baffled and defeated'.[30] But John Cartwright, leader of the Society for Constitutional Information, was critical of Wyvill's moderation. The Duke of Richmond granting his patronage to the society in 1783 changes its fortunes. Members included the aforementioned Jack Milnes, his nephew Richard Slater Milnes the MP for York, as well as John Horne Tooke, John Thelwall, Granville Sharp, Josiah Wedgwood, the famous pottery manufacturer and notable Unitarian, Thomas Walker, the Unitarian minister Rev. Dr Richard Price, Thomas Brand Hollis, Dr Jebb, Capel Lofft, Joseph Gales and William Smith. Joseph Gales, editor of the *Sheffield Register*, was a Unitarian and printed extracts from *The Rights of Man* in his newspaper. It was an organisation of social reformers, many of whom were drawn from the rational Dissenting community, dedicated to publishing political tracts aimed at educating fellow citizens about their lost ancient liberties. It promoted the work of Tom Paine and other campaigners for parliamentary reform. Gales comes to figure in our story in later chapters.[31]

Fox was removed from office in March. It marked the end of the Yorkshire Association. The resulting 1784 general election witnessed the collapse of the Whig party and the coming to power of William Pitt, who rapidly distanced himself from reform. John Pemberton Heywood, a Yorkshire Whig, wrote to Rockingham's nephew and successor Earl Fitzwilliam that he had no option but to vote for Pitt, as he was offered the chance of reform but, foreshadowing what was to happen, noted that Pitt was already calling the Whigs 'Cromwellians . . . levellers'.[32] Pitt believed that the 'people' did not have a natural right to a stake in political power: political office and power were public trusts and the Test and Corporation Acts as well as the constitution were in place to ensure that those who occupied office held political and religious views that were above suspicion. For men like Price and Priestley, political liberty safeguarded civil liberty: all people had the same inviolable natural rights. To achieve this, the state needed to be reformed.

Across the English Channel as 1787 dawned, France was bankrupt and the Assembly of the Notables was called, effectively heralding the end of absolutism and the first stirrings of Revolution. In Britain in the same year an attempt was made to repeal the Test and Corporation Acts.

Chapter 2

# REVOLUTION IN FRANCE

News of the opening events of the French Revolution in 1789 was greeted with widespread enthusiasm by British observers, although some, patronisingly, saw it as evidence that France was abandoning absolutism for a liberal constitution based on the British model. Enthusiasm was most potent among those championing domestic political reform. For these groups and their associated literary, scientific and political circles, events in France signified a much deeper change in government that needed to happen in England, and many were prepared to work to achieve this. The Unitarian minister of Mill Hill Chapel in Leeds, Rev. William Wood, drew parallels between the American Republic and the 'corrupt' British Crown:

> Brethren ye have been called into liberty. The love of civil liberty is an early passion of the human mind. It requires no laboured train of reasoning to demonstrate, that the man who holds his life and his property, and is liable to be restrained in all his actions at the uncontrollable pleasure of an arbitrary sovereign, is a wretch who has lost his native rights, and has little that can render his existence a blessing . . . The patriot heroes fought; the patriot legislator devised the salutary checks of equal laws; the patriot magistrate condemned to banishment or to death the enemy of his country's freedom.[1]

Events in France coincided with the commemoration of the centenary of the English Revolution of 1688. The Society for the Commemoration of the Glorious Revolution, better known as the Revolution Society, set forth a programme of reform, asserting:

1. That all civil and political authority is derived from the People.
2. That the abuse of power justifies resistance.

16

3. That the right of private judgement, liberty of conscience, trial by jury, freedom of the press and the freedom of election ought ever to be held sacred and inviolable.[2]

The commitment to reform placed the society and its members at direct odds with Pitt and his government. Rev. Turner proclaimed from the pulpit at Call Lane Unitarian Chapel, Leeds: 'What duties do we owe our fellow-creatures such as truth, justice, candour, good will and all good offices for which we have ability and opportunity'.[3] A few weeks later he spoke as follows from his own pulpit at Westgate Chapel, Wakefield, in a direct challenge to the British Crown: 'That men are now willing to allow to others that liberty which they would be unwilling to deprived of themselves: I mean of thinking for themselves, seeing with their own eyes ...'[4] This was dangerous talk. Freedom, reason and tolerance became the hallmark of Unitarianism.

As could be readily expected, the leader of the Whigs, Charles James Fox, welcomed the French Revolution, interpreting it as a late Continental imitation of Britain's Glorious Revolution of 1688. In response to the Storming of the Bastille on 14 July 1789, he famously declared, 'How much the greatest event it is that ever happened in the world! and how much the best!' On 26 August, the French National Assembly adopted the 'Declaration of the Rights of Man and of the Citizen'. The declaration directly challenged the authority of Louis XVI, and set out a series of individual rights protected by law, and removed any religious test on civic participation. To mark this momentous moment, the veteran political radical Rev. Dr Richard Price gave a sermon on 4 November hailing events in France as the dawn of a new era:

> Behold all ye friends of freedom ... behold the light you have struck out, after setting America free, reflected to France and there kindled into a blaze that lays despotism in ashes and warms and illuminates Europe. I see the ardour for liberty catching and spreading; ... the dominion of kings changed for the dominion of laws, and the dominion of priests giving way to the dominion of reason and conscience.[5]

Filled with the heady and buoyant optimism that the Revolution in France offered, Price declared that 'The representatives of France work for the world and not for themselves only, and the whole world has an interest in their success', adding:

> The Society for commemorating the revolution in Great Britain, disdaining national partialities, and rejoicing in every triumph of liberty

and justice over arbitrary power ... cannot help ... expressing the particular satisfaction with which they reflect on the tendency of the glorious example given in France, to encourage other nations to assert the unalienable rights of mankind, and thereby to introduce a general reformation in the governments of Europe, and to make the world free and happy.[6]

The sermon reinterpreted the principles of 1688–9 and praised the French Revolution. That evening the Revolution Society's dinner saw expressions of traditional British patriotism combined with support for the French Revolution, and for enlightened and cosmopolitan values. The society called for correspondence with similar groups across Britain and accepted a motion by Price to a send a congratulatory letter to the French National Assembly in which the society, 'disdaining national partialities,' expressed the hope that people in all despotic countries might imitate the French and regain their liberty. The letter was signed by society president Lord Stanhope and Price sent it to the duc de La Rochefoucauld, who read it to the National Assembly. The Assembly's president, Jean de Boisgelin, Archbishop of Aix, sent a reply to Lord Stanhope, applauding the spirit of 'humanity and universal benevolence' that characterised his organisation. This initial exchange of letters heralded the beginning of an extensive correspondence between the Revolution Society and the French National Assembly as well as with various Jacobin clubs in France. One of the first letters received was a congratulatory note from a patriotic society in Dijon which arrived on 30 November 1789.

Support for the ideals of the French Revolution in England and Ireland was most potent among those championing domestic political reform, none more so than members of the United Irishmen and the London Revolution Society. Its membership included Unitarians and high-profile Whigs, though it was Dissenting merchants and tradesmen who formed the bulk of it. Many prominent reformers, such as John Horne Tooke, Thomas Brand Hollis, Capel Lofft and John Cartwright, belonged to both the Revolution Society and the Society for Constitutional Information; these members provided a vital link between the two societies, which were similar in terms of social composition, ideology, and campaign methods.

In addition, the Revolution Society was also in touch with the Whig Club through Richard Brinsley Sheridan, although Charles James Fox, another Whig Club member, distanced himself from the new group. As could be expected, the Society advocated change in the current political system, with a particular focus on parliamentary reform, the repeal of the Test and Corporation Acts and the abolition of the slave trade. With the failed attempt in 1789–90 to repeal the Test and Corporation Acts, the only hope for abolition came through political reform: Unitarian clergy and their circles now took the lead in political reform. Thanks to prompting from John Horne Tookes, the society worked with the Society for Constitutional Information to draft and sponsor Henry Flood's programme of moderate parliamentary reform in the Commons during March and April 1790.[7]

Ultimately Price, and kindred reformist groups, were promoting the rights of man and international revolution. Amongst the good reverend's congregation in Hackney we find John Hurford Stone and his brother William, Mary Wollstonecraft, Helen Maria Williams and Benjamin Vaughan. These people will appear again in our narrative: as a 'Citizen of the World' and 'Friend of Liberty' it was only natural that Price would send a message of congratulations to Paris: indeed, Price corresponded with those directly involved in the events in France such as Turgot and Rabaut Saint-Etienne, the leader of French Protestants, through his sponsor the former Prime Minister Lord Shelburne, ennobled further as the Marquis of Lansdowne. Lansdowne was at the centre of a circle comprising industrialists, commercial entrepreneurs and Dissenters which included Price and his Unitarian colleague Rev. Dr Joseph Priestley: both men who believed government was for the happiness and benefit of all people and that the people had the right to overthrow the government if it acted for a narrow section of society. Similar views would be expressed by one of Price's congregation, Benjamin Vaughan, who was part of this circle. Indeed, beginning in 1788 Vaughan edited his own radical newspaper, the *Repository*, which articulated the political ideology formulated around Lansdowne. Also part of this circle was Jeremy Bentham as well as Etienne Dumont, speechwriter for the comte de Mirabeau and editor of Mirabeau's radical paper the *Courier de Provence*. We must place men like 'Jack Milnes' on the edge of this circle of largely Unitarian clergy and intellectuals. When Price spoke in favour of the revolution, he was doing so on behalf of the 'Lansdowne circle' and for all those seeking liberty. The effect of the French Revolution and the development of clear parties in English politics changed everything.[8]

## The Loyalist Response

Price's sermon attracted the wrath of Edmund Burke who was increasingly uncomfortable with the reformist flirtations of his Whig friends, convinced that reform was destroying the French state and fearful that revolution would spread to Britain. Burke's response, his powerful, deeply conservative *Reflections on the Revolution in France ...* (1791), prophesied the destruction of civilisation in France and the outbreak of European war. Seeing the events unfolding in France, Burke realised that liberalism needed limits and institutions to support the state. Having supporting the American Colonists, he understood that laissez-faire ideals whereby the state did not interfere in economics etc., when tested through the prism of the events in France from 1789, were in need of revision.

In Burke's view, the support shown for the events in France by Dissenters was evidence of their sacrilegious designs on the Anglican Church and the seditious and treasonous nature of their politics. Dissenters were now the 'enemy within': disloyal subjects and above all else republicans. This would spark a wave of violence and counter-protests across the country. Unitarians, Independents, Baptists and reformists were likened by the Tory press to French Jacobins. Handbills were posted across a dozen towns declaring religious dissenters to be 'King Killers' and 'Levellers'. The mob raised the cry of 'The Church in Danger' which combined into a highly organised alarmist agitation, the immediate precursor to the High Tory Anglican reaction of two years later. The British Crown – and inter alia the Tories – believed that the British system of a parliamentary monarchy and the rule of law, combined with a property-based social order and the Established Church, were the bastions which guaranteed British liberties and commercial prosperity. The status quo was to be maintained at all costs; religious toleration was to be disallowed, so too any hint of political reform. The resulting war of ideology against France was also a war against the people of the United Kingdom. The Crown began an effective campaign to stifle the grievances of all those men and women who wanted political reform through repressive legislation and acts of terror and intimidation. Unlike the 1780s where compromise was possible, in the heated atmosphere of the 1790s the middle ground was lost, as both sides rapidly polarised into opposing camps. Those seeking reform and a greater participation in politics were no longer tolerated by the elite: reform was seen as irresponsible revolution.[9]

In April 1791, Fox told the Commons that he 'admired the new constitution of France, considered altogether, as the most stupendous and glorious edifice of liberty, which had been erected on the foundation of human integrity in any time or country'. Burke had initially supported the Revolution, but broke with Fox and the Whigs, favouring national tradition over 'the horrible consequences flowing from the French idea of the Rights of Man'. In his *Reflections on the Revolution in France*, he warned that the revolution was a violent rebellion against tradition and proper authority, motivated by utopian, abstract ideas disconnected from reality, which would lead to anarchy and eventual dictatorship. Fox read the book and found it 'in very bad taste' and 'favouring Tory principles'. Fox continued to defend the French Revolution, even as its fruits began to collapse into war, repression and the Reign of Terror. Fox thought of revolutionary France as the lesser of two evils, and emphasised the role of traditional despots in perverting the true course of the revolution: he argued that Louis XVI and the French aristocracy had brought their fates upon themselves by abusing the constitution of 1791 and that the coalition of European autocrats, which was currently dispatching its armies against France, had driven the revolutionary government to desperate and bloody measures by provoking a profound national crisis.[10]

In defence of privilege, Burke argued 'the poor had to realise that the state should not and could not alleviate their hardships, state intervention went against the laws of commerce, the laws of nature and the law of God'.[11] His vision of the world where market forces led the way (nascent Thatcherism) killed tens of thousands in 1795–6 and 1799–1801 when famine struck. For Burke and his fellow loyalist Tories, the 'swinish multitudes', as he had dubbed the common people, would never have a say in how the country was run.[12] He argued consistently from 1789 till his death, that the French Revolution was a great evil, a cancer in the heart of Europe whose ideals were a direct threat to his vision and understanding of 'Britishness' and thus these ideals had to be destroyed totally before they infected the world. Any threat to the power base of the elite had to be crushed flat, any opposition had to be eradicated: all rather reminiscent of German politics in the mid-1930s!

In this view, he was joined by many in the Whig party. The Earl of Portland led more than half of the Whigs into coalition, forming what would become the modern-day Conservative Party, leaving Fox and the rump of what became known as the 'New Whigs' as the only opposition to William Pitt, the Tories and the pro-war faction that dominated Parliament. Portland and his largely aristocratic and wealthy MPs were as terrified of political change as the Tories and joined the crusade against democracy.

At stake were conflicting visions of society: that of Marat where governance was for the benefit and happiness of the people, and where the government failed to deliver this or was governing for a clique of rich oligarchs, the people were empowered to overturn authority, or Burke's vision of a conservative society, with fixed rules, whereby everyone knew their place and reform was a danger to order and reason.

The debate rapidly escalated to a battle of political rhetoric and mobilisation. Edmund Burke set the stage for what was to come by singling out Unitarians because of their support for the events in France, political reform and religious tolerance calling them 'insect reptiles . . . objects of the greatest terror' who 'fill us with disgust . . . . What would they do if they had power commensurate with their menace? God forbid! . . . I would rather have Louis the Sixteenth than . . . Dr. Priestley . . . their cabals . . . and low-bred insolence.'[13] In the escalating, increasingly vicious and acrimonious clash of ideology, the Unitarian Capel Lofft declared in his pamphlet *Remarks on the letter of the Right Honourable Edmund Burke concerning the Revolution in France*:

> I feel very different emotions from those of pleasure, in being obliged to dissent from MR. BURKE; but I find another point which compels me to express my dissent: his denial of the responsibility of the King to the Public. . . . A King, or Governors of any designation, irresponsible to the community in cases which exclude all other means of redress, would be as monstrous an incongruity, compared with the universal principles and necessary end of government . . . the rights of men, the honour of intellectual and moral agents . . . is an inheritance coeval with the commencement of humanity; its ensigns are the countenance impressed with the divine character of Reason; its gallery the extent of the habitable earth; its monuments, the imperishable memory of the wisest, best, and bravest of the species of every age and country; its evidence, the voice of Nature; its title, our equal relation to the Deity: from whom we derive in common, the powers, the obligations, and the correspondent Rights of man; Reason, Conscience, and Freedom.[14]

Capel Lofft's pamphlet sparked an intense debate on fundamental questions in politics, fought out in over 300 publications – including Thomas Paine's *Rights of Man* which we shall come to in later chapters – Mary Wollstonecraft's *Vindication of the Rights of Woman* and James Mackintosh's *Vindiciae Gallicae*, and spilling over into novels, poetry, popular songs and caricatures.

Joseph Priestley, a bluff, plain-spoken Yorkshireman, had become nationally known as the author of the three-volume *Institutes of Natural and Revealed Religion* (1772–4) which shocked and appalled many readers, primarily because it challenged basic Christian orthodoxies, such as the divinity of Christ and the miracle of the Virgin Birth. He had dared to utter the words that Unitarians were 'laying a trail of gun powder' to explode the superstitions of religion and politics: hence his sobriquet 'Gunpowder Joe'. Priestley commented:

since every private person is justified in bettering his condition, and indeed commended for it; a nation is not to be condemned for endeavouring to better theirs. Consequently, if they find their form of government to be a bad one, whether it was so originally, or became so through abuse or accident, they will do very well to change it for a better. A partial change, no doubt, will be preferable to a total one, if a partial change will be sufficient for the purpose. But if it appears that all attempts to mend an old constitution would be in vain, and the people prefer a new one, their neighbours have no more business to find fault with them, than with any individual, who should think it more advisable to pull down an old and inconvenient house, and build another from the foundation, rather than lay out his money in repairs. Nations, no doubt, as well as individuals, may judge wrong.[15]

Priestley, in backing the abolition of slavery, political reform and the repeal of the Test and Corporation Acts, brought himself to the attention of French radicals: he was honoured by being enrolled as a member of the Société des Amis de la Constitution of Bordeaux. The society wrote to Priestley expressing pleasure at his role in defending the French Revolution, and for seeking to abolish the Test and Corporation Acts which were viewed in France as emblematic of British intolerance.[16] For many Tory loyalists, Priestley was a dangerous man, who posed a direct threat to society, especially so as he was on record in justifying the violent overthrow of an unjust government as 'the generous attack of the noble and daring patriot' in his publication *An Essay on the First Principles of Government* (1768). Many felt that Priestley was planning such an act.

## Blood on the Streets

The controversy over the rights or wrongs of the French Revolution had given renewed energy to metropolitan reform societies such as the Society for Constitutional Information, one of the most famous and most influential radical societies of the later eighteenth century. In the North of England, the society grew rapidly via the Nonconformist, principally Unitarian, political movements in the rapidly expanding disenfranchised mill towns and manufacturing centres, organised by ordinary working people who declined the patronage and control of the wealthy. In June 1791 Priestley attempted to found the Warwickshire Constitutional Society in order to support political reform and demand universal suffrage and shorter parliaments, and took as his model the Lunar Society of which he was a member. As an intellectual talking shop, the Lunar Society was sympathetic to the ideals they saw in the French Revolution. Members were mostly Unitarians like Josiah

Wedgwood, Thomas Day and others, who agitated for increased civil rights, and therefore clashed with the Church of England.

Although this effort failed, it increased tensions in Birmingham over disagreements about public library book purchases, the abolition of the Test and Corporation Acts and the support for the French Revolution shown by Unitarians. Rioting started on 14 July 1791 with an attack on the Royal Hotel, Birmingham. It was here, to mark the second anniversary of the fall of the Bastille, the Lunar Society had – perhaps naïvely – decided to hold a banquet in the revolution's honour. As Priestley would later complain, this gave the authorities the perfect excuse to put an end to their society. Dissenters such as Priestley who openly supported the French Revolution came under increasing suspicion as opposition to the French Revolution grew, fed by the loyalist press: the animus that had been building against Dissenters and supporters of the American and French Revolutions exploded.

Beginning with Priestley's church and home, the rioters attacked or burned four Dissenting chapels, twenty-seven houses and several businesses. Many of the rioters became intoxicated by liquor that they found while looting, or with which they were bribed to stop burning homes. A small core could not be bribed, however, and remained sober. The rioters burned not only the homes and chapels of Dissenters, but also the homes of people they associated with Dissenters, such as members of the Lunar Society. William Smith's house was also targeted and destroyed, as was John Ryland's home, Baskerville House, and the mob drank the supplies of liquor which they found in the cellar. When the newly appointed constables arrived on the scene, the mob attacked and disarmed them. One man was killed. While the riots were not initiated by Prime Minister William Pitt's administration, the national government was slow to respond to the Dissenters' pleas for help. Local Birmingham officials seem to have been involved in the planning of the riots, and they were later reluctant to prosecute any ringleaders. The industrialist James Watt wrote that the riots 'divided [Birmingham] into two parties who hate one another mortally'. The riots revealed that the Anglican gentry of Birmingham were not averse to using violence against Dissenters whom they viewed as potential revolutionaries. They had no qualms either about raising a potentially uncontrollable mob. Had Rev. Dr Richard Price been alive, there is no doubt his chapel, home and school in Hackney would have been destroyed in a similar wave of violence.

Priestley, the intended victim of this arson-terrorism, was lucky to escape with his life. George III was delighted by the events. 'I cannot but feel pleased', he wrote to the Home Secretary, 'that Priestley is made to suffer for the doctrines he and his party have instilled.'[17] In defence of Priestley the 77-year-old Rev. William Turner, Unitarian Minister of Wakefield, hoped that 'it is now too late for persecution ever more prevailingly to lift up its head, and that the horrors of 1791 are rather to be considered as among the last struggles of an expiring daemon, which is not long to be permitted to trouble the peaceful society of men'.[18] Sadly, Turner was wrong.

The rioting spread. In Sheffield a week or so later both 'Church and King' and 'Radical' fury burst into violence. In the days before the riot broke out, one commentator reported that 'the lower classes of the people, both here and in the neighbourhood, are so much enraged, that their common cry is *"Liberty or Death"'*. Local elites reported to the Home Office that 'the many treasonable Inscriptions daily repeated upon walls and doors in several places in this Town for several weeks past give the Friends of Government and of the Peace of Society fear that many here are ripe for mischief' and that 'The peaceable inhabitants of this large and populous Town and neighbourhood are under the most serious apprehensions by the very alarming Riots and Disturbances lately at Birmingham and more so from the arrival here of some of those Rioters who have industriously mixed with the disorderly people of this town'. They believed that the previous night 'several of these Incendiaries . . . used strong endeavours to raise a Riot by . . . inviting them to bring about a Redress of Grievances as they had done at Birmingham'.[19] A visitor to the town noted 'They stuck up all over Sheffield printed bills, with the words No King in large characters. This I suppose is one mode of exerting the Rights of Man.'[20] On the night of the 27th Broomhall, home of the JP and Reverend James Wilkinson was attacked. In a letter of 30 July Vincent Eyre reported that that the burning of Broom Hall had been foiled by the arrival of a troop of the 15th Light Dragoons, but noted that his hayricks had been set on fire and that the mob had set about his own house, again it being saved by the timely arrival of the cavalry.[21] The Duke of Norfolk and Vincent Eyre were from recusant families, and on 27 July the rioters 'broke every window belonging to the house, and also the windows of the Roman Catholic chapel' belonging to the duke.[22]

The Duke of Norfolk, as a Whig and Catholic, was a symbol of everything the 'Church and King' mob hated. Anti-Catholic hatred, ever since the Gordon Riots of 1780, had been a constant political force: many Dissenters supported revolutionary France because it had overthrown the power of the Catholic Church, and fed into the burgeoning ideals of millenarianism.[23] It is easy to see, that Catholics who had been persecuted since the 1540s and made 'enemies of the state' with the events of 1688 and 1745, the later event being in living memory for some, became easy targets. Maintaining the Protestant Reformation from the threat of Catholicism was ever present, and I wonder how linked this anti-Catholicism in Sheffield was to the Irish diaspora and emergence of the Defenders in Ireland and growing religious tension in that country. The rioting has eerie echoes of the Gordon Riots. For Protestant Tories, the Whigs – especially since they supported the repeal of the Test and Corporation Acts to give Unitarians and Catholics the same rights as Anglicans – and Catholics it was feared, would combine lead to 'the total annihilation of all we hold most dear' i.e., the Church of England and the Crown.[24]

The following day witnessed crowds gather outside the Tontine Inn: 150 special constables were enrolled, the Riot Act was read and the crowd was dispersed by the dragoons. It was claimed later that the officers and men had been given secret orders to provoke the townsfolk into attacking the military to justify a crackdown on the people. However, this seems unlikely as the soldiers were reprimanded after the event, but it does seem that the military were responsible for the escalation of violence.[25] On the 29th Norwood Hall, the home of the unpopular lawyer James Wheat, was attacked, the barns and contents being set on fire.[26] This was the last act of almost a week of violence that rocked Sheffield. It is all too easy to blame the dispossessed poor as the instigators of the riots here: a divergent sent of issues all came to a head the legitimate grievances of the poor, anti-Catholic hatred and fears of Catholicism, anti-authoritarianism, political reform, and goading by soldiers all combined to make violence inevitable.

In response, Justice and Parson Wilkinson made sure that high-profile arrests were made: five men were tried at York for taking part in the 27 July riots. Four were acquitted but the fifth, John Bennet, a steel burner from the steelmaking township of Brightside Brierlow, was hanged on 6 September.[27] An example was made to cow the people into line.

What we seem to be seeing here in Sheffield, is working class agitation against enclosures that became hijacked by a radicalised mob of Loyalists from Birmingham who had participated in the Priestley Riots, fuelled by religious hatred, a desire to cause chaos and to also discredit the reform movement, brought terror to the streets of Sheffield.[28] The Loyalist mob gave the magistrates the excuse to 'come down hard' on reform groups in Sheffield and across the West Riding.

Chapter 3

# JACOBIN CLUBS

Despite the rioting in Birmingham and Sheffield, the desire for reform and the Rights of Man was undiminished. The French Republic declared that the 'natural and imprescriptible rights of man' were to be defined as 'liberty, property, security and resistance to oppression'. The Republic demanded the destruction of aristocratic privileges by proclaiming an end to feudalism and exemptions from taxation. It also called for freedom and equal rights for all human beings (referred to as 'Men') and access to public office based on talent. The power of the monarchy was restricted and all citizens had the right to take part in the legislative process. Freedom of speech and the press were declared and arbitrary arrests outlawed. The Declaration also asserted the principles of popular sovereignty, in contrast to the divine right of kings that characterised the French monarchy, and social equality among citizens, eliminating the special rights of the nobility and clergy. Revolution laid aside any tests based on lineage and religion. If this could be achieved in France, why not England, many felt. What had begun as a largely middle-class demand for the right to have a say in how the country was managed evolved rapidly through the 1790s into working-class radicalism. So far, reform had largely been the preserve of the 'middling sort'. Yet the accelerating pace of industrialisation and urbanisation at the end of the eighteenth century was a great driver of social change in Britain in this period. It witnessed the creation of the urban working class. As ever more factories were built in towns like Birmingham, Manchester, Sheffield, Leeds and of course London, so too did the need for a labour force to work in the new factories increase. This was created through an unprecedented shift of labour from the countryside to the towns and cities. Suddenly new urban areas were flooded with an eclectic mix of social and economic classes, including those from other countries – notably Ireland – looking for work in these new industries. The common thread for many of these men was that the social and economic constructs they were so accustomed to had been severely disrupted by relocating to new urban areas which, by and large, tended to fuel the creation of associations, clubs and societies. The formation of these organisations, whether for political, cultural or other reasons, served to connect people of similar interests, but not necessarily the same backgrounds. It was in these new and expanding urban centres that the ideas of equality and the 'rights of man' had the largest impact. The desire for equality, as well as political representation, drove reform.

One of the first regional societies was formed in Sheffield in summer 1791 where '5 or 6 Mechanicks' began to meet to discuss 'the enormous prices of provisions' as well as 'the mock representation of the people'. The meetings in Sheffield said nothing that the Yorkshire Association from a decade earlier had not said, but importantly, political reform was now being debated by working men, who exhorted their brethren to defend themselves against exploitation by the assertion of their natural rights as put forward by Thomas Paine.[1] The leader, William Broomhead, later declared that the society was founded 'to enlighten the people, to show the people the reason, the ground of all their complaints and sufferings' was exploitation by those who denied the people their natural rights.[2] Following the publication of the French Constitution on 3 September, which for the first time granted universal male suffrage, the Sheffield Revolution Club declared:

> As some gentlemen had industriously laboured to thrown an ODIUM on the FRENCH REVOLUTION, and endeavoured to persuade people here, that is in the interest and ought to be the business of Britons to reprobate it; it is therefore judged advisable, in order to remove all unfounded apprehensions . . . We rejoice in the glorious events of the French Revolution . . . and for erecting a government on the Hereditary rights of man – rights which appertain to ALL, and not to any ONE more than the other . . . We say and repeat it, that the French Revolution opens to the world an opportunity in which all good citizens rejoice, that of promoting the general happiness of Man.[3]

The address was printed by John Crome of Sheffield, who we will come to later. With support from both the middle and working classes, the new society grew to such an extent that by December 1791 the alarmed magistrate J. Hunter described the call for political reform as an 'infection' amongst the working men of the town.[4] Leadership was primarily from the Unitarian congregation that met at Upper Chapel on Norfolk Street, notably Joseph and Winifred Gales, David Martin and for a time Samuel Shore, the Rev. Benjamin Naylor and the Rev. James Montgomery.[5] Across the country a wave of Jacobinism was rising. In defence of the French Revolution and Jacobin principles, the Revolution Club of London on 4 November 1791 proclaimed:

> This truly patriotic Society uninfluenced by party, or sinister views, met on this day to commemorate the Anniversary of the Revolution, and with zeal for the cause of Freedom and welfare of Mankind in every part of the World; seem unanimously disposed to assert with proper dignity, the rights of their fellow men in this, and every nation on the face of the earth – Let every man heartily join them until oppression, arbitrary power, and tyranny is rooted out from amongst every enlightened people in the world.[6]

One of those attending was the Mayor of Paris, Jérôme Pétion de Villeneuve, who had arrived in London on 30 October. From his diary the meal was attended by about 350 people and he as guest of honour was sat next to the president, Thomas Walker of Manchester. It was here that Pétion met the Rev. Dr Joseph Priestley – whose chapel, home and library had been destroyed by fire earlier in the year because of his support of 'French principles' by supporters of Edmund Burke – as well as Thomas Paine. Many wore the French tricolour cockade and the orchestra punctuated the proceedings by playing the revolutionary anthem *Ça ira*, an emblematic song of the era: the Rev. Theophilus Lindsey – nominal leader of the Unitarian denomination – remarked that 'the music being happily intermixed with the toast and some excellent songs . . . seemed to inspire the whole company'. The meal provided brotherhood and solidarity between English and French Revolutionaries, and a direct means of contact between revolutionary groups in England and the French state.[7] Patriotic toasts to the King were drunk in an almost gloomy silence, but the company became livelier when a toast declared 'the sovereignty of the people, acting by a just and equal representation'. In defence of France a toast declared 'The Glorious Revolution in France – May it serve as a lesson to the oppressor and an example to the oppressed' with the concluding speeches being:

> The Memory of Dr Price. May we never forget that the end of all Government is to protect liberty, and not to take it away. May the wisdom, courage, and virtue which distinguished the late National Assembly in France be conspicuous in the Present.[8]

A few days later after the London gathering, in Manchester the Revolution Club was chaired by Thomas Walker, with toasts drunk to hope that 'the nations of Europe awake from their lethargy, and assert their birth-right, in daring to be free . . . the memory of Milton, Marvell, Locke, Hollis[9] and Jebb'[10] adding that:

> May every commemoration of the Revolution find the people of England better acquainted with the principles of Liberty, and more firmly determined to support them, the Liberty to the Press, and a speedy Annihilation to every government that shrinks from investigation, May the spirit of Liberty never be Injured by the Spirit of Party.

Closing toasts were drunk to 'the Republic of America and its first Citizen', as well as 'to Dr Priestley' concluding with the solemn words 'may reason and philosophy ever prevail over fanaticism and Ignorance . . . '.[11] In Bath, the Revolution Club wished 'the whole world be one City, and is inhabitants presented with their freedom'.[12] Similar events had been held in Leeds and Wakefield: 'The Leeds Constitutional Society' declared on 17 November 1791:

> I am convinced that the end of society is common happiness – that government is instituted to secure to man his natural rights, which are equality, Liberty, Safety; and Prosperity, – and that ALL men are equal by nature; And I am convinced that the PEOPLE have no part in the government of this County; the Parliamentary Representation as it is called, being inadequate, imperfect and corrupt; I, therefore, will by every constitutional means in my power promote thorough reform in the Commons House of Parliament, namely, universal Right of Suffrage and annual elections.[13]

The Sheffield Constitutional Society – which had emerged from The Sheffield Revolution Society – at its first meeting on 19 December 1791 resolved that:

> That as our constitution from its earliest periods, founded on Liberty, it should not be destroyed by a government of despotism . . . all our political evils, arising from the abuse of the practice . . . the corrupt state of representation . . . a restoration of our liberties is equally due.[14]

By the middle of March 1792, the society had mushroomed to a membership of 2,500: in order to prevent the danger of assemblies 'getting out of hand', the leadership devised a simple and flexible strategy of holding separate meetings or 'divisions' of the society at different public houses in the town on the same night at regular fortnightly intervals: on 27 February the principal meeting was held at the Freemasons Hall on Paradise Square, with 'Divisions' assembling at 'the Fountain' at Town-Head Cross, 'the Tiger' in New Street and twelve other public houses.[15] A plan for an organisation based on 200 'tythings' of 10 members each, 20 groups of delegates and a 'Grand Council' of 20 was proposed in January 1792.[16] The potential of the divisional structure was recognised by John Horne Tooke, the most redoubtable of the reformist leaders, who adopted it for the London Corresponding Society.[17]

It was to the urban working class that Thomas Hardy, a Scottish shoemaker in London who had been convinced of the need for political reform by the ideals of Rev. Dr Richard Price, appealed to in founding his reformist club: the London Corresponding Society. Amongst the papers and pamphlets handed to him by John Cartwright from the library of the Society for Constitutional Information was a proposal from the Correspondence Committee of the Irish Volunteer movement to restore 'the purity and vigour' of the Irish constitution through parliamentary reform.[18]

At the first meeting of his society on 25 January 1792, Hardy led seven friends in a discussion that determined that 'gross ignorance and prejudice in the bulk of the nation was the greatest obstacle to obtaining redress' from the 'defects and abuses that have crept into the administration of our Government' and that to remove that obstacle it should be the aim of those subscribing:

> to instill into [the public] in a legal and constitutional way by means of the press, a sense of their rights as freemen, and of their duty to themselves and their posterity, as good citizens, and hereditary guardians of the liberties transmitted to them by their forefathers.[19]

In contrast to some of Whig-establishment reform clubs, the organisation allowed all subscribers to participate in open debate, and to elect members to leadership positions such as tithing-man, divisional secretary, sub-delegate or delegate, and by May 1792 it comprised nine separate divisions. Membership was 1 pence per week, which made working-class participation possible. High-profile members included John Gales Jones, Olaudah Equiano, Joseph Gerrald, William Skirving and others like John Towgood and John Hurford Stone. It would be Equiano who, drawing on abolitionist networks, brokered connections with the United Irishmen. It was Stone who was the link with France and the foreign minister Talleyrand. Veteran reformer John Horne

Tooke became central to the development of the society and its links with other reformist groups.

## Thomas Paine

On 16 February 1792, the second part of Thomas Paine's *The Rights of Man* appeared. In it Paine advocated, amongst other things, the right of the people to replace their government if they thought it appropriate. For the English Jacobins and political reformers, this was to be achieved through political reform and a greater electoral franchise. When the first volume had appeared in 1791, Paine had repeated the ideas of Marat, Price and Priestley and had written in direct response to Burke's refutation of Price's support of the French Revolution. Indeed, when the book appeared in 1791, it went virtually unnoticed amidst a sea of pamphleteering and it was largely through the Society for Constitutional Information and the London radical John Horne Tooke that the book became nationally known and adopted as the 'bible' of the masses. In Part Two Paine praised the revolution in France, declared that it was futile to petition Parliament to reform itself – as Marat and the Rev. Dr Price had done almost two decades earlier – and echoed Price when he argued that political revolution was always justified whenever the inviolable and natural rights of man were oppressed by the Crown. Like others before him, Paine was making a direct attack on the citadel of aristocratic and upper-class privilege. Unitarian enthusiasts such as Thomas Cooper and Thomas Walker of Manchester, Rev. Thomas Johnstone of Wakefield, Rev. Dr Priestley at Hackney and the nominal head of the denomination Rev. Theophilus Lindsey, spread the 'gospel of Paine' far and wide both in print and from the pulpit. Paine's work also marked a schism in the reform movement: the Wyvillite faction of moderate reformers gathered around Charles Grey as the 'Friends of the People'. Cooper, backed by James Watt Jnr, Walker and others, called those gathered around Grey 'nothing more than men of rank and responsibility' who were 'half-measured reformers' seeking only to enfranchise the rich middle class. Cooper, Watt, Walker and others within the London Corresponding Society and the Society for Constitutional Information fraternised with Jacobins in Paris and sought more radical change and an end to executive tyranny and what we might now call 'sleaze' through the 'virtue' and common good of representative democratic government.

The Whigs had always sought to contain the powers of the Crown and nobility through Parliament. Paine, however, was altogether more democratic; Whigs like Burke, Price and others felt it was their duty to resist imbalance and corruption in the polity through civic virtue, by active participation in political affairs. This was anathema to both moderate Whigs and Tories alike: the radical Whigs had been arguing the same case since John Wilkes 20 years earlier. Paine resolutely believed the British Crown and Parliament was nothing more than a self-interested institution run for the benefit of a landowning elite. In desiring a more equal society, as promoted by the Duke of Richmond in 1780, Paine advocated the proper delegation of powers within a representative democracy but did not advocate abolition of the monarchy, rather a drastic curtailment of the powers of the Crown and the creation of a constitutional monarchy. He was a republican in as much as he wanted the people to rule the country and not a clique of landowners. Paine called for values based on reason, tolerance and understanding rather than institutions: he was a pioneer, along with Mary Wollstonecraft, of the concept of basic human rights, which the Crown rejected. Paine's vision for a new way of government was considered treasonous by the standards of the day. Paine was forced to flee Britain for France and was later convicted of seditious libel in his absence. The idea of regime change, or major constitutional overhaul, appalled Edmund Burke, William Pitt and all those who resisted reform. Crucially it must be stressed that in the early nineteenth century, many radicals conceived themselves as being illegitimately excluded from the public space of political debate and appropriated patriotic language and actions to stress their loyalty to the nation and its history in order to legitimise their claims to participate. Rather than advocating revolution and disloyalty to the state, the radicals stressed their use of constitutional methods and their patriotism – petitioning Parliament and the sovereign, gathering in huge patriotically-saturated mass rallies or joining the Volunteer movement – in which they overwhelmingly wished the state and constitution to remain, but in a fairer and more democratic form. Despite this, reform and religious dissent were now considered by loyalists to be tantamount to French Jacobinism, and therefore both groups were enemies of the state.[20] Burke argued that 'the deceitful dreams and visions of equality and rights of man' had to be stopped.[21]

One of those in full agreement with Burke was the Rev. Henry Zouch, a magistrate living in Sandal Magna near Wakefield. He told Earl Fitzwilliam that he could not 'be indifferent to such dangerous appeals' being made by the reformist societies, and noted that members of the club in Sheffield were:

strangers to me but I understand they are of the lowest classes of manufacturers and amount to several hundred and that they profess to be admirers of the dangerous Doctrines of Mr Payne, whose pamphlets they distribute with industry and support his dogmas with zeal, and these new Doctrines (with much declamation against the supposed abuses of government) constitute great part of their weekly debates.[22]

Zouch feared that the society in Sheffield and allied organisations across the country were planning to ferment revolution as in France, and that the membership would resort to violence to bring about the changes they wanted to see in society.

Apprehensive about the scale of the threat posed by grass-roots activism, the Rev. Zouch sought authorisation to use a spy to infiltrate the society who would collect names of the leaders, and bring them to the magistrates' bench for imprisonment.[23] A spy was duly planted in to the society who informed Sheffield parson, landowner and magistrate Rev. James Wilkinson of every move the 'enemy' was making. On 6 January 1792 Wilkinson informed Earl Fitzwilliam that 200 of the 'inferior sorts of manufacturers & workmen' had gathered to talk politics, which included some of the respectable men of the town as well as some Quakers.[24] The Rev. Zouch informed the Earl that the leading townsmen of Sheffield wanted the magistrates to act quickly to suppress the society and end its meetings.[25]

The use of spies was a marked feature of late-eighteenth-century information-gathering. Purveyors of 'information' were generally working-class, and 'tricked' their way into the confidence of those under investigation. They were paid for their information: it has been suggested by E.P. Thompson and others that the fiscal incentive to provide information made the reports untrustworthy, yet historians Marianne Elliott, Roger Wells and Ann Hone have concluded the reports are generally accurate.[26] The Crown via its spymasters sought to create overlapping sources that would either corroborate or contradict each other: from this, it would 'fumigate' the reports to sift fact from fiction as far as possible. It was in the Crown's best interests if they were to prosecute radicals, and secure convictions, to use reliable information. False information would have been quickly exposed once arrests had been made. The Crown did use agents-provocateurs to secure convictions and also offered arrested radicals the chance to turn 'king's evidence' and escape conviction by becoming a spy. John Moody, who worked for Richard Ford at Bow Street, was one such man. Evan Nepean at the Home Office managed two 'turncoats', William Metcalfe and John 'Citizen' Groves: both had been members of the London Corresponding Society and turned 'king's evidence' to escape gaol. Others included William White, George Orr, James Powell and John Tunbridge. Powell had been assistant secretary to the London Corresponding Society and was a founder member of the United Britons. A member of the United Irishmen, Samuel Turner, spied for William Wickham, the Secretary of State for Ireland, on United Irish contacts in Ireland and Hamburg. It would be evidence from Turner that resulted in the execution of Father O'Coigly.

Getting back to Yorkshire, Henry Zouch reported to Earl Fitzwilliam that, from information passed to him by his spy, the Sheffield Constitutional Society had held a meeting on 30 January 1792, which had been attended by 600 persons. Zouch reported that at the meeting it was declared that 'Who were to obtain a Reform? The Nobility? – No. Would Parliament? – No. It must be the middle-class who pay taxes!' The same cry as John Wilkes – No taxation without representation! The meeting also sought to redress the grievances of the poor against the recently enacted Corn Laws, and began gathering funds to begin a new petition to Parliament for reform. Zouch added that the society was naïve if they thought the legislative body would listen to their appeals and 'the voice of the multitude'. Despite deep misgivings, he wished the endeavour well, but warned that if the petitioning process failed, he feared 'more hostile measures' could be taken as 'the dangerous doctrines of Payne had laid fast hold of the public mind and roused it into active exertion'.[27] As long as the legitimate means of protest established in 1775 were adhered to, then clearly the magistrates could do nothing. If, however, legitimate lines of grievance were ignored by the Crown, the only option left was for direct action. Zouch realised that 'trouble was brewing'.

A second meeting was held in Sheffield on 27 February 1792. No doubt concerned at the direction in which the society could develop, he ordered that his spy was to infiltrate the meeting and report back to him directly what was discussed. With the spy's written testimony Zouch wrote to Earl Fitzwilliam. He noted in his covering letter that the society had 1,500 members, and the meeting was attended by 80 to 90, with speeches made against the Corn Bill, taxes, reform as well as the Test and Corporation Acts. He reported that the motto was '*Vox Populi, Vox Dei*', literally, the voice of the people is the voice of God. Zouch passed on news from Francis Edmunds of Worsborough to Fitzwilliam, informing him that Edmunds was alarmed at a constitutional society being formed in the towns where he lived, Worsborough, and added that 'Dr P' had many friends and supporters in the county.[28] Beyond reasonable doubt 'Dr P' must have been none other than the Rev.

Dr Joseph Priestley. Zouch and Francis Edmunds were clearly linking Unitarianism to anti-establishment activities and therefore the Test and Corporation Acts had to be kept in place stop the likes of 'Dr P' having a say in how the country was governed.

One of the primary activities of the Sheffield society was the dissemination of radical literature: this was welcomed by John Horne Tooke, who suggested a union of reformist groups 'to promote the general cause and shew to the public at large that we are closely united together and are going forward in a systematical manner to obtain for the whole nation a Restoration of Our Rights and Relief from Oppression'.[29] As well as disseminating radical tracts, the Sheffield society, driven by missionary zeal, sought to help the formation of sister societies across the north of England. Zouch's spy reported that the Chairman of the Sheffield society on 27 February 1792 at a meeting in the Freemasons' Hall:

> wished to inform the company that the committee had had personal applications from the adjacent towns and villages at Rotherham, Stannington, Attercliffe, Horton, Ecclesfield, also from Derby and Stoney Middleton, requesting them to take measures for instituting similar associations in those parts.[30]

One member of the Derby group was Henry Redhead Yorke: born in 1772 from a liaison between a slave and her master, he was given his freedom on his father's death and was educated at Cambridge to be a lawyer by men like Dr John Jebb and Gilbert Wakefield (where we also find Benjamin Vaughan and Archibald Hamilton Rowan as students, who like Jebb and Wakefield were Unitarians). Yorke joined the Whig Club in 1790. As a young man he lived in London and Derby and associated with wealthy Derby industrialist reform Whigs. Despite his immediate social circle being opposed to the slave trade, Yorke wrote a pro-slavery pamphlet, published in early 1792, encouraged by the local Tory gentry: Yorke had been forced to reject his own 'blackness' and his early West Indian slave identity through the institutionalised racism he found in England.

William Ward, editor of *The Derby Mercury*, a convert to Methodism and thence the Baptist denomination in 1796, cultivated his skills as an impassioned speaker as a lay preacher. He used his position as a newspaper editor to print editorials about current events rather than merely repeating the 'party line' by printing excerpts from London newspapers. Through his editorials, Ward reveals himself as a moderate, in favour of political reform, who supported the ideals of the Revolution in France and as a fervent supporter of repealing the Test and Corporation Acts,[31] as well as of the abolition of the slave trade. On 13 March 1792 a meeting was held at County Hall, to petition Parliament for the abolition of the slave trade, with the support of Dr Erasmus Darwin, the Strutt family and the Evans family. The petition attracted 3,669 signatures, a considerable achievement considering the population of Derby was just over 8,000. As elsewhere across the country, Unitarians in Derby took the lead: Joseph and William Strutt of Belper Unitarian Chapel, aided by Ward and Darwin, formed the Derby Society for Political Information: its membership being drawn largely from the middle-class Derby Literary and Philosophical Society. The 'Lit and Phil' had written in support of Dr Priestley in Ward's *Derby Mercury* on 29 September 1791.[32] Many of the members of the Derby 'Lit and Phil' were Unitarians who worshipped in their chapel on Friar Gate. The minister there, Rev. James Pilkington, wrote 'The Doctrine of Equality', which aroused local and national opposition to his 'obnoxious doctrine' and he was considered 'a more formidable opponent than even Thomas Paine' to Church and King. Such roused passions caused him to tender his resignation, but at a congregational meeting called to consider the matter it was unanimously agreed:

> That persecution or punishment for speculative opinions would be inconsistent with the principles of the friends of truth and free inquiry, and therefore that the objections urged do not appear sufficient for an acquiescence in Mr Pilkington's resignation.[33]

Clearly, Pilkington was preaching about the 'Church and King' supporters who denounced reform which was promoted by Ward through his newspaper.

Abolitionism and radical reform were 'joined at the hip': where abolitionist societies gathered, they gravitated to radical politics. In wanting to end the slave trade and slavery, radicals understood that slavery existed not only on plantations in the West Indies: at home most taxpayers had no vote, and the state deliberately and clearly discriminated on religious grounds.

Ward channelled this vast outpouring of public feeling into a reform movement and declared at the first meeting on 16 July 1792:

> CLAIMING it as our indefeasible right to associate together, in a peaceable and friendly manner, for the communication of thoughts, the formation of opinions, and to promote the general happiness, we think

it unnecessary to offer any apology for inviting you to join us in this manly and benevolent pursuit; the necessity of the inhabitants of every community endeavouring to procure a true knowledge of their rights, their duties, and their interests, will not be denied, except by those who are the slaves of prejudice, or the interested in the continuation of abuses.

The meeting went on to state that 'we think, therefore, that the cause of truth and justice can never be hurt by temperate and honest discussions, and that cause which will not bear such a scrutiny, must be systematically or practically bad' and asserted that 'We are in the pursuit of truth, in a peaceable, calm, and unbiassed manner; and wherever we recognise her features, we will embrace her as the companion of happiness, of wisdom, and of peace, This is the mode of our conduct: the reasons for it will be found in the following declaration of our opinions, to the whole of which each member gives his hearty assent.' The meeting concluded with words redolent of Paine or Marat, recording that 'That all true Government is instituted for the General good; is legalised by the general will; and all its actions are, or ought to be, directed for the general happiness and prosperity of all honest citizens'.[34]

At nearby Belper, Unitarian merchant Jedediah Strutt, who had backed political reform and the repeal of the Test and Corporation Acts from the 1780s, founded his own Constitutional Society. Membership mostly came from his own congregation and included his immediate family, notably his son William. In a repeat performance of the Priestley riots, loyalist opponents to reform burned the library and home of William, and flooded his cotton mills in November 1792 by blocking up his waterwheel so that the mill race overflowed and virtually destroyed the mills. By May 1793 both the Derby and Belper societies ceased to exist, such was the backlash from loyalist mobs.[35]

Unlike the society in Derby which was largely middle class, the society in Sheffield marked a change in the membership of popular clubs, attracting the city's disenfranchised cutlers, scissor smiths, and other manufacturing workers, and was probably the first British working-class reform association of any consequence anywhere. Magistrate Hunter informed Earl Fitzwilliam that:

It does not yet appear that the better ranks of person in Sheffield are at all infected by the spirit which might be thought to actuate the clubs lately formed there . . . The Club or Clubs, I find consist of a small collection of persons of the lowest order who have hitherto met & discussed some political subjects.[36]

Hunter added that the club in Sheffield was contemptible, and reported that he was not aware of any Dissenters taking part in it. Hunter also forwarded to Fitzwilliam a transcript of Joseph Gales' editorial in defence of the club. Sheffield attorney James Wheat had similar misgivings:

Thinking as I do that all appeals to the Ignorance of the Multitude to sit in judgement on public Regulation is dangerous, and smarting as I do from the Recollection of the mischief arising from the recent violence of the mobs here (many of whom are the professed disciples of Mr Payne), I cannot be indifferent to such Dangerous Appeals for I am apt to suspect both the purity and policy of such designs.[37]

The society declared on 14 March 1792:

This Society, composed chiefly of the Manufacturers of Sheffield, began about Four Months ago, and is already increased to nearly TWO THOUSAND MEMBERS, and is daily increasing, exclusive of the adjacent Towns and Villages, who are forming themselves into similar Societies.

Considering, as we do, that the Want of Knowledge and Information in the general Mass of the People has exposed them to numberless Impositions and Abuses, the Exertions of this Society are directed to the Acquirement of useful Knowledge, and to spread the same as far as our Endeavours and Abilities can extend,

We declare that we have derived more true Knowledge from the Two Works of Mr. Thomas Paine, intituled 'Rights of Man', Part the First and Second, than from any other Author or Subject. The Practice as well as the Principle of Government is laid down in those Works, in a Manner so clear, and irresistibly convincing that this Society do hereby resolve to give their Thanks to Mr. Paine for his Two said Publications, intituled 'Rights of Man', Part 1st and 2d. Also,

Resolved unanimously, That the Thanks of this Society be given to Mr. Paine, for the affectionate Concern he has shown in his Second Work in Behalf of the Poor, the Infant, and the Aged; who, notwithstanding the Opulence which blesses other Parts of the Community, are, by the grievous Weight of Taxes, rendered the miserable Victims of Poverty and Wretchedness.

Resolved unanimously, That this Society, disdaining to be considered either of a Ministerial or Opposition Party (Names of which we are tired, having been so often deceived by both) do ardently recommend it to all their Fellow Citizens, into whose Hands these Resolutions may come, to confer seriously and calmly with each other on the Subject alluded to, and to manifest to the World that the Spirit of true Liberty is a Spirit of Order and that to obtain Justice it is consistent that we be just ourselves.

> Resolved, unanimously, That these Resolutions be printed, and that a Copy thereof be transmitted to the Society for Constitutional Information in London; requesting their Approbation for Twelve of our Friends to be entered into their Society, for the Purpose of establishing a Connection and a regular Communication with that, and all other similar societies in the Kingdom.

By Order of the Committee.[38]

The Rev. Zouch's informant forwarded an abstract of the meeting held on 26 March, at which forty to fifty attended at the Freemasons' Lodge in Paradise Street. It mentions the society had 2,000 members, was in contact with the London radical John Horne Tooke and the London Society for Constitutional Information, into which twelve members in Sheffield were to be enrolled.[39]

The society was conceived originally as organisation of social reformers, many of whom were drawn from the rational Dissenting community, dedicated to publishing political tracts aimed at educating their fellow citizens on their lost ancient liberties. The society was greatly bolstered by the support of Joseph Gales: he was a Unitarian and editor of the *Sheffield Register* and printed extracts of *The Rights of Man* in his newspaper. An out-and out radical beyond the norms of English Jacobinism of 1791, his newspaper had a distribution of 2,000 copies a week and he produced a second publication, *The Patriot*, to further the work of the society. Gales had a vision of a more radical paper, which Samuel Shore initially was keen to encourage, persuading William Wilberforce to support the paper to gain exemption from the recently-levied paper tax.[40]

Gales and the Rev. Montgomery actively promoted the work of Paine and other campaigners for parliamentary reform. Gales remarked:

> Yorkshire and Lancashire, and Warwickshire are particularly aggrieved. Of the first County, neither the East nor North-Riding send Representatives. In Sheffield, nor Leeds, nor Wakefield the population of which at this period is probably 300,000 persons. Manchester in the second County named, nor Birmingham in the last, have either of them a Representative with a still larger population. A few facts will suffice to show the inequality of Representation in the Councils of the Nation.[41]

The lack of political representation, freedom of religion and the vote led to an unheralded upsurge in anti-government protest across the country: for hundreds of thousands of men and women in England,

Scotland and Ireland, the revolution in France gave them a beacon of hope for a better world, and showed the power that the people had against the few. What had begun as debating societies had evolved into radicalised groups: the 'people' wanted their voice to be heard and were prepared to 'take matters into their own hands' to achieve it.

## Chapter 4

# SEDITION AND CENSORSHIP

For the Rev. Thomas Zouch and like-minded men, the spread of the various societies across the North of England, their open declaration of links to Jacobins in France and the rapid growth of what were clearly grassroots Jacobin groups inspired by Thomas Paine was a rapidly escalating threat to the status quo. Yet Zouch could not easily brand the radicals and political reformists as traitors. The Sheffield Society, in its appeal to the monarch, neatly underlined the issue of loyalty and patriotism. So alarmed was he by the events unfolding that Magistrate Zouch requested that steps be taken against the reform societies in the Sheffield area and further afield, notably Leeds, as he and others were convinced that an armed uprising was heading their way.[1]

Keen to demonstrate their loyalty, the radicals in Sheffield, reported Magistrate Bowns regretfully, sang the National Anthem.[2] Whilst the radicals continued to press for political change and sang 'God Save the KING', the magistrates could take no action against them for being disloyal! Yet that was all to change.

Alarmed as much by the emergence of radical groups like the London Corresponding Society as by the events taking place in France, William Pitt and his ministers convinced Parliament and the British people of the need to use new and extreme measures to eradicate the radical threat and protect the political status quo. In the climate and context of the time the Prime Minister and his colleagues believed that political reform was dangerous, French republican idealism intolerable and that both were an existential threat to the nation and its attendant privileges. The British Crown encouraged 'loyal Britons' to help to quell radical activity at home by means of propaganda, loyalist associations, the militarisation of society and intimidation. Using an effective propaganda machine, the Crown enlisted the support of a significant proportion of the population to voluntarily form loyalist associations: if the reformists could harness 'people power' so could the loyalists. This strategy worked.

For the Tories, men like Edmund Burke, William Pitt and the future Duke of Wellington, poverty and inequality were both natural and divinely ordained: hereditary power was necessary to ensure stability and order. The radicals, stimulated by the example set in America and now France, were seen to threaten the social and political order, and the security of property. In support of intolerance, wealth inequality and lack of democracy, Edmund Burke, the arch conservative, declared that:

> The most obvious division of society is into rich and poor; and it is no less obvious, that the number of the former bear a great disproportion to the latter. The whole business of the poor is to administer to the idleness, folly and luxury of the rich; and that of the rich in return is to find the best methods of confirming the slavery and increasing the burdens of the poor.[3]

Conservatives and loyalists therefore came to agree with Burke that the French Revolution was 'the common enemy of all governments, and of all establishments, religious and civil'. Only a complete counter-revolution, restoring the ancient Bourbon monarchy to France, could cure the disease. It was not a forgone conclusion that Britain would declare war on France, but it was a 'dead certainty' that the Crown would set out to destroy the internal threat posed by English Jacobins and radicals. The war was to be nothing less than the extermination and destruction of Jacobinism: for men like Edmund Burke, the people had no say in the governance of the country. Hereditary monarchy, he argued, could not exist if nothing else in society was hereditary or permanent. The governing elites believed themselves to be under direct threat from France and from radical activity at home, and argued that if property and social order was to be maintained in England, nothing short of spreading anti-revolutionary sentiment at the point of the bayonet would do.[4]

Only a total war of annihilation, waged both at home and abroad, would save the country from Jacobinism and inter alia political reform.[5] Burke argued that 'the deceitful dreams and visions of equality and rights of man' had to be stopped.[6] He believed some 80,000 British citizens to be:

> Pure Jacobins; utterly incapable of amendment; object of eternal vigilance; and when they break out, of legal constraint . . . They desire a

change; and . . . If they cannot have it by English cabal, they will make no sort of scruple of having it by the cabal of France, into which already they are virtually incorporated.[7]

Furthermore, he warned darkly that 'Parliamentary reform was the pretext for all the sedition that had been sown for many years in this country' and concluded that Reformists were planning 'more or less than the usurpation, and, in the end, the plunder, of the state'.[8] The common use of the terms 'Jacobin societies', 'Jacobinisation' and 'Jacobinism' in regards to British radicalism was designed to reinforce the supposed similarity between English radicals wanting political reform and Jacobin ideology, particularly the Terror. Burke, Pitt and the government were co-ordinating a very successful propaganda campaign to smear domestic radicalism by conflating it with the horrors and fanaticism of French Jacobinism. So successful was this campaign, via Gillray's cartoons and other pamphlets, that Napoleon is commonly believed to have been a small man, when he was actually of average height: Gillray's constant characterisation of him as akin to a dwarf has grasped hold of the common psyche, so too the hatred of anything French or Jacobin. For Burke and also men like Pitt or Robert Peel, the leader of the Manchester Association for the Preservation of the Constitution, the threat of democracy to the status quo was one that had to be met head on. By calling even limited reform 'French' or 'Jacobin' they closed down the debate on political and economic reform; racist language towards the French by using such words as 'vermin' helped to foster a sense of 'Britishness' and English exceptionalism. It was feared that the democratisation of the common people aligned with consciousness of their rights would result in a loss of respect for the existing institutions of class, authority, constitution and commerce, and ultimately lead to sedition, disorder, social breakdown and finally insurrection cum Revolution. This was to stopped at all costs. To the loyalists, the radicals were traitors and likely to be terrorists. They challenged the very nature of society: they distributed literature that was deemed, to use modern parlance, 'hate speech' and likely to 'cause a breach of the peace'. The literature produced by the radicals at the time, as in modern times with the leaflets and literature distributed by extreme religious radicals, was branded 'hate speech' as it propagated views against the Crown and constitution. The state, then as now, in endeavouring to protect the people from radicalisation, took legal steps to prevent the distribution of such material. The idea of civil rights was anathema to many 'Church and King' loyalists; 'Strong and stable' as well as 'no change needed' became the mantra of the government. The restriction of the electoral franchise to a rich elite was 'the natural order of things'. To ensure the survival of the Crown, Pitt enacted repressive legislation.

On 21 May 1792 the King issued a proclamation against seditious writings, in which he commanded all magistrates to 'make diligent inquiry in order to discover the authors and printers of such wicked and seditious writings'. Originally aimed at banning the publication of any work by Paine, it resulted in the banning of all material that was considered seditious: no more could one satirise the Crown and Parliament or support reform in print. It amounted to the end of a free press: freedom of speech was under direct threat. Official encouragement of spying and informing spread rapidly, resulting in the largest number of trials for sedition and treason in British history.[9] The Proclamation, however, seems to have had one major unintended consequence as Thomas Christie, a prominent Unitarian, explained:

> The people of England had no need of Mr. Burke's book to prejudice them against the French Revolution; they were sufficiently prejudiced before it. Ninety-nine out of a hundred, having access to no better source of information than the newspapers, which in general have been filled with misrepresentations, were persuaded that matters were going on very badly in France; that all was riot, confusion, and bloodshed there; and they would have long continued to hold that notion; for though books had been published to undeceive them, few would have taken the trouble to read them. The affairs of foreign nations have little interesting to the majority of men; and the good people of England, but for Mr. Burke, would have been still going on thanking Heaven, that while there was nothing but war and trouble in France, all was peace and quietness in England. From this state of tranquil unconcern, Mr. Burke has roused them by his ill-judged efforts to plunge them deeper into it. By connecting the affairs of France with matters at home, he has awakened the curiosity of the public, and given to the subject an interest that it never had before.[10]

Christie was perfectly correct about the power of the press: during 1790 he had spent six months in Paris, meeting many important French revolutionaries such as Mirabeau, Sieyès and Necker. Upon his return to Britain, he became a loyal supporter of the revolution and published *A Sketch of the New Constitution of France*. In 1791, he was one of the many who participated in the Revolution Controversy begun by Edmund Burke's *Reflections on the Revolution in France* (1790). His reply, *Letters on the Revolution in France and the New Constitution*, described his impressions of Paris and provided a contrast to Burke's depiction of it as lawless and violent. In 1792 he returned to Paris and was asked by the National Assembly to help translate a polyglot edition of the constitution. Christie was well known to Wakefield Unitarians, having spent time with the Rev. William Turner of Westgate Chapel and the Milnes family in 1787. Turner was close friends with both Price and Priestley and had been a leading player in the Yorkshire Association, as we noted earlier, and had widely disseminated his views across the West Riding.

## I Arrest You for Sedition!

The radical press became the target for the loyalists. The press was now forced to print what the Crown wanted it to say, or the presses were broken. The Unitarian and therefore pro-Jacobin virtual monopoly of the printing firm J. Johnson, of St Paul's Church Yard London, created a print culture of abolitionist and libertarian material that helped change the world: yet it was all now in jeopardy as the loyalists sought to close down the debate. Unitarian-edited reviews included *The Analytical Review* published by Johnson and founded by Thomas Christie, *The Monthly Review* founded by Ralph Griffiths and the *Critical*, as well as *The Sheffield Register* edited by Joseph Gales, *The Cambridge Intelligencer* edited by Benjamin Flower, a member of the extended Milnes family through marriage, *The Leeds Mercury* of Edward Baines, the *Wakefield Star* of Milnes and Lumb edited by Martin Naylor and lastly the *New Annual Register*. Rev. George Walker FRS, the minister at Nottingham who we encountered earlier, Rev. Joseph Towers, Rev. Dr Priestley, Rev. Dr Price, Rev. Dr Abraham Reece and many other influential ministers dominated the popular press for the cause of religious toleration and abolitionism, making them easy targets for the mob and legal challenges. In Birmingham, the Unitarian printer John Belcher was arrested, along with John Thompson who was Priestley's printer and bookseller. In Leicester Richard Phillips, a member of Unitarian Great Meeting, editor of the *Leicester Herald* and the *Monthly Magazine* was gaoled for two years for printing excerpts of Thomas Paine's *Rights of Man*.[11] The radical newspaper the *Manchester Herald* was silenced by the 'Church and King' mob, while the *Newark Herald* printed by Daniel Holt who was active in the Nottingham Constitutional Society found its press closed by loyalists after he had refused to withdraw Painite and other radical works from his bookshop: this was just the beginning of what became known by the radicals as the English Reign of Terror. Through the efforts of the Crown, the liberal press was either forcibly closed down and the presses smashed by loyalist attacks or acquiesced to their demands. The *Anti-Jacobin Review* described Unitarianism as a 'virus' to be stamped out as nothing more than 'Jacobin insolence'.[12] In Liverpool, the Literary and Philosophical Society, of which William Roscoe and William Rathbone were members, was silenced by anti-Jacobin violence. Broadly speaking, loyalists hoped to close down radical space through prosecution or intimidation.

Equally important was the active propagation of loyalism, by addresses, sermons, tracts and other means of dissemination. Claiming reform was 'Jacobin' or 'French Treason' gave the loyalists control of the debate. It placed the radicals in a defensive position, having constantly to defend their position and declare their loyalty, whereas the mobs themselves got 'carte blanche' to do what they wanted: they were in de facto control. As in the McCarthyite witch-hunts in 1950s America, the victims of this unregulated 'hegemonic' blacklisting were found disproportionately in academic and cultural arenas. National religious and educational bodies purged liberals, and promising literary careers were nipped in the bud. The loss to British culture is immense, if inestimable.

Pitt had been elected in 1784 on a platform of political reform: yet he was now the arch-conservative, who had instigated a 'reign of terror' against all those who objected to his rule. The Rev. Wyvill acidly remarked to the Rev. Dr Towers, a Unitarian minister whose sobriquet was 'Pamphleteer' for the number of reformist tracts he issued, that:

> Mr Pitt is not the person to whom the Nation will owe, in any great degree, the renovation of its Constitution ... his principal objective is not to improve the Constitution, and meliorate the condition of his Countrymen, but to secure the permanence of his power, the duration of which, for a single day, he seems unwilling to hazard for the attainment of that Political Reformation he formerly though of such might importance.[13]

The lawyer cum politician Thomas Erskine had recently '. . . returned from Paris a violent democrat', noted a fellow MP, who wrote 'he has had a coat made of the uniform of the Jacobins, with buttons bearing this inscription "Vivre libre ou mourir",[14] and he says he intends to wear it in our House of Commons'.[15] Such were Erskine's pro-French ideals, that on 30 April 1792 in defence of free speech he stood up in the House of Commons and declared:

> The rights of man are the foundation of all government, and to secure them is the only reason of men's submitting to be governed; —it shall not be fastened upon the unfortunate prisoner at the bar, nor upon any other man, that because these natural rights were asserted in France, by the

destruction of a government which oppressed and subverted them . . .
The rights of men, that is to say, the natural rights of mankind, are indeed
sacred things; and if any public measure is proved mischievously to
affect them, the objection ought to be fatal to that measure, even if no
charter at all could be set up against it.[16]

Through repressive legislation, a wave of arrests took place across
the country starting in late spring 1792. One such was in Wakefield,
West Yorkshire, and was typical of hundreds of similar episodes
which marked the beginning of a bitter conflict over personal freedom
and liberty of conscience. Alarmed by seditionist meetings, Zouch
convened a meeting of the magistrates in Wakefield on 31 May:

At the General Quarter Sessions of the Peace . . . Bacon Frank, Esq, Henry
Zouch Clerk, Pemberton Milnes Esq, John Blayds Esq, John Beckett Esq.
Justices of the Peace there & C.
    It was resolved . . . that Constables, Peace Officers and Parish Officers
do exert themselves in lodging information against all publicans and
guests, who shall be found offending in the premises . . . that they do not
permit any working persons to sit drinking in their ale houses without
special business.[17]

The legislation was clearly intended to stop groups like the Wakefield
Constitutional Society, which like that in Sheffield met in public houses,
from assembling, such was the fear that working men talking together
in public houses would lead to sedition. Working men were to be
stopped from consorting together, and when they did landlords were
to spy on drinkers in case they were speaking treason. Thomas Hardy
later recalled that the loyalists 'overawed the publicans so much than
none of them would admit us into their houses', forcing the London
Corresponding Society to meet privately and continually to shift its
rendezvous. The magistrates' actions further radicalised the reformist
groups, who were now driven underground and carried on 'just as
before', so much so that Zouch held a second meeting on 11 June:

Henry Zouch, a Justice of the Peace in the Chair, It was resolved,
    That it is with the utmost indignation and concern we have observed
divers seditions and inflammatory writings industriously published
throughout the Kingdom, and which, professing to inform and
enlighten the people, have conducted to exercise groundless jealousies
and discontents amongst them.
    The under the specious pretence of Equality among Mankind
(A doctrine however physically true, we hold to be politically false and
dangerous) different associations have been established, some of them

promoting visionary or impracticable plans of general reform, others entertaining principles tending to annihilate all civil society, nay even to the pillars of the constitution itself . . . have taken upon themselves to recommend the revolution in France as a model of Government to be adopted in this free and happy country.

That we rely upon the good sense of the People of England that they will resist the idea of being dictated to by any foreign assembly upon Earth, most of all by the Emissaries from the Jacobins of France.[18]

Zouch again urged neighbour to spy on neighbour, to root out sedition and to destroy Jacobin books and pamphlets. He thanked King George for enacting legislation to safeguard the nation from sedition. The Rev. Dr Coulthurst, parson and magistrate of Halifax, issued a similar charter.[19]

As could be expected, the Wakefield Constitutional Society, dismayed by the repressive legislation, began to take action against the new law. A counter-petition appeared in Wakefield, arguing that the demands of the magistrates to enact the Sedition Acts was 'a charter of spying' and went against the constitution. The Bill of Rights of 1689, the petitioners stated, cemented into law freedom of speech and of the press, and the new legislation in effect ended both. Therefore, the petitioners argued the loyalists were hypocrites as they were not supporting the constitution but were championing tyranny and repression and change to the very constitution they pledged to preserve! The Wakefield Constitutional Society stuck up handbills across the town, much to the outrage of the loyalists. These, in very blunt terms, reminded the literate public at large that loyalists like Zouch, Pemberton Milnes and others were hypocrites: Richard Milnes and his cousin James were all too well aware of the 'traitors' in their midst as they probably viewed their uncle Pemberton and the Rev. Zouch. Both men had publicly supported reform in 1775, 1780 and 1783 as part of the Yorkshire Association, but with the onset of the French Revolution, terrified by the forces it had unleashed, had abandoned their principles and were now considered to be 'aiding the government in enacting harmful legislation' which the radicals considered to be against 'the spirit and intent of the constitution'.[20] Indeed in 1783 Pemberton Milnes had been libelled, being accused of being a supporter of a 'Republic state . . . levellers and king killers . . . desirous of a false rebellious and designing son of Cromwell'.[21] The handbill declared:

An infamous and calumnious falsity having been affected in the Wakefield Resolutions on the 11 June, respecting the state of the French

Nation; and a most glaring and designing misrepresentation of the principles of the Society of the Friends of the Constitution at Paris, called Jacobins ... in order that the TRUTH may have its proper influence on the minds of those on whom imposition has been practised ... whether the friends of reform are not the real friends of the human race; and whether those may not be concluded enemy, who, by thanking HIS Majesty for his proclamation, evinces themselves supporters of Ministerial Hypocrisy – and impudently proclaim to the world, not only their own apostacy from the cause of Freedom, but their wish to persecute those with whom they formerly acted, because (as honest men) they cannot (liker them) submit to a versatility and duplicity of conduct which is a disgrace to human nature.

For the Public ought to be informed that the Leaders in Addressing His Majesty, both at Wakefield & Rotherham were Associators for a Reform of Parliament in the year 1783: and then declared 'that the Commons House of Parliament ought to have a common interest with the nation; and that, in the present state of the Representation of the people in Parliament, the Commons of this Realm are partially and inadequately represented and consequently cannot have that security for their liberties which it is the aim of the Constitution they should have!'.—These men are now giving themselves the lie direct.

Englishmen, think for yourselves!

Beware of sycophants who fatten on the produce of your labours!

Study your own interest and put implicit confidence in no man.[22]

The indignation felt by the members of the Yorkshire Association who had remained true to reform is palpable. The response from the magistrates was swift and merciless.

The Rev. Zouch noted that the 'Jacobins' were led by James Milnes – we met him earlier as a member of the Yorkshire Association – who with 'one or two more, led a very feeble attempt to throw difficulties in the way'.[23] Zouch informed Earl Fitzwilliam that the printer and writers were well known, and noted that one was 'a dissenting teacher & a man born & bread a quaker but latterly converted by a young wife of strong mind and will ...'. Zouch added that Pemberton Milnes 'will FIND the teacher'.[24]

Who were these men? Of the accused, the first man, reported as 'the teacher' and not even afforded the title of Reverend or minister of religion, is without doubt the Rev. Thomas Johnstone, the minister of Westgate Chapel 1792–1834 – where Pemberton Milnes worshipped alongside his nephew James – and the second is Robert Bakewell who was, as Zouch states, born in 1767 in Nottingham into a Quaker family. On his marriage Bakewell converted to Unitarianism: as the law dictated, he married Apphia, daughter of Thomas Simpson and Apphia

Aldcroft on 24 September 1790 at an Anglian ceremony at Wakefield Parish Church. Leaving Quakerism, depending on his meeting's rules, could have meant Robert was totally estranged from his siblings and parents by the act of rejecting their faith. This was a brave act, with no way back. Clearly, Apphia was a major and dominant influence on her husband. She had been born in 1791 and was 29 when she married, Robert being just 22. Thus, there can be no doubt about the identity of the two wanted men. For Apphia to be mentioned as a 'bad influence' on Robert, she must have been strong and outspoken. She was not alone in the congregation at Westgate: she worshipped alongside Rachel Milnes who talked politics and the abolition of slavery with William Wilberforce and Ann Hurst, who would go onto to dominate radical politics in Wakefield as a printer, abolitionist and newspaper editor.

Disgusted by the magistrate's action the Wakefield Constitutional Society, in what would be its 'swansong', printed a highly inflammatory handbill and nailed copies of it to the door of the parish church, the Moot Hall and Cross Hall. Copies were also pasted to the house doors of the local magistrates and on walls throughout the town:

Fellow Townsmen,
    We are strongly impressed with veneration for the genuine Principles of the constitution, and are no less loyal in our Attachment to the reigning family than you – but will you assemble to prove that loyalty which can never be suspected and give any indirect sanction to the infringement of your inestimably privilege – the Liberty of the Press?
    What is really good can never suffer by investigation, and they are the greatest enemies of the state, who would conceal from the public eyes its principles or prevent an Enquiry into the conduct of governors.
    Before you sanction a measure, which strikes at your dearest privileges – We address you in the language of Galgacus the intrepid Briton, when marching to resist the Power of Roman Despotism – Countrymen, look back on your Ancestors – look forward to your posterity.[25]

The handbill went on to urge the townsfolk to resist the government's Sedition Acts, the sole purpose of which, it was felt, would be to criminalise political reform and membership of reformist political clubs. The writer went on to state the act would expel the principles of John Locke whereby the people had the power to change the government as they saw fit for the happiness of all men, and would create a spirit of distrust and jealousy. The handbill concluded that the government's actions were an unconstitutional exercise of power and would turn neighbour against neighbour and friend against friend through a network of spies and informants.

Galgacus is recorded by Tacitus, and is the first Scot we have a name for – assuming he is not fiction – and is reported as giving a rousing speech to the Caledonian tribes before the Battle of Mons Graupius: the Caledonians could either die fighting to protect their ancient liberties or become slaves and allow the Romans to rule through oppression: the inference is clear here, and was obvious to the educated middle classes. William Pitt was the new Roman Emperor, seeking to destroy ancient liberties. For good reason, Jack Milnes – then in Paris – called his son Alfred Mirabeau Washing Milnes on his birth on 21 April in that city: Alfred the Great was seen as the 'godfather' of ancient British values and liberties that had been usurped by the Normans. Alfred and Galgacus were beacons of hope against new tyrants that a better world could be created by regaining lost liberties stolen by an aggressor from the people.

At this new display of hostility to the new laws and the open call for armed defiance, the magistrates redoubled their efforts. Thanks to an informer, the printer of the handbill and petition against the West Riding magistrates was arrested. He was John Hurst of Wakefield.[26] With Hurst arrested, all that remained was to arrest Rev. Johnstone and Robert Bakewell, who were still at large. The pair had dared to publicly ridicule the magistrates for calling a meeting whose sole purpose, they argued, was to interfere with freedom of expression: they were wanted men.[27]

General Loftus Anthony Tottenham led the local 'Church and King' mob, backed by Henry Peterson who we will meet again later.[28] In a blatant act of intimidation, the windows of Westgate Chapel parsonage were smashed: one can only imagine the terror that Martha Johnstone and her young children felt as the mob vented their anger at her husband. The chapel windows were smashed as were those of nearby homes of James and Richard Slater Milnes, in what could be described as Wakefield's 'Kristallnacht'. With a writ in hand, Pemberton Milnes aided by Tottenham and Peterson broke open the chapel doors during morning service and dragged Johnstone down the pulpit steps and out to the waiting magistrates, guarded by special constables. Bakewell tried to flee the town but was caught at Lupset Bar.[29] We can only imagine the fear of Apphia Bakewell, pregnant with her second child, and with a toddler at her heels, felt: we assume there was a tearful parting as Robert left his wife and unborn child – was he fleeing Yorkshire or leaving town on business? What must it have felt like to witness the doors of your place of worship broken open, and your minister taken away and friends arrested? Terror is a good word: daring to stand up to an unjust law placed your life in danger, as we shall see.

The Rev. Zouch recorded the arrests of those speaking out against the Acts in a letter to Earl Fitzwilliam from second week of June 1792.[30] Against the Rev. Johnstone and Bakewell, the magistrates recorded 'indictments for seditious libel re freedom of religion, equal rights, favouring invasion by France'.[31] Both men were taken to York Assizes and put on trial on 9 June 1793 for 'seditious libel in form of an address to the inhabitants of Wakefield'.[32]

As could be anticipated, the arrests in Wakefield aroused much local opposition: the magistrates declared that protest against the arrests was 'a riot', and the Rev. Zouch informed Earl Fitzwilliam that he had recourse to call out the Militia against 'riotous behaviour'. He added that when arrests were made in Sheffield for similar reasons to Wakefield, he had recourse to take the same action in order to 'keep the peace after inflammatory addresses' had been made against the seditious writing bill. Wanted by the bench in Sheffield for sedition were two men, one an engraver and the other a printer identified as 'Crome'. Zouch also expressed alarm at the Rev. Wyvill's continuing demands for reform and also the support given to the reformists by the Bishop of St Asaph.[33] The engraver was certainly the Unitarian David Martin, who was a member of the London Corresponding Society and its sister organisation in Sheffield and an avowed Jacobin. Francis Edmunds[34] of Worsborough estimated that the 'mob' that had assembled outside the Tontine Inn, Sheffield, where the magistrates sat, was several thousand strong. The 'mob' chanted slogans and waved placards, to object to the steps taken by the magistrates to prevent seditious meetings. The 'riot' was broken up by the Militia after the Riot Act was read and the crowd had not dispersed after an hour had passed. In their reports neither Zouch or Edmunds mention any acts of violence to warrant the reading of the Riot Act and calling out the Militia: we assume therefore that they overreacted when confronted by opposition to the state's plans to curtail freedom of speech and assembly. Edmunds noted – no doubt in direct response to the heavy-handed acts of the magistrates – that as 'the mob' dispersed, violence broke out across Sheffield with windows being smashed. Edmunds failed to understand that a good percentage of the population of Sheffield objected to the curtailment of freedom of expression, and failed to realise that his actions in breaking up the protest would beget violence. Edmunds called for aid from the Wakefield bench, requesting Bacon Frank and his 'kins man' Pemberton Milnes to attend.[35] Three days later, Zouch admitted that the garrison in Sheffield had instigated the rioting by goading the townsfolk with inflammatory addresses against reform.[36] Had the garrison been given orders to be provocative, in order to cause a riot so that the authorities could 'come down hard' on the radical groups in Sheffield? It does seem very likely indeed. A week after the arrests in Sheffield, the *Leeds Intelligencer* reported:

> Anonymous inflammatory writings were lately dispersed through the town of Wakefield; the constable and some gentlemen who were at the meeting there handed them up to the Chairman when being loudly called for to be read, they were heard with disdain. Enquiry, it is said, is making after the publisher . . . on Friday last a small parcel was brought by a post boy to one of the first Inns at Wakefield, addressed to a gentleman who usually dines at the ordinary there on the Market day – On opening it, there were found (curiously wrapped up) a number of inflammatory handbills, and an anonymous letter requesting the gentlemen would dispose of them amongst his acquaintance – the letter being read, and also one of the bills, there well all exhibited on the table after dinner and unanimously ordered to be burnt, which they immediately were, to the great pleasure of near twenty gentlemen who were then present.[37]

The suspect package was six copies of *The Rights of Man*.[38] Book-burnings marked a significant escalation of the campaign against reformist ideas. The only printer producing copies of *The Rights of Man* in Yorkshire was Joseph Gales in Sheffield who distributed them through his newspaper delivery network. Clearly the system that forced landlords to act as spies was working very well indeed. As the Crown had intended, radical activity rapidly dissipated in Leeds, Wakefield and Sheffield following the Seditious Meetings and Writings Act. Freedom of speech was 'all but dead' and every landlord in the country was now a government spy.[39] The Rev. Zouch congratulated himself and the government on the acts in a letter of bombastic Toryism to Earl Fitzwilliam dated 25 June.[40] Zouch congratulated himself that the resolutions across the West Riding were having a good effect in silencing the 'revolutionaries'.[41] Magistrates now advocated the formation of 'Loyalist Associations' to bolster the state and to encourage publicans to spy on their customers or else lose their licences. Judging by the number of loyalist declarations by the alehouse keepers themselves, this warning was taken very seriously. In Wakefield sixty publicans signed a solemn oath of loyalty to King and Constitution to seek out sedition.[42] Between May and September 1792, councils and boroughs across the country issued 386 loyal addresses saying they would do more to fight radicalism.[43] The Horbury Loyalist Association declared: 'the government of these realms, consisting of a King, Lords and Commons, in whom are combined the advantages of monarchy, aristocracy and democracy, is the most perfect form of all governments'.[44]

The vicar of Horbury, the Rev. Taylor, and the parish clerk William Rayner were at the forefront of crushing sedition and Jacobinism at home.[45] Besides attempting to disrupt the activities of the radical societies by clamping down on public houses, the loyalist associations answered the government's call to sniff out sedition, corresponding with Whitehall on cases which seemed to merit Crown intervention, but also prosecuting some themselves. The creation of associations to co-ordinate and finance private prosecutions was not new; similar societies had been formed throughout the eighteenth century, sometimes in response to royal proclamations. But their extension into the political sphere was new. 'The Friends of the Liberty of the Press', for example, claimed that such unauthorised sedition-hunting intruded upon private opinions and intimidated juries to acquiesce to the forces of reaction, thereby undermining any libertarian gains made by the Libel Act of 1792. The provincial press, in particular, was severely weakened, with the *Manchester Herald* and other radical newspapers in the Midlands and North succumbing to either prosecution or intimidation.[46]

# Chapter 5

# LOYALISM

Following the French victory over the army of George III's brother-in-law the Duke of Brunswick at the Battle of Valmy on 20 September 1792, a new wave of Gallic euphoria spread across the country: French freedom was extolled as being 'far superior' to British; toasts were raised to 'the Virtue of Revolutions'. In London two radical societies burnt the Duke of Brunswick in effigy. On 27 September the Manchester Constitutional Society, represented by Thomas Walker and Samuel Jackson, the Manchester Reformation Society, the Norwich Revolution Society, the Friends of the People and London Corresponding Society sent a message of congratulations to the French government.[1] From Newington Green on 31 October came a separate address in support of the Republic. The Sheffield Constitutional Society followed suit, as did the London Revolution Society on 5 December, and the Nottingham Constitutional Society and the Derby Constitutional Society a few days earlier at the end of November.[2] The emissary from Derby was Henry Redhead Yorke. He travelled to Paris in November 1792 and transitioned from Whig to Revolutionary and became a passionate abolitionist. In Paris he engaged with the exciting atmosphere of the revolution, attending the Convention and the trial of Louis XVI, and was accepted as a 'Citizen of the World' rather than having to conform to the exclusivity of 'Britishness'. His politics and cosmopolitanism were in direct conflict with the nationalistic politics of William Pitt and Edmund Burke in England. Yorke wrote his first radical pamphlet in Paris, *Reason urged against Precedent; A Letter to the People of Derby*, which was published on his return to England in February 1793 accompanied by John Frost who he had met whilst a member of the London Corresponding Society. The address was strongly radical and revolutionary in its language and promoted French humanitarian and universal ideology. Yorke would become one of the leading revolutionaries in England. For men like him and those who were excluded from 'Britishness' due to the illegality of their religion, Paris was a beacon of hope, and the gatherings of English exiles at White's Hotel in Paris offered a new vision for the world based on freedom, reason and tolerance.

Earl Fitzwilliam, who would shortly become the Lord Lieutenant of the West Riding, wrote to Zouch on 5 June that the reform societies in London, Sheffield, Manchester and Norwich were:

> hitherto contemptible, but they took a very different aspect when they were headed by a new Association, formed by some of the first men in the kingdom in point of rank, ability and activity—when members of Parliament began to tell the lowest orders of the people that they had rights of which they were bereaved by others; that to recover these rights they had only to collect together, and to unite; that if they were anxious to vindicate those rights they had the power of doing so, and to effect this, advocates and leaders were ready at their call . . . Now there is nothing but revolutions, and in that of France is an example of the turbulent and the factious instigating the numbers . . . to the subversion of the first principle of civil society . . . the protection of the individual against the multitude. . . . The French Revolutionists are just as anxious to bring into England their spirit of proselytism as they have been to carry it into every other part of Europe.[3]

In Sheffield, 5,000–6,000 supporters participated in a parade through the streets on 15 October in which a banner was displayed condemning Burke's contempt for popular radicalism and the government's prosecution of Paine. Tom's 'Truth' had become 'Libel' at the hands of the Crown, the banner declared, and British liberty was now in peril. It was a defiant assertion of popular rights in the face of government censure. On 27 November, to mark General Dumouriez's triumph in Belgium and the Netherlands, a procession marched through Sheffield. French republican banners were displayed, the tricolour cockade was distributed and the bells of the parish church rang out in support of the French Revolution.[4] Joseph Gales trumpeted 'The French by their arms have conquered tyrants and by Just laws, Liberty and reason will conquer the world'.[5] The Sheffield and Derby radicals, as well as the London Society for Constitutional Information, regretted their inability to actively participate in the defence of liberty in France, but declared that they would solemnly oppose the reactionary forces in Britain.[6]

If Pitt declared war, representatives of the Manchester Constitutional Society and the London Corresponding Society who met at Ambassador Chauvelin's house in London declared that anti-war addresses and protests would be forthcoming.[7] In Sheffield, the Rev. James Wilkinson opined that 'the late very alarming appearances and extravagant behaviour of the lower classes of people here by tumultuously expressing their joys on the success of the French Armies and their rich applause of French Principles'.[8] Magistrate Athorpe, having participated in the loyalist rioting in Birmingham, echoed similar sentiments 'to oppose every effort' made in the cause of reform.[9] Magistrate Charles Bowns of Pontefract was of similar mind, stating he was an 'avowed enemy to Republican and Levelling principles'.[10]

At the end of the month, Captain George Monro, who was spying on the English radicals in Paris, noted that the group at White's Hotel 'would stand at nothing to ruin their country'.[11] He was correct. The British Crown was now aware of the French plans and the threat from 'the enemy within'. Yet the plot spread further than Monro, nor for that matter William Pitt, could realise. Monro's reports in December accentuated the conspiratorial streak in British radical politics in France and confirmed in the mind of William Pitt that the group in Paris was an ultra-violent fringe in the radical underworld whose members had little sense of loyalty to their country. It is undeniable that the intermixing of British and Irish radicals in the French capital caused concern to the British Crown as it marked the beginning of an ultra-violent culture of more organised Irish resistance which in turn had influenced the British radical movement.

## Reeves' Association

In order to counteract the spread of Jacobin societies, the Crown had supported the creation of loyalist clubs across the country. A week before Pitt mobilised the Militia, John Reeves, a lawyer, former governor of Newfoundland and paymaster of the Westminster police magistrates, had announced the formation of a loyalist association to counteract the groundswell of sedition and encouraged like-minded souls to do the same. Within months, assisted by the government's press network, his call was answered by 1,500 local societies, creating a movement of prodigious proportions. Reeves campaigned against Jacobinism by founding at the Crown and Anchor tavern on 20 November 1792 the Association for Preserving Liberty and Property against Republicans and Levellers. Reeves was backed by Pitt and his government, who had conceived a programme of deliberate persecution of the voices of opposition.[12] This was to be achieved in three ways. In the first instance the loyalist associations sought to enforce public conformity to the campaign against republicanism by mobilising local authorities and employers against radical sympathisers, sometimes to the point of pressuring all local householders to declare their allegiance. This strategy was buttressed by a strict surveillance of taverns and alehouses, whose landlords were threatened with the loss of their licences if they permitted radical groups to meet on their premises.[13] The public, stirred by Reeves' populism for 'Church and King' and 'John Bull and England', was roused to opposition against political reform and 'the other' i.e., Unitarians, Jews, Catholics and the nascent trade unions. Reeves even declared that the King could rule without the Lords or Commons.[14]

This was a step too far for many, even loyalists, who sought to preserve the constitution from reform, and above all else to defend inequality of rank and religion and preserve wealth. Republicanism in the form of political reform, and Parliament freed from the shackles of aristocratic patronage, were seen as an existential threat to commerce and wealth accumulation and wealth inequality. The defence of wealth inequality and property was a key factor in attracting cross-party support for Reeves' ideals: both Whigs and Tories understood that broad ideas of liberty and equality were explosively incompatible with wealth accumulation. The rich 'bourgeois' had as much to lose from Jacobinism and reform as the aristocracy.[15] The spectre of 'levelling', as well as a 'fair day's wage for a fair day's work' was anathema to many. Charles James Fox denounced the Association's publications and claimed that had they been printed earlier in the century they would have been prosecuted as treasonable Jacobite tracts due to their advocacy of the divine right of kings. In a speech on 10 December 1795, Fox described the Association as a system designed to run the country through 'the infamy of spies and intrigues'. Reeves' project was preeminently a policing operation.

Magistrate Charles Bowns of Pontefract warned Earl Fitzwilliam and his fellow magistrates in December 1792 that:

> with respect to the state of the neighbourhood, we seem to be quiet and peaceable and everyone that I have heard speak of public affairs . . . think their ought to be a more equal representation in Parliament so that a reformation without a revolution, forms what I am able to judge from what I hear in this neighbourhood, seems to be a general wish. The Barnsley people made a collection of coals, and would have burnt Mr Paine in effigy, but were prevailed to desist by Mr Beckett who thought it more prudent to be quiet – At Leeds and Wakefield there has been public meetings where I hear resolutions have been entered into.[16]

In Leeds, a meeting was held on 26 December 1792 to form an association to defend the constitution and actively encouraged neighbour to spy on neighbour with the lure of reward:

> That a reward of TEN guineas be paid on conviction by the committee, to be appointed by this Association, for apprehending any person within this town and Neighbourhood, distributing or pasting up any papers, for speaking anything tending to encourage sedition and treasonable subversion of the Laws of this land ... it be earnestly recommended to all inn keepers and publicans within this Town and Neighbourhood, to discourage to the utmost of their power, any seditious meetings or inflammatory discourses at their respected houses.[17]

A similar group emerged in Dewsbury whose aim was 'in discouraging all seditious publications and endeavour to bring to justice the Authors, Printers and Publishers thereof'.[18] Sheffield followed suit in January 1793.[19]

The Church of England, jealously guarding its privilege as the national church, became the mouthpiece of government. The slave-owning Tory Rev. Richard Munkhouse, vicar of St John the Baptist, Wakefield, ranted:

> the general principles of the Gospel is in direct opposition to the systems of modern innovators. They will there learn, that God himself makes one man to differ from another; that the distinctions of high and low, rich and poor, are the appointments of divine Providence, and are made the sources of various duties ... The evangelical virtues of compassion, gratitude, and humility, can be practised only where there is a diversity of ranks; and a contentious and turbulent spirit can never be reconciled with the Gospel graces of gentleness, forbearance, and contentment.[20]

For Munkhouse, Burke and others wealth inequality, class distinction and lack of political representation were all by divine providence and society had reached a state of perfection and could not change. In Scotland, it was feared that the influx of French émigrés was an 'invading army' who would be 'provided with arms and ammunition by their British friends' and that the French had no need to land.[21] Anti-French and anti-reform hysteria was on the rise.

## Thomas Walker

For a while, members of the Manchester Constitutional Society were fairly successfully in persuading the local newspapers, the *Manchester Mercury* and the *Manchester Chronicle*, to publish their articles on parliamentary reform. However, by the summer of 1791, the editors of these two newspapers became much more reluctant to give the reformers publicity. Thomas Walker and his fellow radical Thomas Copper decided to edit their own newspaper, the *Manchester Herald*. A local firm, Faulkner & Birch, agreed to print their radical newspaper, and the first edition was published on 31 March 1792. Thomas Cooper was connected with the Jacobin Club in Paris, and had published his own reply to Burke's reflections on the revolution. He had been in Paris in July 1791, taking a highly visible and symbolic part in the procession on the Champ de Mars, carrying a bust of Algernon Sidney and accompanied by James Watt Jnr carrying the British flag.[22]

What happened next was perhaps predictable: Thomas Walker was to become the first victim of Reeves' Association. The 'Church and King Club of Manchester' gathered in St Ann's Square, to welcome the proclamation against seditious writings in December 1792. Peel and his allies viewed the ending of freedom of the press as a good thing, and welcomed the clampdown on opposition politics and reform. Those assembled to participate in the celebration of ending of free speech were driven into fury by addresses against reform, the radical press and hatred of all things Jacobin. The assembly became an armed mob, out quite literally to remove the 'fifth columnists' in their midst, with the most obvious target being Unitarians. The mob marched on Cross Street Unitarian Chapel, crying 'Down with the Rump' and 'Church and King'. The mob endeavoured to break down the doors: driven by a lust for destruction, unable to break in and to 'trash the place' using the modern vulgate, the mob tried to set fire to the chapel. Even after attacking Cross Street Chapel, the mob's bloodlust was still not satiated, and it made a similar attempt on Mosley Street Unitarian Chapel to destroy the 'nests of Jacobins and vipers'.

In a second night of violence, the mob turned their attention to Thomas Walker: his warehouse was firebombed and his home threatened. On a third and fourth night of rioting the premises of the *Manchester Herald* were broken open and the presses smashed. It was recorded at the time that magistrates and constables refused to act and indeed had connived in the riot! The Tory loyalists sought to destroy radicalism in Manchester. Scared for their lives, Birch and Falkner, the printers of the radical Manchester newspaper, left for America in the spring of 1793, and the last issue of the *Manchester Herald* appeared on 23 March 1793. As Thomas Walker pointed out, the leaders of the Manchester Constitutional Society 'preferred a voluntary exile to imprisonment'.[23] Thomas Cooper fled for his life.[24] This was state-sanctioned terror or at least, as in Birmingham, the Crown and its representatives the magistrates turned a very blind eye to mobs fighting for 'Church and King'. Yet those who objected to such actions were arrested! Justice and equality before the law no longer existed: terror against 'the other' had been in essence legalised.

## Burning Thomas Paine

It is undeniable that the noisy demonstrations by the reformist and Jacobin groups in support of the French Revolution and the ideals of Thomas Paine as well as their addresses of loyalty to the French government provoked an overwhelming conservative reaction. The target for the mob was 'the other'. Reeves' Association was the catalyst to a nationwide spate of public burnings.

Thomas Paine never advocated armed rebellion and insurrection in his writings, yet this is exactly what Edmund Burke read into them. Paine's publisher was arrested for sedition, Paine himself fled to France, and became a representative in the French National Assembly. For the loyalists this was a 'red rag to a bull': here was proof the English radicals sought revolution, and had contacts at the highest levels with the hated Jacobins. Paine was put on trial *in absentia* – it was a public event aimed at defaming all those who supported him. It was perhaps hoped it would intimidate the radicals into silence. The trial was finally held on 18 December 1792: the result was a foregone conclusion. Pitt's administration took the guilty verdict as a sign that further prosecutions for sedition were possible: in the 17 months following the trial, eleven publishers of *The Rights of Man* were prosecuted, receiving prison sentences of up to four years.[25] The trial also unleashed unprecedented acts of violence and public displays of loyalism: you either supported the mob or faced the consequences. *The Leeds Intelligencer* reported:

> The meeting at Halifax on the 22nd inst. Were unanimous in expressing their sincerest attachment to the King and Constitution – The Dissenters came forwards in the most handsome way, in particular the Rev. Mr Ralph and Mr Swaine, both of whom, in a very spirited and explicit manner declared their earnest loyalty and love for the great principles of the constitution, and added that they did not merely speak for their own sentiments, but the sentiments of every individual in their communion; the declarations of these gentlemen were received with the loudest applause![26]

In the wake of the Priestley riots and the firebombing of Cross Street and Moseley Street Unitarian Chapels in Manchester, the trustees of Northgate End Unitarian Chapel where the Rev. John Ralph was minister 1767–95, took no chances and backed the loyalist mob. So effective was government propaganda that religious dissent equalled political dissent and therefore Jacobinism, that a Mr Read, on behalf of the congregation at Mill Hill Unitarian Chapel, was forced to declare before Leeds Corporation that he and his fellow Dissenters were not traitors, but loyalists. The corporation felt that such a meeting and declaration was 'indispensable'.[27] This has undoubted parallels with what occurred in Halifax to the congregation at Northgate End: the threat of violence in both cases is obvious.

Henry Peterson, a wealthy Anglican Tory merchant living in Wakefield, at a meeting of the clergy and loyalists in the Moot Hall in Wakefield, declared:

> the deceptive, seditious doctrines which are propagated among us with such malicious industry that it is high time for every sober man and loyal subject to use his best endeavours to counteract this EVIL tendency by uniting heart and hand in support of our most excellent constitution of government in aiding and assisting the Civil Magistrates in the execution of the laws against all traitors, rebels and seditious persons who endeavour to or attempt to subvert the government.[28]

The declaration in support of King and Constitution set up in the Moot Hall attracted 1,660 people.[29] Henry Peterson, a native of Wakefield, had moved to America where he owned a slave-worked tobacco plantation. He exported slave-produced goods to Europe. With the American Revolution, he settled in Utrecht, until the creation of the Batavian Republic forced him to return to Yorkshire. He despised democracy, political reform and all those who were not 'Church and King'.[30] In his crusade against all things reformist, he was backed by John Naylor and his son Jeremiah Todd Naylor, who had gone from house to house for six days collecting 17,000 signatures to their resolutions to sniff out sedition, reporting to John Reeves that 'the friends of Tom Paine were crestfallen' at the strength of the support they received.[31] The Naylors had been supportive of reform, but the unfolding chaos in France resulting in their allegiance shifting to militant loyalism and rejection of their Unitarian faith. How many signatures were obtained under intimidation we cannot say, but it seems likely coercion was indeed used: refusing to sign marked one out immediately as a traitor, a target for the loyalist mob. Therefore, it took those of firm resolve not to sign and be stigmatised by the wider community. A reward of £20 was placed in the Wakefield bank for any person who provided information to the loyalists and magistrates about distributors of Paine's writings.[32]

Part of this public display of loyalism was an orgy of destruction and outpouring of hatred against 'the other' symbolised in the burning of effigies of Paine:

> On Thursday last, the inhabitants of Rawden, eager to shew their loyalty and great abhorrence of a levelling disposition burnt Tom Paine . . . after being hanged and shot they burnt him . . . on Thursday last upwards of five hundred of the inhabitants of Batley and Birstall assembled at Thomas Thompson's, the Black Bull Inn, in Birstall, and adjourned from thence to the church, where they came to several patriotic resolutions. 'God Save the King' accompanied on the organ was sung in the church and each stanza followed with three cheers, after which the company returned to the above inn, where an elegant entertainment was provided . . . the effigy of Tom Paine was carried through the town and afterwards destroyed by the populace . . . Paine's effigy was carried through all the streets of Wakefield on Monday morning last, and being hung upon a gallows out of the town, was next burnt in the Market place a little past two o'clock . . . 'God save the King' was incessantly repeated . . . at Barnsley, there was a procession of a great number of the inhabitants of the place, accompanying the effigy of Tom Paine; who was hanged on a pitch fork, held up by a stay-maker standing upon a butchers block, and afterwards burnt amidst the acclamations of an immense number of spectators. We are also favoured with accounts from Halifax, Rochdale, Baildon, Bramley, Heckmondwike and a multitude of other places where meetings have been held during the last then days for the purpose of the inhabitants declaring their loyalty.[33]

Effigies were also burnt in Leeds, Pontefract, Wetherby and Horsforth.[34] These burnings were a nationwide phenomenon: a mass outpouring of hatred for 'the other', resulting in vigilante violence at a minimum of 208 events and was a spectacle witnessed by hundreds of thousands of Englishmen and women. Even allowing for journalistic exaggeration, the numbers reported in the press are impressive: 5,000 in Marlborough; 3,000 in Leeds; 2,000 in Changford, Dukinfield and Nettlebed; 1,000 in Bridport and Croydon; 300 in the Hampshire village of Cosham, just outside Portsmouth. When we read the newspaper reports, very few give any figures at all, but of the thirteen reports that do, the average attendance at each burning was an average of 1,500 people per burning: this suggests that something like 302,432 people took part nationwide. It is, however, misleading to regard these events as 'spontaneous demonstrations of loyalty'. Such a spectacle took time to organise: the bonfire had to be built, the 'guy' made, the fireworks purchased, beer and food obtained: this all took time. These events – street theatre designed to bring a diverse community together to foster a sense of 'we are in this together' – were highly ritualised imitation trials with the punishment the loyalists felt Paine deserved being meted out, had he been present at his actual trial.[35] Taking part in these patriotic events, and joining loyalist clubs, for the participants, had wider social connotations. The carnival atmosphere of a burning would have been a welcome break from the 'everyday', and can be seen as a social event and not primarily ideological. The loyalists had a clear target for their persecution, and in expressing their anger, helped to foster a sense of community, and also localism. Every town and village was compelled through 'peer pressure' to burn an effigy and take part in 'this orgy of loyalism' in case they were seen as 'the enemy' and became a target of the mob. Such 'bonding activities' of mass participation is little different to the 'crowd' at a football or as Terry Pratchett calls in 'the shove': the attendees get subsumed into the single entity of the mob, the mob only dissipating when its anger has been quelled; the mob could not be controlled; the mob does not think other than to hate 'the other', being it an opposing football team, or those of different race, religion, gender etc, which we see writ large with the MAGA phenomenon in America or Brexit in the UK. The mob is dangerous: we wonder how much coercion the Rev. Ralph and his trustees at Northgate End were put under to back 'Church and King'? Mark Philip argues that the loyalists clearly intimidated many they canvassed to sign their petitions: this placed radicals and reformists on the defensive. Failure to sign such loyalist declarations shows to the world their 'disloyalty' and therefore their French and Painite leanings, and marked them out for vigilante retribution. We can also easily see how merchants and business owners could bully their workforce to support the burnings and tracts with the threat of unemployment: the face-to-face nature of the burnings and signing loyalist petitions made non-compliance no an option: the fear of immediate public denunciation as 'a traitor' no doubt terrified many moderate reformers into acquiesce.[36] The level of support for such petitions cannot therefore be used to judge public perceptions, despite some historians arguing that the state was indeed unified by an abhorrence of the events in France.[37]

The Jacobins were now the mortal enemies of 'Church and King'. By December 1792, the Prime Minister, William Pitt, was sufficiently concerned about the possibility of a revolutionary uprising in Britain that he recalled Parliament, called out the Militia and ordered the

Tower of London to be re-fortified.[38] The use of informers and spies as well as the mass-participatory loyalist associations of Reeves were for radicals a blight on the free-born Englishman, incompatible with his ability to exercise his supposedly inalienable rights and liberties. This was an attack against the constitution, but saying so openly would result in imprisonment. The presence of informers obliged community members to react and choose sides, turning communities and even families into divided battlegrounds. In the 1790s it was argued that the support afforded to spies by government and loyalist groups had tipped the balance in the spies' favour. In the words of a letter-writer to the *Morning Chronicle*, the employment of government spies had 'armed one portion of the community to beat down the other'.[39]

Chapter 6

# HENRY REDHEAD YORKE

In Paris Henry Redhead Yorke had socialised and discussed politics with the English exiles who gathered at White's Hotel, amongst whom were Thomas Paine, John Oswald, Sampson Perry, John Hurford Stone and his mistress Helen Marie Williams, Rev. William Jackson, Lord Edward Fitzgerald, William Duckett, Henry and John Sheares, Bernard MacSheehy and lastly Nicholas Madgett, who would all go onto endeavour to bring revolution to England and Ireland.[1] The activities at White's Hotel did not go unnoticed. Captain George Monro documented the activities of British radicals in Paris in late 1792 and early 1793 for the British Crown. He reported that 'The party of Conspirators have now formed themselves into a Society, the principles of which I have the honour of inclosing'.[2] On 21 December 1792 Monro wrote to Lord Grenville at the Foreign Office that the group York was part of were 'such that I am however sure they would, with the assistance of France, put anything in execution that could injure their country' adding that 'England ought to be on their guard against such parties'.[3]

Yorke was now a wanted man, but until he actually broke the law, the Crown could take no action against him. In company with John Frost, Yorke returned to London in February 1793, enthused by his experiences in France and desiring to 'export revolution'. After a public disagreement with John Frost in London, he headed to Derbyshire and joined the radical group in Sheffield, aligning himself with Joseph Gales and his sister Winifred. Henry became engaged to Gales' sister. Gales and Yorke worked tirelessly writing and printing reformist propaganda. He now began to advocate immediate parliamentary reform and the abolition of slavery.

In April, Yorke chaired a meeting in Sheffield to celebrate the acquittal of Thomas Bower on charges of seditious libel for selling copies of *The Rights of Man*.[4] That same month he declared from Sheffield that 'the voice of the great body of the people ought not to be smothered by the voice of a partial interest; but should be fairly and fully heard'. An informant for the Crown reported on 28 May 1793 that the Constitutional Society in Leeds had informed J. Adams, Secretary of the London Society for Constitutional Information, that according to the proposal of the Sheffield Society, headed by Henry Redhead Yorke, they were ready to act with other reform societies not only in England but also in Scotland. The spy added that the Leeds and Sheffield societies shared a similar political outlook, and advocated an annual Parliament, universal manhood suffrage and expressed a common opinion about the 'inappropriate and destructive war' then being fought and lost.[5] It seemed to the Crown that a vast wave was about to break: the reformist groups were now a clear and present danger to the government. The national convention – which had originated with a plea by Gales dated 16 January 1793 for co-ordinated national action for reform – had to be stopped and the leaders arrested. National petitions for reform were drafted to be sent to Parliament: that backed by the London Corresponding Society received 6,000 signatures, that from Norwich 3,700, whilst those from Nottingham and Sheffield were rejected by Parliament due to their language and disrespectful tone. Charles Grey led a motion in Parliament for reform on 7 May: he lost 282 votes to 41.[6] The chance of reform through petition had passed, and the Crown began arresting leading radicals.

Due to his outspoken criticism, Yorke was put on trial in June 1793 on a charge of conspiracy against the government. The jury acquitted him. Joseph Gales noted Yorke was 'a strong and determined enemy' of the government.[7] Undaunted, he plunged back into radical politics, supporting the Derby Constitutional Society which declared:

> That all true Government is instituted for the General good; is legalised by the general will; and all its actions are, or ought to be, directed for the general happiness and prosperity of all honest citizens.
>
> That we feel too much not to believe, that deep and alarming abuses exist in the British Government ... We are certain our present heavy burthens are owing, in a great measure, to cruel and impolitic wars, and therefore we will do all on our part, as peaceable citizens, who have the good of the community at heart, to enlighten each other, and protest against them ... We think it a deplorable case when the poor must support a corruption which is calculated to oppress them; when the labourer must give his money to afford the means of preventing him having a voice in its disposal ... we view, with the most poignant sorrow, a part of the people deluded by a cry of the Constitution and Church

in danger, fighting with the weapons of savages, under the banners of prejudice, against those who have their true interest at heart;—we see with equal sensibility the present outcry against reforms, and a cruel proclamation (tending to cramp the liberty of the press, and discredit the true friends of the people) receiving the support of numbers of our countrymen;—we see the continuation of oppressive game laws and destructive monopolies;—we see the education and comfort of the poor neglected, notwithstanding the enormous weight of the poor rates . . . the present outcry against reforms and improvements is inhuman and criminal. But we hope our condition will be speedily improved, and to obtain so desirable a good is the object of our present Association; a union founded on principles of benevolence and humanity; disclaiming all connection with riot and disorder, but firm in our purpose, and warm in our affections for liberty.[8]

A stark warning emanated from Derby in July, again from the pen of Yorke:

Are we in England?—Have our forefathers fought, and bled, and conquered for liberty?—And did not they think that the fruits of their patriotism would be more abundant in peace, plenty, and happiness?— Are we always to stand still or go backwards?—Are our burthens to be as heavy as the most enslaved people?—Is the condition of the poor never to be improved? We invite the friends of freedom throughout Great Britain to form similar Societies, and to act with unanimity and firmness, till the people be too wise to be imposed upon; and their influence in the government be commensurate with their dignity and importance.[9]

The threat was obvious and did not go unnoticed.

## The First Arrests are Made

In the unsettled circumstances of the time, Pitt was no longer content to address radicalism as merely a political or ideological issue. Instead, in print, pamphlet, sermon and loyalist address, the Crown and its sycophants portrayed radicalism as an existential threat to national security, unworthy of a place in political and civil society. It had to be exterminated: a war had to be won, and 'fifth columnists' at home had to be gaoled.

On 12 September 1793 Rev. Thomas Fisher Palmer, Unitarian minister in Dundee and pro-reform agitator, was arrested and charged with writing a seditious pamphlet, the 'Dundee Address to the Friends of Liberty'. The authorities claimed that Palmer was guilty of 'writing or printing seditious or inflammatory writing, calculated to produce a spirit of discontent in the minds of the people against the present happy constitution and government of this country, and to rouse them up to acts of outrage and violence'. Thomas Muir had ill-advisedly returned from exile in Paris whence he had fled earlier in the year after the first Convention of the Scottish Friends of the People – which had met in Edinburgh on 11 December 1792 – had been quashed by Lord Dundas. Muir was arrested for treason and put on trial. With news of the arrests becoming public, a demonstration gathered outside Joseph Gales' house in Sheffield: the mob was accompanied by a recruiting party with drums and fifes. Musket shots were fired outside the house. These drew perhaps 500 Sheffield radicals to the scene, who sang to the tune of the national anthem 'God Save Great Thomas Paine', and whose weight of numbers forced the 'Church and King' mob to leave.[10]

Despite the arrest of Muir and Palmer, at the end of 1793 Yorke was to travel to Edinburgh where a National Convention of British Reformers assembled. He had been elected to be delegate for the Sheffield Constitutional Society, and was to attend with the delegate from the Leeds Constitutional Society, 'Citizen' Matthew Campbell Brown. On 1 November Brown declared:

> It appears to me, that if the societies do not become more active and more united in their efforts in time to come, what they have done hitherto will be rendered useless, and arbitrary power will trample on all that is dear and valuable to men . . . incompatible with a free constitution as fire and water . . . I am staunch democrat and speak my mind freely . . . we are both strenuous to support and forward the cause of freedom.[11]

Even before the convention met, Brown was a wanted man both locally and nationally: he was editor of the militantly Jacobin *Sheffield Patriot* newspaper, owned and printed by Joseph Gales and Rev. Benjamin Naylor. He was secretary to the Sheffield Constitutional Society, an actor by trade and something of a spendthrift, having squandered his Irish wife's substantial dowry. Placed in debtors' gaol, he was released by a coterie of Sheffield radicals.[12] Yorke failed to attend due to illness: this saved him from imprisonment when those attending the convention were arrested. Browne became the delegate for both Leeds and Sheffield, and Yorke's place was taken by Charles Sinclair from the Edinburgh Constitutional Society: he turned king's evidence to avoid imprisonment, incriminating his fellow reformers to 'save his own neck'. The two London delegates were Joseph Gerrald and Maurice Margarot. The meeting declared itself a British Convention and appointed a secret committee to act in case of emergency.

The authorities broke up the meeting and put Gerrald and Margarot and the Scottish secretary William Skirving under arrest. Margarot was accompanied to his trial in early 1794 by a procession holding a 'tree of liberty' in the shape of a letter M above his head. He was sentenced to 14 years' transportation and Gerrald received the same sentence a month later. Matthew Campbell Brown was arrested for high treason.

At his trial, the prosecutor called Palmer 'the most determined rebel in Scotland' and he was found guilty and sentenced to seven years' transportation, as were Thomas Muir and William Skirving. The men were placed aboard prison hulks on the Thames. They were to be transported to Australia, their only crime being the desire to introduce universal suffrage. Radicals in the House of Commons immediately began a campaign to save the men now being described as the Scottish Martyrs. On 24 February MP Richard Sheridan presented a petition to Parliament that described the men's treatment as 'illegal, unjust, oppressive and unconstitutional'. In defence of the accused, Charles James Fox pointed out in a passionate speech to the House that Palmer had done 'no more than what had done by William Pitt and the Duke of Richmond' when they had campaigned for parliamentary reform. Attempts to stop the men being transported failed: the Crown wanted to make examples of these men. On 2 May 1794, the *Surprise* left Portsmouth and began her 13,000-mile journey to Botany Bay.

## Sheffield Climax

Despite the Crown's best efforts to silence the voice of the people, it drove Yorke to a new level of fury against it. In London, John Horn Tooke presented a stark picture to radicals: 'we must now choose at one either liberty or slavery for ourselves and our posterity'.[13] Tooke's protégé John Thelwall, an extraordinary orator, now stepped onto the scene and along with Fox, Grey and Sheridan began a campaign to convince the Crown of the illegality of the sentences handed out to Palmer and others. In response the Crown believed the country to be at a tipping point and authorised the formation of volunteer corps to guard against French invasion and also from reformist ideals. For more on the Volunteers, see the author's forthcoming volume on the subject, also to be published by Frontline.

Yorke's fiery rhetoric now became the focus of attention in Yorkshire. A friend of Thomas Walker – he had appeared as a witness at his trial – he wrote and published at New Year 1794 *Thoughts on Civil Government: Addressed to the Disfranchised Citizens of Sheffield*. From the first lines it assumed an audience rather than a readership:

As a Man, I rejoice that I have lived to be a witness of these times, which seem, to me, peculiarly marked out by the finger of God, as promotive of the happiness and improvement of my Fellow-Creatures. As a CITIZEN, I glory to see the insolent and rapacious dominion of Kings about to be supplanted by the mild rule of Laws, and that mass of Disfranchised Human beings, with whom I am associated, about to be protected by Equal Laws, the result of the will of all.

PEOPLE OF SHEFFIELD, to you I address myself because I know your virtues, your constancy, your unshaken firmness and integrity. You hate Tyrants, because you love Justice; you adore Liberty, because you cultivate Reason: Hearken then to one of yourselves, who, knowing that he is addressing Men, who are too wise to be flattered, and too well informed to be alarmed – who have numberless wrongs to avenge, and numberless rights to regain . . . The foundations of all human societies are laid in Justice; no pretended arguments of political expediency ought to be allowed to shake its immutable and eternal principles. Its perversion and abuse have cajoled men into servitude; they have been excluded from a participation in the common interests of their country, although they are sure of feeling its common misfortunes . . . Citizens! the day of account and retribution is at hand. Then will the People be called upon to exert all the severe energy of Justice; then will they be called upon to practise those lessons which History and Patriotism have been long preparing for them. They cannot, therefore, be too deeply rooted in their minds. Let Despots calculate on the consequences. If, then, our principles be just, their efforts are never to be feared.[14]

Like the words of Mirabeau and Desmoulins, these were not intended for the page: this was the ardent, forthright speech of a skilled orator. Whilst in Paris, Yorke had clearly imbibed the form and language of Revolutionary speechmaking, shaped by the oratory of Mirabeau and Robespierre: the tract is a fine example of the breast-beating, sob-provoking declamations then in vogue in Paris. Yorke, throughout his radical writing and speeches, took command of the theatre of eloquence, deploying 'virtue militant', adding in for good measure a sense of patriotic martyrdom. The threat was clear: working men wanted their voice heard, and would fight to be heard, even if it meant armed insurrection.

In order to build on the groundswell of protest against the arrests in Scotland, a mass open-air meeting was held on 28 February on open ground on West Street. Yorke was to the fore and did not hold back from censuring the government, declaring the national fast day a 'solemn prostitution of religion'. Building on Thelwall's dystopian vision which prophesied that barracks would be built in every town and village manned by Hessian or Hanoverian mercenaries to enslave the people.[15] Yorke, with arm outstretched pointing to the recently completed Sheffield barracks, declared to the thousands listening to him, that the Crown would house mercenaries there who would 'massacre the people'. In drawing to a close, Yorke reminded the assembled crowd of the fate of Thomas Muir, Palmer, Skirving and Margarot, who he called the 'Scottish Martyrs!' as an example of the way in which the Crown acted in arbitrary and unjust ways. The 'take-home' message was that the people had to arm themselves should the government endeavour to curtail their freedom and turn foreign troops on them. The speech drew largely from Desmoulins' famous speech of 1789.

Gales and Yorke began 'ramping up the pressure' in March and April, distributing handbills across the West Riding. One of these declared:

> You have minds that should be instructed, as well as bodies that should be provided with food and cloaths . . . Those men, whose duty it is to make your situation as easy and comfortable as your lifes of care and toil will allow of, endeavour to prevent you from enjoying your RIGHTS as Men, as Citizens, and having helped to bring you into your present oppressed state, upbraid you in your wretchedness – call you 'Low Bred – A vile herd – A Swinish Multitude' . . . Fellow MEN! Respect yourselves – vindicate your own dignity – You are rational Beings . . . you have rights . . . the constitution of your Government allows you to express your grievances, and claims redress – Do this, and enjoy all that happiness which is due.[16]

Buoyed by their success, Gales and Yorke published their radical address to Sheffield on 1 April 1794:

> 1st. That the people being the true and only source of government, the freedom of speaking and writing upon any subject, cannot be denied to the members of a free government, without offering the grossest insult to the majesty of the people. 2d. That, therefore the condemnation of citizens Muir, Palmer, Skirving, Margarot, and Gerrald to transportation, for exposing the corruptions of the British government, was an act better suited to the maxims of a despotic than a free government. 3rd. That the Address which has now been read, be presented to the king, in behalf of the above persecuted patriots. 4th. That in every country where the people have no share in their government, taxation is tyranny. 5th. That therefore a government is tyrannical or free, in proportion as the people are equally or unequally represented. 6th. Convinced of this truth, it is the opinion of this meeting that the people ought to demand

as a right, and not petition as a favour, for universal representation. 7th. That therefore we will petition the House of Commons no more on this subject. 8th. That the committee of the Sheffield Constitutional Society be desired to see that the above resolutions be carried into effect; and that they prepare an address to the British nation, explanatory of the motives which have induced its meeting to adopt the resolution of no more petitioning the House of Commons on the subject of reform.[17]

Gales and Yorke surely must have known they were 'skating on thin ice' and would likely become targets for arrest; despite this, the pair organised another open-air meeting on Castle Hill, Sheffield for 'the Friends of Justice, Liberty and Humanity' on Monday 7 April 1794. Contemporary reports put attendance at 10,000–20,000 but that number may have been inflated by Gales and his newspaper in order to enhance the political importance and impact of the Sheffield group. Ever the skilled orator, Yorke boldly declared in an impassioned speech:

Fellow Citizens, the day has at length arrived . . . the energy of Englishmen will no longer endure the strange uproar of injustice. I trust they will demand the annihilation of all corruptions and abuses and a restitution of the original rights of human nature . . . . the Machine of State should be guided by the polar star of reason alone, which is never seen but when the Majesty of the People is resplendent.

Citizens! I repeat my former assertion. Go on as you hitherto have done in the culture of reason. Disseminate through the whole of your country, that knowledge which is so necessary to Man's happiness, and which you have yourself acquired. Teach your children, and your countrymen, the sacred lesson of virtue, which are the foundations of all human polity. Teach them to respect themselves, and to love their country. Teach them to do unto all men, as they would that they should do unto them, and their love shall not be confined to their country, but to the whole human race. When such a revolution of sentiment, shall have dispersed the mists of prejudice; when by the incessant thundering's from the press, the meanest cottage of our country shall be enlightened, and the sun of Reason shall shine in its fullest meridian over us . . . government is tyrannical or free in proportion as the people are equally or unequally represented . . . the people ought to demand as a RIGHT and not petition as a favour for universal representation.[18]

Yorke's speech was met with rapturous applause: 'virtue militant' was set to triumph over 'Church and King'. At the conclusion of the meeting 'when Yorke got into the Coach, the horses were taken out and the people drew him through most of the public streets in Sheffield amid the acclaim of thousands'.[19]

The Sheffield magistrate the Rev. James Wilkinson declared the meeting seditious and ordered the ringleaders arrested.[20] Knowing that he was a wanted man, Gales produced two handbills: *National Debt* was an attack on borrowing for the purpose of war rather than public benefit, a theme taken from *The Rights of Man*, while in *To poor and labouring men* Gales bemoaned the fact that education was for the rich elites and not the poor man, and encouraged the working man to demand political representation and a reformed parliament.[21] Gales' demands may seem innocuous to us today: we have the right to vote, we have free compulsory education to the age of 16. In 1794 only the elite had the vote – perhaps 250,000 voters from a population of three million – and only the rich could afford education. Demanding radical social change was treason, and the Crown wanted to crush any hint of social and political reform to keep 'the plebs in their place' by arresting all those they considered a danger to the Crown, Church and constitution.

Chapter 7

# THE NET CLOSES IN

At the very moment that Yorke was whipping up support in Sheffield, the Crown uncovered links between British radical groups and a planned French invasion of Ireland and England which implicated an Irish priest called Richard Ferris, an Irish Presbyterian minister by the name of William Jackson, and three Unitarians: Benjamin Vaughan MP, and brothers William and John Hurford Stone. In his own lifetime, John Stone was considered highly intelligent and cultured. His Unitarianism had evolved into the Deism of Paine and he lived in an open relationship with Helen Maria Williams and his wife. In October 1790 he presided at a dinner given by the Society of Friends of the Revolution to a French deputation from Nantes. In September 1792, he had been in Paris and presided at a dinner of British residents at White's Hotel to celebrate French victories. Stone was arrested, together with his wife Rachel Coope and his mistress, under the decree of 9 October 1793, but they were released on 30 October. Stone immediately plunged back into politics: a week later he was in London talking to radical groups.[1] He had written to now 'Citizen' Rev. Dr Joseph Priestley in March 1790 forecasting that he would live to see 'the Empire of falsehood, religious and political, overthrown and the world free and happy'.[2] With the arrest of Jackson, the Crown now had hard evidence that reformist groups were planning to overthrow the state.[3] In response it embarked on a campaign of repression: all radicals and reformists were to be rounded up.

At 6.30 in the morning on Monday 12 May 1794, Thomas Hardy, the secretary of the London Corresponding Society, and Daniel Adams, the secretary of the Society for Constitutional Information, were arrested in their respective homes and was later charged with treasonous practices. Thomas Walker in Manchester was also arrested along with the leadership of both national bodies and regional affiliated societies. As could be judged by the fate of Thomas Hardy, Thomas Fisher Palmer and others, the Crown wanted Gales and Yorke 'dead or alive'.

Following the arrests in London, the Crown formed two secret committees to study the papers they had seized from the radicals' houses. After the first committee reported its findings, the government introduced a bill to the House of Commons to suspend habeas corpus; thus, those arrested could be held without bail or charge until February 1795. The Secret Committee furthermore asserted that on the evidence they had uncovered, the radical societies had been planning at least to 'over-awe' the King and Parliament by the show of 'a great Body of the People' and establish a French-style republic. The Crown, fearing a revolution, redoubled its efforts to find proof.

The Crown's fears that radical groups were preparing for an uprising seemed to be proven when a spy identified as 'D' reported that pikes were being made in Birmingham to arm the London Corresponding Society and its affiliated branches.[4] A week later another spy reported that the Sheffield Constitutional Society had armed themselves with pikes and spears.[5] With 'evidence' to hand of the reformist groups being a front for armed insurrectionists, the Rev. James Wilkinson ordered arrests to be made and wrote to the Home Office gleefully with his news. He had found the evidence the Crown was looking for to charge Tooke, Hardy, Thelwall and the others with treason for aiding and abetting France.[6] But the true extent to which the English radical societies were arming themselves to aid the French has been an unanswerable question since 1794.

Blacksmiths and carpenters in Sheffield were now wanted men: these men, the Crown argued, must have made the pikes, and therefore were guilty of arming the rebellion. Wilkinson managed an extensive spy network, which reported to him that Frederick Jackson, an iron founder, had been observed to be grinding spear heads. Another witness, William Greene, an employee of Jackson, reported under cross-examination, that he had spent '2 days grinding 12 dozen or more spear heads, which were delivered to the lodgings of George Hill and the aforementioned Jackson'.[7] Were these for self-defence, as Winifred Gales would later argue, or for the offensive in a uprising planned by the French secret service?[8] The Home Office was informed that the Sheffield Constitutional Society had armed themselves with pikes and spears.[9] Another spy reported that pikes were being made in Birmingham to arm the London Corresponding Society.[10] In Hampshire Josiah Webb of Pamber, noted as being 'a dissenter and a Francophile with 3 brothers in London whom he visits', was arrested for the illegal manufacture of weapons. An informant reported 'thousands of pike handles have been made by Josiah and conveyed to Newbury in George Webb's waggons, and from thence to London'.[11] North of the border in Scotland the 'Pike Plot' (a plan to stage a coup in Edinburgh as the start of a general insurrection) was uncovered and its architect, Robert Watt (a former government spy), was hanged and suffered the ignominy of post-mortem decapitation after twelve pike heads were discovered in his house. His alleged co-conspirator David Downie was tried but was pardoned.[12] The authorities believed they had nipped revolution in the bud.

Wilkinson requested the Secret Committee at the Home Office to arrest Joseph Gales, Henry Redhead Yorke, Robert Moody, William Camage, William Moult, Gale's journeyman Davidson and a man known as Broomhead for high treason. Gales decided to flee the country as ever since he acclaimed the victory of 'our French brethren over despots and despotism' in 1792 he was aware that he would not receive a fair trial. Gales addressed Sheffield, invoking the spectre of patriotic martyrdom: '. . . could my imprisonment or even death serve the cause I have espoused – the cause of peace, liberty and justice – it would be cowardice to fly from it'.[13] Yorke, following Gales' example, also fled Sheffield.

In response to Wilkinson's demands, the Home Office granted warrants of arrest to William Ross and George Higgins, King's Messengers, authorising and requiring them to find and arrest Joseph Gales for 'treasonable practices' and 'to bring him and all his papers for examination according to law'.[14] Soldiers, special constables and the magistrates began a manhunt to arrest 'the traitors'.

Early on 21 May George Higgins and William Ross, having received warrants to arrest Joseph Gales and others, went to Dinnington Hall, the home of Colonel Robert Athorpe, acting magistrate for the West Riding. They eventually found him in Pontefract, and all three rode immediately to Sheffield. Reaching there in the morning, they had a meeting with Wilkinson, and when the mail coach arrived they learned of the arrest of several other suspects. At midnight they received a note from a Mr Foljambe that Gales was staying with William Moult[15] at his home about 10 miles from Sheffield. Ross and Athorpe and others arrived at Moult's house between 3.00 and 4.00 in the morning but could not find Gale 'after conducting the search of utmost delicacy'. Moult had written attacks on the government under an assumed name: he was an associate of Gale and believed in the ideals of the French Revolution. Indeed, so disgusted was he at the magistrates basically breaking into his house, Moult gave the magistrates 'a piece of his mind', to use Yorkshire language. King's Messenger Ross reported to Evan Nepean that it was:

> unfortunate that Moult is a high minded and avowed friend to favour, as he calls it of Liberty; declared his attachment to Gales, declared his approbation at the attempt made by the government to search the few [illegible]. He speaks of Liberty belonging to all Englishmen. Says he should sell his estates and soon depart for another Country. He betrayed symptoms of fear on our approach. We afterwards learnt that this Moult has been at Gales House, writing subjects for the press and has constantly written attacks upon government under feint names such as Aristotle.[16]

He too was arrested for high treason.

By midday, Athorpe was certain that Gales had made good his escape, as had Henry Redhead Yorke and Davidson.[17] Gales was thought to be in Tickhill, according to Edward Miller, the organist of Doncaster Parish Church. Miller furthermore informed the Secret Committee at the Home Office that as a true 'Church and King' man he had organised a loyalist meeting in Doncaster 'to detect the disaffected and enlighten the ignorant' and had been applauded for taking the initiative. He believed that he could have had Gales arrested but lamented that the magistrate's opinion was such that the information against him had not yet justified a warrant.[18] Once the warrant was issued, the suspected safe house was raided, but Gales was nowhere to be found. The Rev. Wilkinson opined that none of the magistrates had warrants to seize Gales and Yorke, only the King's Messengers could do so, and if he had the power of arrest, he could have arrested Gales before he fled.[19]

The King's Messengers, on advice from 'the beak', looked for other conspirators. Wilkinson identified these men to be William Camage, William Broomhead and Robert Moody. As Higgins and Ross didn't trust the town constables, they asked Athorpe and the Rev. James Wilkinson to swear in eight or nine respectable inhabitants as special constables. The moves against Gales and Yorke did not go unnoticed and 'a mob gathered in the town centre' around midday 'amongst them the friends of the party' i.e., the Sheffield Constitutional Society, Wilkinson lamented. The King's Messengers and the magistrates, having missed Gales, were 'determined to make arrangements for attack on all their houses with the same time' to ensure they arrested Broomhead and others. At 06:00 the following day:

We sallied forth. Mr Higgins commanding William Needham, Thomas Matthews, John Wilkinson and William Thomas all assailed to arrest Camage – William Ross commanded Joseph Sergeant, Josh Hicliffe, William Cundle and William Wheeler for Broomhead. Mr Athorpe commanded Samuel Hall, John Staniland, and James Eyre for Moody.

At 7 o'clock we took all the premises and thankfully found them to be in. We ordered immediately carriages for their departure. We are particularly indebted to Captain Birch of the 16th Dragoons whose indefatigable zeale to prosecute our object does him infinite credit and provided us 12 light horse to conduct the prisoners to the seat of the Robert Athorpe Esq 15 miles distant. We got them clear of the area before 8 o'clock tho the mob got wind of us and assembled in great numbers.[20]

Unsurprisingly, a large crowd had assembled outside the Tontine Inn protesting at the arrests and Athorpe feared they would break in and snatch away his prisoners.[21] Higgins and Ross were informed by a Mr Brookfield that Davidson, Gales' journeyman printer, who had apparently offered to sell pikes to the London Corresponding Society, 'might be hiding in Gales' house'. Ross reported that 'a mob which had gathered in great numbers' blocked the magistrate's way to Gales' house. To gain entry magistrates Athorpe and Rev. Wilkinson ordered the street cleared by the 16th Light Dragoons. Once this was done, the house was ransacked to search for incriminating papers.[22] Rather than seditious papers, according to a third party a cache of spears, pikes and caltrops 'to be thrown in the lane to lame the horses' were found in the house. One thankful loyalist, who believed full well that an armed rebellion had been planned and that the good Rev. Wilkinson had averted disaster, wrote 'this is a most horrid conspiracy against both church and state, under the pretence of reform . . . it is a mercy the plot is discovered'.[23] The loyalists congratulated themselves that the rebels had been foiled and that they could 'sleep safely in their beds'.

Recovered from Gales' house was an invoice for 500 copies of *Locke on Government* for the sum of £9.[24] Locke we recall was a seventeenth-philosopher who advocated 'the right of revolution', which was used as a basis for the Glorious Revolution of 1688, if the people felt that the government was not defending their natural rights. It was this argument that Rev. Dr Price had advocated in the 1780s and had been advanced by Jean Paul Marat in his seminal text *Chains of Slavery* a decade earlier. Locke's writings were considered at the time to be as dangerous as those of Thomas Paine. Quite clearly the government had no intention of allowing the middling sorts and working class to discover they had as much right to overthrow the monarchy and government as the men of 1688, of 1775 in America or 1789 in France. Democracy, freedom, reason and tolerance had to be stopped, and William Pitt threw the weight of government behind his ambition to stop reform, which became the de facto political aim of the Tory party for the next 40 years.

In returning to Sheffield in 1794, at some stage during the day, two more prisoners were brought in by the Rev. Wilkinson, George Wideson/Widdison and Henry Hill.[25] Henry Dundas signed the latter pair's arrest warrants on 21 June for 'treasonable practises'.[26] The Rev. Wilkinson examined men identified as Widdison and Hill, both named as members of the Sheffield Constitutional Society, who had been arrested but not charged. Widdison confessed that had made pikes, but refused to say how many, but did reveal that he had sold twelve to a man identified as 'Booth'. Wilkinson was convinced that 'Booth' was none other than Joseph Gales, and demanded that Widdison confirm this. Widdison refused to do so under further cross-examination by the priest, telling Wilkinson 'You better go ask Booth'. Wilkinson clearly was clearly trying to 'fit up' Joseph Gales![27]

The next man interrogated was Hill, who admitted to buying a pike for his own defence, declaring he had the right to own such a weapon. Wilkinson, displaying his trademark disdain and hatred of political reform, caustically remarked 'he was one of the society & held that the people have a right universal [illegible] in electing members for the commons house of Parliament'.[28]

Athorpe was a worried man. He already held four men in Sheffield Barracks and requested that they be 'escorted to London without delay as their maintenance in custody without evidence or charge was inflaming the local seditious spirit'.[29] Imagine being arrested for believing all people had the same universal human rights! Yet History would have us believe, that William Pitt was a great man 'who saved the nation':[30] but from what? The answer is democracy.

Once in London, under examination by Evan Nepean, Robert Moody confessed that the Sheffield Constitutional Society had been making arms 'for defence in case of molestation at their meetings or where force may be needed to achieve a reformation'.[31] The Crown had at long last uncovered the true nature of the insurrectionary threat that the country faced from the reformist societies, or at least so they thought.

Chapter 8

# I ARREST YOU FOR
# TREASON!

Despite key members being arrested, the Sheffield Constitutional Society was not cowed into submission. The Rev. Montgomery was still in Sheffield and was still an avowed friend of reform – so too Winifred and Sarah Gales. Joseph Gales wrote a farewell address, which was published on 22 June: he denied the charges levelled against him and that he was planning a revolution. He fled to Germany, his passage paid for by Samuel Shore. In 1795, he travelled to Philadelphia, Pennsylvania, where he worked as a printer, bookkeeper and as a journalist covering the United States Congress. He then established the *Independent Gazetteer* newspaper. Having moved to Raleigh, North Carolina, in October 1799 he published the first issue of his *Raleigh Register*. This Whig-supporting paper was influential throughout the state for the next 60 years. He died in 1841 and is buried in Raleigh's City Cemetery.

With her husband en route to Germany, the undaunted Winifred Gales published the last edition of the *Sheffield Register* with Montgomery's help on 24 June. As soon as the paper hit the streets, she too left Sheffield for Germany, having sold the business a few days earlier to James Montgomery and Rev. Naylor. Her last publication read:

Those of our members who apprehended, by what appear to us a groundless alarm of government, might have escaped if they had not believed themselves to be innocent of the breach of any existing law ... this society continues to believe a radical reform would be best effected by universal suffrage and annual parliaments ... well-meaning but mistaken Britons ... recollect that a nation having once got its liberties in view, will never lose sight of them till they are obtained ... by the dogma of the Bayonet it was found impossible to subdue the spirit of America, or even Belgia, by what means do you intend to enslave opinion in BRITAIN?[1]

How right Winifred Gales was! The working man never gave up on his dream of the vote, nor later would the Suffragettes. They had a goal in sight, and were determined to achieve it, regardless of the 'slings and arrows of outrageous fortune' the Crown would throw at them. The idea of 'one man one vote' could never be crushed, nor could the ideals of the French Revolution as articulated by Thomas Paine.

Yorke, like Gales, fled Sheffield. He was thought to be hiding in the home of the Manchester radical Thomas Walker. The Rev. James Wilkinson informed Henry Dundas MP on 13 June that 'Yorke, the runaway black demagogue' was likely in Manchester with Mrs Henstock 'his natural mother'.[2]

At no stage had Henry Redhead Yorke's ethnicity been commented upon prior to this letter: the radicals in Sheffield conceived a different form of Britishness to the Tories. Wilkinson supported a Protestant – i.e., Anglican – white, slave-owning, exclusionary vision of it. The radicals, being anti-slavery, embraced a diversity of religion and ethnicity. Yorke had declared that exclusive concepts of Britishness were outmoded, and that the minority had no right to rule the majority or make slaves of other human beings. Wilkinson's response to Joseph Gales and Yorke is remarkable: Gales, a white, middle-class Unitarian is never slandered for his religious beliefs, yet Yorke, being a middle-class, black Unitarian is seen as 'degenerate' and 'black', as if somehow the very notion of him being black explains his politics as he 'not like us'. Wilkinson had no need at all to mention Yorke's skin colour, yet he did. Wilkinson is the only person involved in the whole sorry affair who was overtly racist: as a man of God, he championed the right of the rich to treat the poor as slaves, supported the institution of slavery, was disgusted by the ideas of democracy and that all people were equal, and loathed any suggestion of religious tolerance. Above all, he was a man who could not conceive of anyone apart from a white Anglican taking part in society. Wilkinson, who is honoured to this day in Sheffield Cathedral, was not just a man of his times – I say again that no one else in the arrest or trial of Yorke made racist comments – he was a racist.

Yorke's mother, Sarah Anne Bullock, had married Edward Henstock, a linen draper, in 1787. His son or nephew, another Edward who was working in Wakefield at the end of the 1770s as he had been taken on an apprenticeship with Thomas Smith in 1776. The household in Manchester included a daughter, a son who was a physician who had lived in London, who had fled to Switzerland. Mrs Henstock was described in 1794 as a mulatto and 'as a freed slave from Barbuda'.[3] The family were in England by 1784 and on his death, Sarah inherited all the contents of his London house and £1,500 in cash. Despite having been slaves, the household included slaves: a 'Negro Hester' and 'Mulatto William' passed to Sarah Ann Bullock; Joseph and Henry each received £1,500 and ownership of two Antiguan slaves, Stephen and John.[4] These are likely to be their own half-siblings!

In getting back to the tumultuous events of 1794, a trade directory printed in 1795 tells us that Edward Henstock lived at 23 Faulkner Street, Manchester, with a warehouse on Market Lane. Regarding Henry's brother Joseph, the letters written in 1794 tell us he was a physician, living in Bartlett's Buildings, Holborn, London, and he travelled or fled to Switzerland to join the French army.[5] He presumably died fighting for the French Republic as Henry collected his ashes in 1802 from France.

John Brookfield, solicitor, of Sheffield, in a letter to Dundas records that Rev. James Wilkinson JP had sent him to Manchester to apprehend Yorke, but had failed to do so. The letter also tells us that letters of arrest with a description of Yorke – 'a black' – had been sent to the chief magistrates of Liverpool, Newcastle, Sunderland, Shields, Hull and Carlisle by Wilkinson with a view to prevent him leaving the country. Wilkinson suggested that Yorke had come from France explicitly to 'sow seeds of discord'.[6]

Yorke was caught in Hull trying to board a ship to sail to France.[7] His servant, John George Powell, evaded arrest in Hull, but was caught in North Lincolnshire, and was arrested 'as a suspicious person and committed to Kirton gaol'.[8] Yorke was put on trial for 'a conspiracy and unlawful meeting for seditious purposes at Castle Hill, Sheffield, Yorks, 7 April 1794'. Gales and Davidson were tried at the same time in absentia. Yorke was found guilty of conspiracy and sedition on 10 July 1795 and sentenced to two years imprisonment in Dorchester gaol.[9] At the trial he was described as 'Mr. Henry Redhead Yorke, a Mulatto, by birth, and equally tropical, and verging to extremes, in disposition'.

During the course of the trial, in which he defended himself, Yorke first presented himself as an apologist for the ancient English Constitution. He changed tack, and became a romantic martyr for liberty before finally reaffirming the natural rights of men in a universalist and very Painite challenge to the Establishment. Yorke endeavoured to use his trial as a public forum to legitimise his radicalism. On 4 July, Rev. James Montgomery thundered in a letter to the press that the Crown and Anglican clergy wrongly 'represent every reformer as Jacobin, and every advocate of peace as an enemy to his King and country' and argued that such views were 'unworthy alike of Britons, of Christians or of men'.[10]

The imprisonment of Yorke was met with outrage across the country. Sheffield residents had attended the trial, and loudly disagreed with the verdict, as a result of which the gaoler had locked Yorke in a room adjacent to the court until the castle yard was cleared of the mob. Sheffield and Newcastle radicals met on 10 August in Newcastle. The meeting agreed that, on the basis of the evidence given at the trial, Yorke was not guilty; furthermore, they unanimously agreed that any punishment would be 'illegal, cruel and unjust'. The meeting resolved that a subscription was to be opened to buy 200 copies of the trial report for free distribution in York, Sheffield, Leeds and Hull and that they would publish their resolutions in the York, Leeds, Newcastle and Sheffield newspapers.[11] Yorke's trial and arrest appears to have galvanised the radicals in Yorkshire and the North East into action, and cemented links between groups throughout the area. Others rejoiced at the arrests. The news was greeted with enthusiasm by the Sheffield loyalists, and John White, a Sheffield lawyer, informed the Home Office 'that many respectable inhabitants are Volunteering for military service in case such people [Camage, Broomhead and Moody] are set at liberty'.[12]

After his imprisonment, Yorke seems to have been a changed man. He forgot his engagement to Joseph Gales' sister, and married the daughter of his gaoler. He abandoned radical politics and became a 'Church and King Man'. He was named lieutenant colonel of a regiment commanded by Colonel Tyndale, late of the Life Guards, for service in the West Indies, and toured the north in October 1798 with a recruiting party. He was booed and hissed in Sheffield and other places. Yorke complained 'of the adverse, violent and turbulent behaviour . . . and the unfriendly disposition & declared opposition' shown to him and Colonel Tyndale. Yorke's reformed behaviour was no doubt due the fact that he had been informed by the Attorney General that if he displayed loyalty to the Crown, he would promote his intentions of being called to the Bar.[13] Unlike Thomas Muir and the Scottish Martyrs, Yorke had not been deported, but had been held in England: for what reason was his punishment less severe than Muir? This is perhaps an unanswerable question.

## Leeds and Liverpool

The arrests in Sheffield were part of a nationwide year of persecution against radicals. Across the Pennines, Yorke's arrest prompted a crackdown on Liverpool radicals. John Shaw, Mayor of Liverpool, informed the Home Office that seditious papers and handbills in defence of Yorke had been posted on walls in Liverpool and

Manchester. Shaw added that he believed a number of persons were involved in 'this most flagitious business', and that he was trying to discover 'the whole combination'. He added that Yorke had met with radicals in Manchester, amongst whom were Thomas Oulton of Messrs Phillips, Wilkinson and Wood of Spring Gardens, Manchester, and a Frenchman called Wiesche who were both arrested and seditious papers seized and sent to the Home Office.[14] In the Midlands, William Finch, Joseph Priestley's son-in-law, was arrested, and the homes of leading Unitarians were searched because of their 'violent anti-government attitudes'. The windows of Dudley Unitarian chapel were broken by 'Church and King' supporters who sought to remove the 'nest of traitors'.[15] It was to the house of this William Finch that Dr Priestley fled after the riots in Birmingham for assistance to get him to London. William's uncle John had married Jane Shore, daughter of Samuel Shore of Sheffield, and was linked to the radical Milnes family of Wakefield and also the radicals of Sheffield through Unitarianism. It seems undeniable that Unitarianism was a conduit for anti-government radicalism.

Almost simultaneous to the events in Sheffield and Ireland on 21 April 1794, at Wharley near Halifax, societies from Leeds, Wakefield, Bradford and Almondbury met at a large open-air meeting. It was infiltrated by a spy, paid for by Cookson.[16] So concerned was Leeds magistrate William Cookson that the Sheffield plot had links to Leeds, that he requested from the Home Office a warrant to seize arms and seditious papers to close down the Leeds Constitutional Society. With the warrant in hand, Cookson organised raids on the homes of known members and seized papers that stated that the society was working towards political reform, equality, liberty and the 'natural rights' of man. The documents gave details of the structure of the radical movement, which was divided into districts, each headed by a delegate with an oath book to record members. Each delegate was a member of the central committee which comprised a secretary, treasurer and seven delegates. Membership was accepted only by two existing members vouching for the new member, the swearing of an oath and paying 1 penny a week for their ticket. The seized oath book implicated:[17]

No. 153 Luke Broughton
No. 205 John Broughton, William Walton, Joseph Ross, James Ross
No. 206 Joseph Coper
No. 207 Thomas Broughton

Other members who paid for their ticket that we have names for were Joshua Ross, John Atha and Abraham Tancred. Did over 200 Leeds residents share the same ideals and values and the membership list truly counted over 200? Or was it a small clique of radical extremists? It is impossible to say.

Broughton was arrested but released in July, as the evidence against him was considered insufficient. We do note he was arrested again in April 1798 for cultivating 'sedition and is a focus of correspondence'.[18] Even with arrests taking place, in the summer of 1794 the Lord Mayor of Leeds, Alexander Turner wrote to the Home Office stating that:

> We have in this town a few disaffected people, some of whom are very active & we apprehend would do mischief if they could; they meet frequently at public houses & it is notorious that their object is to promote sedition, but they are so much on their guard it is impossible for the magistrates to lay hold of them; there are two of three attorneys in the number, but the most notorious is Mr I P Idestein, a foreigner, against whom I have had many complaints.[19]

Turner noted that Idestein was raising money for the trial fees of Mathew Campbell Brown as well as other radicals imprisoned in Edinburgh. Turner stated furthermore he would like Idestein deported and other 'British Constitutionalists' arrested.[20] His arrest brought the treason trials and accusation of treason directly into Leeds. William Camage of Sheffield took £10 from Sheffield and £10 from Leeds towards the costs of Thomas Hardy's trial for treason, at which Camage also gave evidence.[21] Moody, Camage, Broomhead, Hill, John Edwards and Isaac Saint were still imprisoned without charge as autumn turned to winter. All the men would give evidence in the trial of Thomas Hardy.[22]

After several months, a number of those arrested were formally charged with treason; they therefore faced the prospect of being hanged, drawn and quartered if convicted. The government propagated the notion that the radicals had committed a new kind of treason, which they called 'modern' or 'French' treason, aimed at overthrowing the government, and for that purpose the radical societies had attempted to assemble a large armoury, but no evidence could be found of either the armoury or plans to take direct action against the state. Amidst considerable tension, the trial of Thomas Hardy, the secretary of the London Corresponding Society, began on 28 October. After nine days he was acquitted and released. Due process of law ridiculed the Crown's evidence and it became increasingly obvious to the Crown that they would not get any convictions. Moody et al were released at the end of October.[23] The only victim of judicial anger was Henry Redhead Yorke who was gaoled.[24] Does this show the state was getting worried that it could longer deport and hold without charge with such abandon as in the case of Thomas Muir without facing legal challenges? Possibly.

As E.P. Thompson comments, the trials, although they were not government victories, served the purpose for which they were intended – all of these men, except Thelwall, withdrew from active radical politics as did many others fearful of governmental retribution. Few took their place.[25] Pitt's own oppressive legislation against reform, freedom of speech and the press, gave English Jacobins an ever-increasing array of grievances against the Crown they wanted redressed. Pitt's own actions empowered the radicals, and turned simmering anger into burning rage.

Chapter 9

# PACTE DE FAMINE

As 1795 began, the British Crown felt itself secure: loyalists were busy forming Volunteer cavalry and infantry associations to aid the magistrates in their duties in clamping down on radical societies. Over 1,000 Volunteer units were levied by 1800, drawn from the 'property-owning class' and representing a mobilisation of the middle class against the working man. As could be expected, Whigs and reformist radicals took a dim view of the militarisation of society:

> It would be a miracle indeed, if, during the present rage for Battle and Murder, certain inhabitants of Sheffield were outstripped in quixotic loyalty by any town in England. A number of heroes have accordingly agreed to form themselves into a Military Corps, to be called The Independent Sheffield Volunteers; to be armed, accoutred, clothed and disciplined at their own expense, with the charitable intention, we are told, of being ready, when required, to embrue their hands in the blood of those of their fellow-townsmen who are so audaciously rebellious as to SPEAK AS THEY THINK!!![1]

The goal was to be suppression of all those opposed to 'Church and King'. Yet a perfect storm was brewing.

Rising unemployment, a major economic downturn and the frightening prospect of starvation loomed over tens of thousands of people all across Britain. Cereals were the basic foodstuffs: from the start of the century the staple crops had been oats, barley and rye, but from mid-century wheat was the favoured cereal. Loaves made from wheat by and large replaced barley and oat bread by 1800. The working man spent between 60 to 80 per cent of his income on food, bread being 80 per cent of that for the poorest. Any increase in price flung not only the working man into food poverty but also took away much of the disposable income of the middle classes, who would be unable to buy their usual amount of foodstuffs, thus taking much-needed money away from the merchant. This was a lose-lose situation except for the rich. It is not surprising therefore to note that there were frequent allegations of wheat merchants and millers hoarding grain to inflate prices still further or depriving local markets of their produce in order to sell it in places where a higher price could be obtained. Throughout the country, mills and grain warehouses were broken into by crowds of desperate people, farmers' carts were seized, riots broke out and ever more lurid rumours fanned the flames of discontent. A steady stream of reports of hunger and disorder arrived in Whitehall from the government's representatives out in the counties, to the alarm of ministers who were all too aware that similar events in France had played a big part in sparking the revolution of 1789 – even if Marie Antoinette never actually did say 'let them eat cake' ... Cut off from imports of grain from Russian ports in the Baltic, prices rose from 52s a quarter in April to 80s by July, and then reached 150s a quarter by August! The previous year's harvest had failed owing to drought, then a severe winter followed which saw the River Thames freeze over in temperatures as low as –20 degrees centigrade. The cold weather and the floods which followed the subsequent thaw meant neither large-scale farmers nor the multitudes of smallholders with their strips in village fields were able to prepare their land properly for the following year's crop, after which a cold, wet spring came as the final blow. Poor harvests were by no means a rarity during the eighteenth century but the usual expedient in such circumstances, of importing grain from the Continent, was impossible because Britain was at war with France. After the exporting and importing of corn between France and Britain was banned in 1793, Pitt was accused that his main aim was to starve both France and Britain into submission.[2]

Not only that, but since the government's priority was to supply the army and navy with bread, the civilian population was left even more at the mercy of shortages and of rocketing prices. The national harvest in 1795 was poor but in Yorkshire it was a catastrophe: the corn was too wet to be harvested, much of it never having fully ripened. At Sledmere, 250 loads of barley were left in the fields to rot.[3] It is a common myth that Britain has always been self-sufficient in food. This is blatantly untrue. This stems from propaganda of the 1940s and 'Dig for Victory'. Since the 1770s the country has relied extensively on imported food from Europe and further afield. Nothing says privilege quite like holding banquets for the great and good of the land whilst people were starving. Food inequality, just like wealth inequality both today and 200 years ago, was a major issue in society. With depressed wages, the working classes had to make a choice between paying ever-increasing rents and starving, or eating and being made homeless. Increasing prices and decreasing wages thrust millions into poverty. Unlike today, food banks did not exist: thousands starved to death. Food banks are a modern phenomenon driven by the same capitalist greed that created issues 200 years ago: the rich elites were and are insulated from the real world. The poor had no voice, and when they found it through direct radical action, the liberal and radical elites had little or no intention of helping the working man: the fight for rights was for the middle class to be the equals of the rich and powerful oligarchs and not the labouring man.

On average 8 per cent of an artisan's wage was spent on accommodation, the remainder went on food: cheese, mutton, beef and pork cost 4d a pound, bacon 7d a pound, butter 8d a pound, milk 1d a pint and oat bread 1d, or wheat bread 4d. On an average weekly pay of 9s, 90 per cent was spent on food, and as we have said 8–10 per cent on housing. It left nothing for illness and unemployment, or for price increases of bread and other essentials. No work meant destitution. Price rises meant starvation.

It was estimated in 1790 that in Leeds a woman spinning could earn 2s a week, and labourer 5s–9s, artisans could earn 15s and the croppers – the 'kings of the working-class' who finished broadcloths – the unheard-of sum of 30s a week. A clothier was reckoned to be of the 'good sort' to earn £50 a year, the price of a two-bedroom cottage to buy. In comparison, in 1796 a Mrs Arthington sold a pair of houses in Park Place, Leeds, for £3,000, while John Dennison spent the unheard sum of £6,100 on constructing Denison Hall in 1786. Most merchants who comprised the 'middling sort' had an income of £200–£600 a year: in 1790 the Leeds Street Commissioners noted an income of £400 a year would allow a merchant to rent a town house 'with five servants and a princely table'. In comparison, the merchant princes like Benjamin Gott, Thomas Lloyd and William Cookson had incomes in excess of £10,000 a year: they were the billionaires of the era. The gulf between the rich, the middle class and the poor, then and now was staggering. The world of the elite is enshrined by Jane Austen: the real world was 'hellish, nasty and brutal'.[4]

With the bulk of the townsfolk of Leeds, Wakefield and Halifax – like pretty much anywhere in towns and cities across the country – being never more than a week's wage away from being in the workhouse or living on the streets, life was hard. This was made worse by the changing nature of the workplace with the onset of the Industrial Revolution.

Wheat which in 1790 had cost around £2 10s per quarter rose to around £3 in 1794 and by 1795 was selling at anything from £4 to almost £5 per quarter, while the same year a 4lb loaf of bread cost a shilling, almost double its price 12 months previously.[5] A loaf of bread cost the same as the average workman's daily pay!

## A War for Food

What happened next was all too predictable. The *Newark Herald* reported 'Battles are fought – blood is spilt – money is exhausted – taxes are multiplied – debt is doubled – trade at a stand – bankrupts increase – the *poor* cannot maintain the *poor*'.[6] The poor rate – a fund designed to pay the poor of a parish 6s a week, barely enough to live on – was paid mostly by the working poor: as the newspaper said, it was impossible for the poor to feed the poor.

Food riots broke out. As spring buds blossomed, Birmingham was the centre of an explosion of rioting in the Midlands, which encompassed Leicester, Dudley and Wolverhampton.[7] Riots also broke out in Chester and Shropshire.[8] In May 1795 an anonymous writer had informed the local authorities of a plot to seize arms from the barracks when the soldiers were away on drill, and to 'butcher' local interests and aristocrats.[9]

Magistrate Pemberton Milnes wrote to his patron the Earl of Portland on 7 June informing him that 'the population of Wakefield were invited to impose popular prices on commodities brought to market'.[10] The fear of a food riot so concerned Milnes in his capacity as magistrate that he wrote on 15 June 1795 requesting permission from the Secretary of State for War for orders to call out the Volunteers:

> The general discontent that prevails in the minds of the manufacturers and common people in this populous part of the country is very great, and rather alarming on account of the high price of corn and other necessities of Life, presuming the different corps of Volunteers raised in this town & others in this neighbourhood falls within your department, in case I am right in my convictions, my request is, that you'll be pleased to give orders to the commanding officers of such corps to be ready to aid the Civil Magistrates should they be called upon by them to quell any riotous proceedings that may arise.[11]

Even with the power to call out the Volunteers, the threat of rioting did not abate. Milnes wrote to Portland at the close of the month noting that the following handbill had been nailed to the door of the Parish Church of All Saints:

To Give Notice. To all woman and inhabitance [*sic*] of Wakefield that they are desired to meet at the New Church in Saint John Field on Friday next at Nine O'Clock in the morning to state the price of Corn and other Articles that come to the Market. By desire of the Inhabitants of Halifax, who will meet them there.[12]

The women of Wakefield, like in many other towns and villages throughout the country, were not prepared to see their families starve and took direct action to rally the people of the town to their side. Milnes feared a riot and we suppose the presence of the Royal Wakefield Volunteers prevented a general disturbance. Milnes and his fellow magistrates, who never felt the pangs of hunger or had to worry about where their next meal and wages were coming from, had been given the 'green light' to maintain the peace by whatever means necessary.

The Tory, Anglican *Leeds Intelligencer* sounded remarkably Jacobin in summer 1795:

The deficiency of corn that is now felt over great part of Europe should be borne with this country with fortitude ... sympathy for our fellow countrymen whose lot is fallen here where the quantity of corn is always insufficient for their consumption, and who are therefore at this period more than commonly dependent on those districts that produce a surplus. We should bear each other's burdens and fulfil the obligations of brotherhood by permitting the free communication of one part of the Kingdom with another ... The state can possibly not see one part of its subjects pining with want, whilst another part shall in the same moment of distress be fully supplied.[13]

The Pontefract troop of the West Riding Yeomanry was called out at the end of April 'for apprehending riot and disturbance in the market of Pontefract' and to guard against 'a mob coming from Knottingley' who it was feared would enflame matters in Pontefract.[14] The corn mill at Rotherham, holding a stockpile of milled wheat and other grain, was an obvious target for the starving masses to obtain flour to make bread. A mob arrived outside the mill and stoned the windows some time on 24 June. The Riot Act was read and the Rotherham Volunteers opened fire to disperse the mob.[15] In July an anonymous Leeds resident wrote to the Home Office. The writer noted that the high price of corn was not caused by its scarcity, but was entirely due to the corn factors, hucksters and mealmen who were profiteering by withholding grain from the market if it did not reach their chosen price. The writer quoted the current prices being paid in

Leeds, which they noted put grain beyond the reach of most of the poor, and pleaded for the Home Secretary's intervention. The writer concluded that corn factors were buying up the standing crops from the farmers and therefore he did not expect the poor to fare any better in the following year. The writer concluded that there were many hundreds of families in the neighbourhood of Leeds with wages of 9 shillings a week or less, noting that due to the inflated price of corn, four loaves of bread was costing 10 to 12 shillings a week, corn being sold at £6 8s 0d a quarter.[16] On 29 July, John Gale Jones of the London Corresponding Society addressed a crowd of 10,000 in London, stating 'if they could not find relief for their grievances by legal and constitutional representation, they should take the law into their own hands'.[17]

To offset the scarcity, the government implemented a scheme of grain imports to provide relief to famished communities. The system, perhaps all too predictably, proved a disaster and actually served to increase rather than ease shortages. Government purchases of grain from abroad discouraged independent trade by grain merchants, and thus reduced overall imports and the amount of grain available. The grain shortage was exacerbated, and the Home Office was inundated with requests from town relief committees for access to government stocks. If a request for grain was successful, it had to be transported from Newcastle, Bristol, Hull and Liverpool to where it was needed along rivers and canals. This made the grain very vulnerable.

Paranoia and anxiety took hold across the country. For the starving masses, the rich elites and the Crown had entered into a conspiracy to starve them to death for daring to challenge them. The rising prices were seen by thousands as a direct punishment of the poor by the rich. The King, seen as the father of his people, was doing nothing to help, nor were his ministers. The starving masses wanted justice and above all else food. A handbill simultaneously appeared in Sheffield, Wakefield and Leeds on 4 August:

Treason! Treason! Treason!
Against the People!
The Peoples' Humbug'd! A Plot is discovered!
Pitt and the Committee for Bread are combined Together to starve the poor into the Army and Navy!
And to starve your widow and orphans!
God Help ye labourers of the nation!
You are held in requisition to fight in a bad cause; a cause that is blasted by heaven, and damned by all good men!

Every man to his tent O Israel: Sharpen your weapons, and spare not! For all the Scrats in the nation are united against your blood! Your wives and your little ones! Behold good bread at Six shillings per stone, and may every wearer of a bayonet be struck with heaven's loudest thunder and refuse to help you!

Fear not your lives! Aristocrats, Scoundrels, Cowards! Cursed be the farmers and promoters of the Corn Bill! And let the people say Amen![18]

The same night as the handbills appeared, the starving and disaffected took direct action to redress their grievances. The MP for Pontefract, John Smythe of Heath, wrote to the Home Secretary suggesting that enclosures should be halted, and that wheat had sold at Sheffield on the recent market day for above a guinea a bushel and that people believed it to have been hoarded to enhance the price, and he feared that the riot at Knottingley might spark others due to the high price of corn.[19]

Barges bringing grain into the West Riding were supremely vulnerable to attack. Late on the night of 4 August, grain barges in Wakefield and Knottingley were seized: the nature and scale of the attacks implies a degree of planning by an underground movement. The attackers clearly knew when the barges would travel along the River Calder, and where they would stop. This was not a spontaneous event, but one weeks in the planning. As the barges waited in Heath Lock on the canalised portion of the River Calder near Wakefield, a crowd stormed them but was dispersed by the presence of the Barnsley troop of Yeomanry.[20] The same night, barges were stopped in Knottingley. In the early hours of 6 August 1795, John Smyth wrote a desperate letter to Lieutenant-General Scott, the military commander of the West Riding, from his home at Heath Hall near Wakefield. He informed Scott of 'the great disposition to riot of the lower orders of the people in many different parts of this County' and suggested 'the utility of your sending a Regiment of Dragoons to Wakefield or the neighbourhood if you can with propriety do so'. He added that 'a great riot is now existing at Knottingley' and that several smaller disturbances had taken place 'all relative to the high price of corn'.[21] Magistrate Joshua Wilson wrote to the Home Office:

Since Wednesday evening, the fifth instant, the passage of corn along the rivers Aire and Calder, the one leading to the prosperous District of Leeds and Bradford, the other to that of Wakefield and Halifax, have been interrupted by the inhabitants of Knottingley, and of Batley and of Castleford. The corn [illegible] after being detained by Mobs have been [illegible] by the stead exertions of the Magistrates and by the Yeomanry

Cavalry of the Pontefract District and the Corps of Infantry Volunteers of Wakefield. There is not at this hour any obstruction that I know of in either river, the Calder Navigation being opened today by the united efforts of the Gentlemen and the Volunteers Corps of Wakefield and Pontefract. I am desired as Chairman of the gentlemen assembled yesterday at Castleford to [illegible] your grace with the facts above mentioned, and to add, that it is their opinion, that efforts so constant and [illegible] as those that have been made for four days . . . will not be continued and that the peace and welfare of these trading and prosperous districts require the temporary support from Government, they therefore intreat your Grace to lay before his Majesty these circumstances . . . in order that some regular forces be ordered to these quarters.[22]

The Royal Wakefield Volunteers were called out by the magistrates, the Riot Act was read – and a riot duly ensued as soldiers and civilians battled for possession of the barge.[23] Chief among the protagonists was a collier by the name of Michael Sidebottom: having yelled at the troops that they would not escape alive, at one point he grabbed the reins of a Pontefract cavalryman's horse, tried to drag it towards the river and kept hold until the bucking animal unseated its rider.[24] Also in the thick of the action were two women: Ann Sharp, the wife of a Castleford boatman, and Margaret Wilson, from Methley. Sheircliffe Smith, a Pontefract sadler, was charged with assault of George Pearson, a trooper in the Pontefract Yeomanry.[25] In all, a dozen people were arrested. Of the villagers arrested, Michael Sidebottom, Ann Sharp and Margaret Wilson were remanded in York Castle (the two women on the word of David Dunderdale, who must have observed with real fear the events happening outside his premises, and Sidebottom on the oath of a Captain Jeremiah Naylor) while another three were sent to Wakefield prison. Sidebottom was charged with riotous behaviour and threatening the lives of the soldiers, while Sharp and Wilson were accused of aiding and assisting the detention of the vessel;[26] the latter two were released on bail but Michael Sidebottom remained in custody at York, with all three set to stand trial at York Assizes the following spring.[27] On 12 August the Justices of the Peace for the West Riding convened at Ferrybridge where, the *Leeds Intelligencer* reported:

The late obstructions of the navigation of the rivers Aire and Calder at Knottingley and Castleford are totally removed, owing to the ready assistance afforded to the Magistrates and Gentlemen of the country by the Wakefield Volunteer Corps of Infantry, and the Pontefract Troop of the West Riding Yeomanry Cavalry. The public may rest assured that the same exertions will not be wanting (tho' we trust they may not, in future, be necessary) to protect all property passing those rivers ... the Magistrates unanimously voted their thanks to Colonel Tottenham, and the corps of the Wakefield Volunteers; and also to Lieutenant Torre, (the commanding officer) and to the troop of the Pontefract Yeomanry Cavalry, for their recent meritorious conduct in assisting the magistrates in the suppressing and dispersing a tumultuous assembly of men and women at Knottingley and Castleford.[28]

It is undeniable that groups in the West Riding were in that communication with radical groups that existed further afield: the simultaneous seizing of grain barges on the river Calder on the night of 5 August is proof of this. The degree of synchronisation implies that the radicals knew when the barges would be travelling along the river, and had a good idea when they would enter locks and which locks were the most vulnerable to attack. The plan seems to have unravelled, however: the Wakefield group, it seems, had planned on the local Volunteer force being sent to Knottingley, leaving no troops in Wakefield, to allow the barge held at Heath to be seized and the grain taken. Knottingley was clearly intended to be a diversion for the attack on Heath. What had not been accounted for was the unexpected presence of the Barnsley Yeomanry in the town, which is when things went badly wrong. This degree of planning, assuming this hypothesis is more than 'wishful thinking', shows the extent of underground communications in the West Riding. The people of Wakefield were appalled at the actions of their own townsfolk in putting down the demonstrations: appearing in the *Leeds Intelligencer* of 16 November 1795 we find an article, that states on 8 August 1795 with the return of the Volunteers to the town, they were verbally abused.[29] John Goodchild reports that at some stage in 1795 Pemberton House, which stood less than 20 yards from the home of radical Rev. Thomas Johnstone and his place of worship at Westgate Chapel, was attacked by a mob – was it now? Certainly, Milnes left Wakefield that summer and died later in the year whilst living with his sister in Liverpool. Westgate Chapel trustees' accounts report some £9 8s 6d was spent repairing glass windows in the parsonage 'broken in the disturbances' and likewise £17 5s 2½d was spent fixing damages to the chapel. In retaliation for his actions at Heath lock, Colonel Spencer Stanhope of the Barnsley Yeomanry received a death threat: 'No tyrannical laws shall take place ... whee joined the French and fight for Liberty ... life is sent to all men as well as you ... Canonhall shall NOT stand.'[30]

The same day as the Yeomanry galloped into action outside Wakefield, in Sheffield Rev. James Montgomery had organised a meeting in Norfolk Street to raise a petition for an immediate peace and to demand a lowering of the price of wheat to 36s a quarter and a loaf to 8d. Prophetic words. At the same time, Colonel Cameron had been recruiting in Sheffield for the 132nd Regiment of Foot. Some time in the early evening, he drew his recruiting party and new recruits up on Norfolk Street, perhaps less than 20 yards from where Montgomery was speaking outside Upper Chapel. Cameron was seemingly trying to intimidate those listening to Montgomery through force of arms. When Cameron ordered his men to return to their billets, the men mutinied, refusing to do so, and complained their bounty had been withheld. The men proclaimed that they would obey no orders till they had received their bounty. Solidarity between the recruits, relatives, friends and onlookers led to a rapid escalation, with cries of 'Shame, shame, shame' being directed at the officers.

The crowd that had gathered to observe the military spectacle became agitated. Disaffected soldiers and the new recruits supported by onlookers and Sheffield radicals attending the peace rally combined into a single body of about 4,000. Fearing a riot Wilkinson panicked, and sent word to Colonel Athorpe of the Loyal Sheffield Volunteers to call out his men. Athorpe was then at Wentworth Woodhouse dining with Earl Fitzwilliam. As a magistrate Athorpe carried with him at all times a copy of the Riot Act. He rode hell for leather to take command of the situation rapidly unfolding in Sheffield – at such a pace his horse dropped dead – but when he arrived he found that in his haste he had forgotten to transfer the Riot Act card to his uniform: unable to read it and thus unable to act, he found a new horse, rode back to Wentworth, found the card, and then returned to the unfolding events on Norfolk Street. During his absence, the Loyal Sheffield Volunteer infantry had arrived, supported by the Yeomanry, and were drawn up three ranks deep across Norfolk Street. Some in the crowd, notably a man called Eyre, shouted to the soldiers to desert and rise up against their officers and another reportedly cried 'Knock him off his horse', referring to Colonel Cameron. Many of the recruits filled their pockets with stones, some fixed their bayonets, and others made their muskets ready to fire.

Athorpe read the Riot Act, and on receiving comments to the negative from a self-proclaimed leader of the crowd, the aforementioned Eyre, Athorpe 'lost his head' and 'plunged with his horse among the unarmed defenceless people, and wounded men, women and children promiscuously' in attempting to arrest Eyre for sedition. In order to defend Eyre, and fearing a military crackdown, the crowd started to hurl bricks at the Volunteers. Some of the soldiers joined in.[31] The situation rapidly escalated: one of Athorpe's officers, intending to disperse the crowd and to prevent further injury from bricks and stones being thrown at them, gave the order to open fire at almost point-blank range: two in the crowd were killed and over fifty were wounded, many of whom died later. As the gun smoke cleared, Norfolk Street was now filled with 4,000 terrified men and women: some screaming from horrendous gunshot wounds, being tended to by friends and neighbours; others were no doubt stunned into silence, no doubt others began to pick up stones and bricks to hurl back. Before the crowd could retaliate, in order to clear the street Athorpe ordered the Yeomanry to charge. With their 'blood up', the cavalry charged along Norfolk Street and chased men and women into alleyways 'hacking them to pieces'.[32] Earl Fitzwilliam later wrote on 9 August: '. . . the Volunteer corps have shewn their readiness to act in support of Law and Order, in a manner that must give great satisfaction to all those, who wish to see them maintain'd . . . in the manner, in which it has ended, I trust it will be productive of good, and tend much to the future quiet of the place'.[33]

After the event Athorpe callously remarked that lives of those who he butchered were not 'worth a moments purchase'.[34] One of the wounded was Mary Needham, who showed her scarred face and breasts to the jury convened to investigate the riot. The magistrates reported that the surgeons in the town were stretched to the limit to treat all the victims found lying in Norfolk Street following the charge by the Yeomanry: this was one of the largest losses of life at military hands before the 'Peterloo' massacre of 1816 and is almost totally forgotten today. In defending Athorpe's actions, magistrate and parson Rev. Wilkinson stated the success against the mob was down to the actions of the cavalry and sent a letter of congratulation to them. He was totally unrepentant for his and his fellow magistrates' conduct. Soldiers who had joined the 'Jacobins' were arrested for treason. The following day, after minor disturbances overnight, a huge crowd assembled outside Athorpe's house who quite rightly were protesting at his actions. Perhaps the protestors should have learned the previous day what happened when Athorpe felt he was threatened. The Loyal Sheffield Volunteers backed by cavalry and artillery were deployed and the crowd fled.[35] For the second time in under a year, Sheffield townsfolk had been cut down by soldiers from the barracks on the orders of the vicar.

Reverend Montgomery opined through his newspaper 'the widowed wives and children of the unfortunate deceased have had occasion to lament the untimely loss of their husbands and loved ones'.[36] Athorpe was taken before the bench charged with murder: tried by his own colleagues, including James Wilkinson, the bench was more concerned with gathering evidence of a Jacobin plot and the bench of his peers unanimously agreed that Athorpe faced no charges. The magistrates, led by Rev. James Wilkinson, rather than show any remorse for the death of the civilians, congratulated Athorpe for his conduct.[37] Letters of support for Fitzwilliam for deploying the Yeomanry cavalry to disperse the mob came from MP Michel Angelo Taylor.[38] Wilkinson thanked the Volunteers for assembling to do their duty.[39]

The deaths were recorded by the magistrates convened to investigate the episode as 'justifiable homicide'. Through the press Athorpe was accused of murder by the Rev. James Montgomery. In reply Athorpe charged Montgomery with sedition: once more he faced the stark choice of moderation or martyrdom. He was found guilty of seditious libel and sentenced to six months in York gaol by Athorpe himself. Sheffield has a fine public monument to Montgomery, yet no memorial to those who died, nor any memorial or even mention of Montgomery's more radical associate Henry Redhead Yorke. Has Sheffield turned a blind eye to its radical and black past?

Despite savage reprisals in Wakefield, Knottingley and Sheffield, the war for food continued. A week later on 17 August 1795, Halifax was the scene of a riot led 'principally by women' at the corn mill. The vicar, the Rev. Dr Coulthurst, and leading townsmen addressed the crowd and ordered them to disperse. J.A. Busfield, magistrate, read the Riot Act. The Halifax Volunteers were called out and remained under arms all day, but were not compelled to act.[40] Discontent with the way the government was handling the famine led desperate people to contemplate desperate acts. At the height of the famine, the Halifax magistrates, aided and abetted by the churchwardens and the Rev. Dr Coulthurst the vicar, endeavoured to reduce the poor rate, and had actually attempted to force poor and unemployed men to enlist in the navy![41] Nothing says 'Christian compassion' like forcibly removing the poor from the parish! Riots broke out in Birmingham – where the militia opened fire and killed protesters – Nottingham, Newcastle, Bristol, Leicester and London: all across the county famine drove a wave of violence. In London at the height of the rioting on 14 August, the High Sherriff of Surrey reported that a carefully prepared handbill was passed to soldiers policing protests in St George's Fields, with a persuasive call to the cause of 'liberty', as well as an attempt to seduce the soldiery from their duty: 'let soldiers protect the Rights of Citizens and Citizens will avenge the wrongs of soldiers'.[42] On the same day, Downing Street was attacked and several of Pitt's windows were smashed, leaving one undersecretary in fear of bloody revolution.[43] The rioting in London was fuelled by famine, coin crimping and the Londoners' instinctive hatred of soldiers, increasing disenchantment with the war, and first-hand knowledge of coercive recruiting. Yet some viewed the rioting as symptomatic of the existence of religious dissent. Teesdale Cockell of Pontefract, writing to Earl Fitzwilliam, expressed his fears of 'fifth columnists' in the West Riding who met under the guise of religion:

> I've great apprehension from the vast increase in the Presbyterian sect who are indefatigable in making converts: every Priestleyite becomes a Republican, a leveller & an innocuous enemy to our Established religion. I am about my Lord to advance a bold operation, but I can support it. After this, that what are called the well educated & higher classes of the Presbyterians are not Christians. They deny his divinity & in so doing they must deny his veracity in which case my Lord, what opinion can they form of our Saviour & his revealed truths ... I don't hesitate to say that if this turbulent sect of infidels continues to gain strength in other parts of the kingdom as in this neighbourhood, they will (unless properly looked after) plunge the nation very shortly into the most imminent peril – Divest the lowest order of the people of a belief in the Revealed religion & other sacred truths & I will venture to assert that land of Happiness will speedily become the same chaos of horror, slaughter & misery that France has & still groans under.[44]

Cockell was clearly describing the Unitarian congregations in Wakefield and Pontefract and making references to Rev. Dr Priestley, perhaps the most famous, or infamous, Unitarian in the country. Repression was seen as the cure-all.

## The 'Gagging Acts'

After stones were thrown at the King's coach at the opening of Parliament on 29 October 1795, the government responded by introducing the 'Gagging Acts' on 6 November (consisting of the Seditious Meetings Act and the Treasonable Practices Act). This body of legislation placed further restrictions on the movement for radical reform in Britain. The state viewed the English Jacobins as terrorists, and indeed modern legislation used to hold suspected terrorists works in the same manner: guilty until proven innocent. Earl Fitzwilliam felt it did not go far enough, however:

I could not help thinking what a feeble and futile effort to keep down Jacobinism this bill must be, when compar'd with the effect to be produc'd by all the consequences arising from compromising with its existence under color of a peace with the Nation—what is to be done with all their Com[missioner]s Ambassadors, Consuls, and Citizens? Are they to range at large, in every town and every house, preaching their doctrines, and perhaps even buying proselytes?—are Englishmen to be sent to Paris to be witnesses of the successful result of audacious usurpation, and of the elevation of Tom Paine, from a Staymaker to a fine Gentleman, from an Exciseman to a Sovereign, as the reward of the Rights of Man and the Age of Reason—I fear Restriction and Coercion will avail little against the influence of example—but our Ministers have made up their minds, to save Jacobinism, at its last gasp, and the experiment of shaking hands with it.[45]

In protest at the actions of the Crown, the London Corresponding Society called a 'monster meeting' for 12 November 1795 at Copenhagen Fields, Islington. Veteran reformers Joseph Priestley and Charles James Fox joined Irish republicans John and Benjamin Binns, John Ashley, John Gales Jones and John Thelwall in addressing crowds estimated at upwards of 100,000. For the Society, Binns and Ashley declared that in the face of 'the continuation of the present detestable War; the horrors of an approaching Famine; and above all, the increased Corruption, and Inquisitorial measures' of the Government, the British nation 'should demand strong and decisive measures'. To do so they declared that the London Corresponding Society would be 'the powerful organ' ushering in 'joyful tidings of peace . . . universal suffrage and annual parliaments'.[46] In the House of Commons Fox spoke ten times in the debate on the bills. He argued that, according to the principles of the proposed legislation, Pitt should have been transported a decade before in 1785, when he had been advocating parliamentary reform. Despite this, parliament passed the acts. When the 'Gagging Acts' came into law, it is undeniable that the London Corresponding Society was in its death throes: only a hardcore Jacobin element remained, who would become the United Englishmen. The Binns brothers would figure prominently in this new society bound by a secret oath.

Support for the Acts was 'by popular demand'. The West Riding was divided: Leeds Corporation, with the backing of the Anglican merchants, was unanimous in support of government actions in the suppression of 'republican and levelling principles'. The corporation backed a county meeting at York to support the government's repressive agenda and was 'the largest assemblage of gentlemen and freeholders which ever met in Yorkshire'. A newspaper advert ran:

Are you not tired of Jacobins and their detestable practises? Come then to York and let us encourage the legislature to suppress sedition, which stalks through the land. Britons are and will be free; but they likewise should be secure. The abuse of our valuable privilege of free discussion wants some restraint. It is be no retrained, the privilege itself and our whole constitution will be lost.[47]

Burke correctly recognised that 'we are a divided people' and remarked that the radicals were 'utterly incapable of amendment . . . on these, no reason, no argument, no example, no venerable authority, can have the slightest influence. They desire a change . . . this minority is greatly formidable.'[48] One of those men that Burke was thinking of was the Rev. Wyvill, the indefatigable champion of reform, who called a meeting of the 'honest and industrious clothiers' to assert their independence from the merchant class – who were mostly Tory Anglican loyalists – his call being backed by men like Walter Ramsden Fawkes, Richard Slater Milnes and Jack Milnes as well as the Unitarian clergy and leading merchants of the county like Samuel Hamer Oates of Leeds. As might be expected, with public opinion running in favour of the Crown, Wyvill's meeting was virtually ignored, largely through government propaganda and coercion.[49] Wyvill thought it did Walter Ramsden Fawkes, derided as a Jacobin by the Tory press, much credit that he 'stood forward with great spirit in opposition to the unconstitutional measures of Mr Pitt's administration from 1795 to 1801 etc'.[50]

The 'Gagging Acts' were quickly followed by the Newspaper Publication Act which required that all printing presses were to be registered in order to prevent the publication of material that criticised the government. The government claimed to be defending the constitution, when in fact its own actions were infringing upon it and placing it at risk. Rev. Wyvill warned his fellow Yorkshiremen that they were witnessing the implementation of a:

system of a State Inquisition, begun by the employment of spies and informers, in every corner of the kingdom; you have witnessed the growth of that system, in its natural consequences, the most violent State prosecutions, and the most rigorous and unprecedented punishments.[51]

The writing and publication of even vaguely political pieces became an extremely hazardous business, with informers being ever ready to report any potentially seditious content to the authorities. The Unitarian minister Rev. Joseph Towers lamented that it was now considered unsafe in 'England, once considered as a free country, to

103

speak of kings or ministers of state, or to converse on any political subjects'.[52] Towers was quite correct, as this is what they were designed to do. The 'Gagging Acts' greatly contributed to the stifling of political debate, by attempting 'to be judges of what was, and what was not, seditious conversation' and by preventing 'freedom of speech from being enjoyed in inns, in taverns, in coffee-houses, in alehouses'.[53] Basically, the Crown led by Pitt understood free speech to mean what they dictated it to be!

Amelia Opie, whose father was a noted Unitarian minister, meditating later in life on the changes wrought on the country by Pitt and the 'Gagging Acts', wrote 'I knew, in the secret of my heart that my own prospects for life would be changed and darkened . . . when even innocent men were accused of treasonable intentions, practices and talk'.[54] In Norwich the radicals declared that this was 'the institution of a system of TERROR almost hideous in its features, almost as gigantic in is stature, and infinitely more pernicious that its tendency than France ever knew'. John Gale Jones and William Godwin spoke of Pitt being the 'English Robespierre'.[55] Fox described Pitt's government as despotic and tyrannical. He regarded Pitt's suspension of habeas corpus, the restriction to the right of free assembly and the Treasonable Practices Act which made it an offence to criticise the constitution, monarchy and government, as an attack on the constitution itself. He argued the power of the Crown had corrupted politics, and drew parallels between the extreme Jacobins in France and the 'Church and King Loyalists'.[56]

Chapter 10

# THE UNITED THREAT

In the wake of the treason trials, the moderate members of the remaining constitutional societies began to withdraw: the reformist movement was splintering between those who wanted to continue to press for reform via constitutional means and those who sought direct action. What had been reformist groups now became revolutionary movements in England, Ireland and Scotland.

The government's closure of peaceful avenues for reform agitation, as well as the withdrawal of the middle-class moderates from the ranks of the reformist societies to apathetic stoicism – gone were the likes of Cartwright, Muir, Palmer, Gales, Johnstone, Bakewell et al either through banishment, imprisonment or fear of arrest – further radicalised the remaining members: with the prospect of French assistance, many hoped to achieve their goal of universal male suffrage and annual parliaments by direct action. This was a watershed moment in the development of working-class political activism. The new generation of radicals found willing allies among the Irish radicals seeking to liberate Ireland from the British Crown with the aid of French soldiers.

Hoping to build on disaffection generated by the famine, Irish radicals – the United Irishmen – emerged as the leaders of radical groups in England, Scotland and Ireland. The Irish Catholics and Unitarians wanted the same rights as the small Protestant minority that ruled Ireland and made them second-class citizens. The desire for reform led naturally enough to thoughts of home rule. One of the founders of the movement, Theobald Wolfe Tone, arrived in Paris at the beginning of 1796 and along with others in France sympathetic to the cause of Irish home rule, developed a bold plan that would see a French army land in Ireland and English radicals rise simultaneously as a diversion.

Protest meetings and food riots had been a common feature of class conflicts in the eighteenth century but now, on the dawn of the nineteenth, the events starting in winter 1795 represented a different phenomenon – a national movement, formulating its propaganda with a clear political ideology and agitating for resistance against the ruling class and the state. The United movement was born with a unified system of communication between Dublin, Glasgow, Manchester, London and Paris.

## The United Englishmen

When we look at documents created by the United Englishmen, without a shadow of a doubt sections of the 'Declarations, Resolutions, and Constitution of the Society of United Englishmen' printed by the Manchester radical William Cowdray reflect the reformist ideology of the democratic movement of the early 1790s, presenting the United Englishmen as the heirs of the Society for Constitutional Information, in a network of 'societies in every quarter of the kingdom, for the promotion of constitutional knowledge, the abolition of bigotry in religion and politics, and the equal distribution of the rights of man throughout all sects and denominations of Englishmen'. It is difficult to distinguish between the agenda of the United Englishmen and the politics of the London Corresponding Society, its sister groups in Manchester, Sheffield and Leeds and the policies of John Horne Tooke and Major Cartwright.[1] Maybe that was the point! Historian, Jenny Graham asserts that 'the fundamental ideology of the United Englishmen . . . and even their personnel, can arguably be interpreted as a further development of a movement wholly frustrated in all its previous attempts to alter the political system by means other than force'.[2] The new organisation became known as 'The United Englishmen', the core ideology of which was built on the works and ideals of Thomas Paine. The United Englishmen's appeal to knowledge and education was not just hollow rhetoric: free national schools were identified as an objective in the society's constitution, so too old-age pensions and a commitment to a minimum wage and a highly regulated economy.

The United Englishmen directly modelled their strategic aims and organisation on the London Corresponding Society, and like the United Irishmen, members of the new group were sworn in and given a membership card bearing the motto 'Liberty, Justice and Humanity' and a small eight-page pamphlet outlining the aims of the organisation and its constitution. Each group was to be organised in a cell system where members were known only to the 'conductor' of the organisation, one conductor managing a group of ten.

Organised in secret, we know very little about the United movement. Consequently, how far this was a cohesive, coordinated organisation is impossible to ascertain. Also how far this was organised and driven by the French Secret Service or the United Irishmen (or indeed both!) it is almost impossible to judge. Certainly, French money flowed into London, and agents travelled around the country in winter 1795 to establish a network of radical groups across the country. On 1 January 1796, one spy returned to Paris and reported on the public mood in England, Scotland and Ireland. The people 'cried out for revolution' he reported, adding that the Irish, Scots and English wanted to 'be free from the yoke of Tyranny and the extremist Pitt'.[3] Clearly radical links to France lay to some extent behind the United Englishmen: it is undeniable that many tens of thousands of British subjects were seemingly prepared to take direct action to bring about the replacement of what they felt was a corrupt regime with a new mode of government based on more egalitarian enfranchised values.

Living in squalor, made increasingly 'economically redundant' thanks to the Industrial Revolution, starving, seeing family and friends die of typhoid from drinking contaminated water, is it little wonder that the working class rose up against the elite and bourgeois? What had been a largely middle-class crusade for reform of Parliament and an end to religious tests in public life became a cry for a total reformation of the nation: the working man wanted a say in how their county was run. No more would the poor accept the huge wealth disparity that existed.

## Lancashire and Yorkshire

In Manchester, one of the earliest United Englishmen cells was established in late 1795 or early 1796. It was here that we find the first English use of the United Irish branch system. Each branch comprised a minimum of fifteen members. When a branch had grown to thirty-six members, it divided into two divisions. Each division elected a treasurer and secretary. Linking the divisions was what was termed a baronial committee, to which each division sent its secretary and two other divisional members. This was clearly a deliberate use of a noble title reflecting the power of the barons to curb the power of King John. An elaborate network of baronial, county, provincial and national committees provided a nationwide organisation – underpinned by a code of secrecy to ensure the names of committee members were not known to persons other than those who elected them. The divisional structure was later reduced to ten members to further hamper government interference and the detection of meetings. So that members could identify one another, secret signs were taught to members by their Irish compatriots, while immigrants from Ireland, like James Dixon, was responsible for distributing Irish oaths and radical literature to English democrats.

The Manchester branch aimed to abolished taxes and the Test and Corporation Acts and to reform Parliament with an equal and fair representation by giving ever man the vote. In addition, the United Englishmen were 'to learn their exercise and join the French when they invaded this country and make it a free nation'. Membership of the United Englishmen was by swearing an oath of allegiance.[4]

The Rev. Dr Coulthurst, Jacobin-hunting magistrate vicar of Halifax, reported to the Home Office information from one Hayton, a surgeon of Elland, who had found that Jacobins had sent an agent from London to meet with the Halifax Jacobin Clubs 'to carry on their *wicked* designs'. On further enquiry a local man referred to as 'A' had found that agents were being sent to all parts of the country to sound out the level of support. On gaining majority support, they would carry out a nocturnal massacre, attack the Tower of London and replace Parliament with their Convention and 'come upon the nation like a clap of thunder'. Their leader the spy had reported was a captain in the Navy, called a '2nd Cromwell'. The good Reverend noted furthermore that the Jacobins had been sending signals at night by a telegraph. What grounds, we ask, did the Reverend have for suggesting that radicals around Halifax were able to assemble a telegraph tower, send a signal and then disassemble the tower, and co-ordinate with other groups by other means of communication other than by telegraph, to make sure people were on hand to see the message? Surely, a 30ft tall wooden telegraph was not, to be honest, secret! Such was his conviction that Halifax was the centre of sedition, Coulthurst reported any and all news about 'secret messages' to the Home Office, no matter how ludicrous it may have seemed. We assume Coulthurst only made this suggestion because telegraph technology was French and he was linking activity in his parish to France and no doubt 'Frenchness', i.e., Jacobinism. Furthermore, driven by hysteria rather than common sense, Coulthurst suspected that Jacobins would buy up all the provisions and sell them to the poor at a high price thereby increasing general discontent. In a final conciliatory tone, he hoped the 'Gagging Acts' would solve the immediate concerns.[5]

The same month as Coulthurst wrote to the Home Office, so did fellow magistrate J.A. Busfield with rather more solid and troubling news. Busfield, like Coulthurst, was a scared man. He reported that due to the lack of jobs and the famine, he had observed an increase in the numbers of the disaffected in Bradford, and was increasingly concerned about their intentions. Busfield sought Government instructions on how to best to deal with the rapidly-changing situation. Furthermore, he informed the Secret Committee of the Home Office that a disciple of John Thelwall had been sent from London to Halifax, and had attended seditious meetings at several places in the West Riding, noting furthermore that this individual was organising delegates to attend a national convention. One of the local Jacobins, a man named Shaw, he told the Home Office, had been arrested and had been brought before him for defaming the King, the Government and the Legislature. Busfield noted that individual was well known to the Home Secretary, but without sufficient evidence to hold him, Shaw had been discharged with a reprimand and a warning.[6]

Busfield added that upon talking with the town constable, Luke Townsend, he had learnt that a box of arms had recently arrived in Elland from Birmingham, and noted that the Jacobins met in large numbers to practise drills at all-night meetings. He noted that 'Friends to Government' were fearful for their own safety and Townsend thought a public search for arms would initiate an armed insurrection.[7] The arms, consisting of 'guns, bayonets & swords' were lodged at the home of Joseph Bottomley of Elland, as well as those of Phineas Lumb and Robert Brearly.[8]

Who was 'Shaw'? Why was he known to the Secret Committee of the Home Office? This was certainly James Shaw, who history tells us gave political lectures in Manchester, and who would become a known associate of the Manchester radicals Thomas Walker and Joseph Hanson and of Father O'Coigly, a United Irish ambassador to the French government.[9] Clearly West Riding radicals were in contact with their counterparts in Manchester, London and Ireland which shows how well organised the United Irishmen were in 1795 and that support of their aims, and of the United Englishmen, had increased due to the famine.

Yet whatever was being planned went underground during 1796: the lack of Home Office papers that identified the United Englishmen as a threat does not mean that the threat was not real. We only know about what happened next when arrests were finally made two years later. A French agent was in the Midlands during late summer 1796, and his mission was centred on making contact with reformist groups and the 'disaffected' to organise sporadic revolts, promote popular unrest at the bread shortages, food prices, low wages and other grievances to turn the workers against their masters.[10] A French spy reported in summer 1796 that John Horne Tooke 'was a special man, who would lead the people in a united effort with the movements of the French Army'.[11]

The United Scotsmen can be seen as an extension of the Scottish constitutional radicalism of the early 1790s. The influence and involvement of United Irishmen in the development of the United Scotsmen was considerable. David Black, a Dunfermline weaver and member of the United Scotsmen, believed that 'persons from Ireland . . . were the original founders of the Society of United Scotsmen'.[12] In July 1796, two delegates from the Belfast United Irishmen, Joseph Cuthbert and Thomas Potts, were sent to Scotland. They carried with them a copy of the new constitution of the United Irishmen 'for the inspection and approbation of the Scots'.[13] Poor harvests, grain shortages and price rises lead to sporadic outburst of violence in Scotland and were 'the recruiting sergeant' for the United Scotsmen. By the end of 1795 it was estimated that there were more members in the United Scotsmen than the actual Scottish electorate – about 3,000. The United Irish delegates reported that 'the Scotch were willing and ready to act with the Friends of Liberty in Ireland'.[14] The Irish wanted political reform, so did the English; the Irish wanted a redistribution of land and a fair and simple economic system, so did the English. Ireland wanted to be free of her English lords and ladies, and the English for their part wanted rid of the King and their overlords: so too the Scots. All three groups shared a common goal, and willingly took French gold to achieve it.[15]

But when the French did arrive in Ireland in December 1796, no uprising in England occurred. Yet it did not mean that threat was not real.

Chapter 11

# THE MISSION OF FATHER O'COIGLY

Despite the Bantry Bay landing in December 1796 being a debacle, and the landing in Fishguard by the French also ending in failure, they acted as the best 'recruiting sergeant' the radical underground could ever have wished for. In Manchester Father James O'Coigly and a cotton spinner from Belfast, James Dixon, helped convert the town's Corresponding Society into the republican United Englishmen. Bound by a test that promised to 'Remove the diadem and take off the Crown ... [and to] exalt him that is low and abuse him that is high', sister groups were established in Stockport, Bolton, Warrington, Birmingham, Leeds and London. The regicidal nature of some branches was given expression at Stirling, where members referred to George III as 'George Whelps' and toasted 'The Old Dog's head cut off, the Bitch hanged, and all the Whelps drowned'.[1]

O'Coigly was ideally placed to promote this alliance. His charismatic personality made him an effective missionary; he was no stranger to the English radicals, nor was this his first attempt to elicit French assistance. He had been to Paris in 1796 and on that occasion had carried with him an address from the 'Secret Committee of England' to the French Directory. In addition, O'Coigly had a radical social philosophy close to the egalitarianism of Thomas Paine which made him a powerful emissary amongst the disaffected textile workers of Lancashire. In London he attended meetings at Furnival's Inn Cellar where the United Englishmen's central committee met in 1797. One of O'Coigly's informants in Manchester was a man called Shaw, who was a cobbler by trade working on Deansgate. He had moved from London to help found the Manchester Corresponding Society.[2]

In exile, O'Coigly served a vital if precarious role, not merely evangelising the British radicals but also acting as a link between United Irish factions in Dublin and Paris. In Manchester he made contact with James Dixon. Dixon had travelled to Belfast in January 1797 to liaise with the United Irishmen and Wolf Tone. He was, according to a paid informer, away in Ireland about a month, and that when he returned, he brought news that the French were to invade Ireland, where a delegate from France had just arrived. Furthermore, the spy reported that Dixon had brought back from Ireland 400 copies of the 'Oath and Test for the United Englishmen'.[3]

It was here too that he first met Robert Gray, who became an informer in March 1798. At this meeting, O'Coigly described himself as an emissary of the United Irish executive, on a second diplomatic mission to Paris where he hoped to secure French assistance for a revolt by 30,000 men. Beyond the city, O'Coigly assisted the spread of the United system to Stockport, Bolton, Warrington and Birmingham, while further north, contact had been made with the United Scotsmen. From Manchester, O'Coigly travelled on to London where he joined the leading activists in the radical conspiracy: Colonel Edward Despard and John and Benjamin Binns, key figures in the republican transformation of the London Corresponding Society into the United Englishmen. Despard was an Anglo-Irish officer in the British army and an experienced colonial administrator. He had joined the army in 1766 and attained the rank of colonel. After serving in Jamaica, he was sent to Central America in 1781; there he was made governor of Roatán Island, off the Honduras coast, and soon afterward of the British Mosquito Coast and Gulf of Honduras. In 1784 he took over the administration of Belize. There he supported the land claims of recent immigrants from the Mosquito Coast against those of earlier settlers, on whose complaints he was recalled in 1790. Charges against him were dismissed in 1792, but the British government refused to employ him further. He then went into radical Irish politics. In London, O'Coigly also met the radical printer John Smith, John Gales Jones and others at the house of Thomas Evans in Plough Court, Fetter Lane.

From evidence recovered in 1798, Richard Ford of Bow Street informed John King, Undersecretary of State, that membership of the Constitutional Society had decreased because of a quarrel, which began at the Coopers' Arms, between the gentlemen members and the mechanics and working-class artisans. In order to bring some order to the prevailing chaos, John Shaw had come from Yorkshire, where he had been giving political lectures, to rally the society at a meeting near St John's Churchyard with Thomas Walker. It was now that the United

Irishmen James Dixon became a member. He had been introduced by William Spence, landlord of The Five Houses near The Seven Stars public house. It was this point, Ford reported, that the Society then split into two: one group met at The Buck and Hawthorn in St Anne's Square and the other at Perins's [Perrins] in Lees Street. A third group emerged, led by Robert Gray, at the White Hart in Sugar Lane.[4]

Isaac Perrins was a bare-knuckle prize-fighter and one-time employee of James Watt and Matthew Boulton. He was an early convert to the ideals of the United Englishmen and kept a public house in Manchester called The Engine. It was here that meetings of local United Englishmen divisions regularly took place.[5] In June 1797 O'Coigly brought a copy of an address from the United Irishmen to the radicals of Manchester, that encouraged the assassination of 'the petty tyrants of Manchester . . . and the rest would fear as they did in Ireland'.[6] Whilst in Manchester O'Coigly lodged at The Engine. Perrins, a man of huge stature and renowned fighting ability, ensured that his pub was a safe house, and that at all times O'Coigly had 'a private parlour, & would suffer none but his associates to come to him'.[7]

While the exact number of United Englishmen is not known, the organisation's expansion in Manchester and environs during 1797, primarily among Irish émigré communities, appears to have been rapid. About fifty divisions were in existence during the spring of 1797, and a spy reported that a further seventeen divisions had been established with societies in Leicester, Leeds, Nottingham, Sheffield, Wolverhampton and Birmingham. In Lancashire Robert Gray reported that there were 900 members in mid-1797, and over 600 in Stockport.[8] Having met with the Directory, and agreed on requesting French aid, and accompanied by Arthur MacMahon, the Presbyterian minister from Holywood, O'Coigly left London for Paris. Having passed on his information to Talleyrand, he met the United Irishmen in Paris. James Napper Tandy dispatched him back to Dublin to bring Arthur O'Connor back to France.

Subscriptions were raised to finance O'Coigly's travels to and from France, with, according to Robert Gray, the express 'Purpose of giving Intelligence to the King's Enemies'.[9] In December 1797 O'Coigly returned from France with news of French plans for an invasion. On 3 January 1798 he met the national committee of the United Englishmen with advice that 'France is watching for an opportunity to be given from hence by some popular commotion as anxiously as their friends here wait for some direct assurance of force to warrant their showing their faces'. Within days O'Coigly and Benjamin Binns were travelling to Dublin with an address from the United Englishmen to the United

Irishmen. O'Coigly returned to London in the first week of February. He met with the North of England radicals en route, informing them that this would be his last visit; if he returned it would be to see 'the Tree of Liberty planted in Manchester'. In London he met with O'Connor at the home of Valentine Lawless where they planned their mission to France.

## Spies and Arrests

On 30 January 1798, by then its death throws, the London Corresponding Society issued an Address to the United Irishmen, declaring that 'If to Unite in the Cause of Reform upon the Broadest Basis be Treason . . . We, with you, are Traitors'.[10] The Parliamentary Secret Committee attributed wide success to this movement especially amongst the working class:

> Many ignorant or inconsiderate persons throughout the country were gradually involved in these transactions and the influence of the destructive principles from which they proceeded was still further extended by the establishment of clubs among the lowest classes of the community which were open to all persons having one penny and in which songs were sung, toasts given and language held of the most seditious nature.[11]

The fears of the ruling class were expressed in the committee's summary of the aims of the republicans in both Britain and Ireland as:

> the entire overthrow of the British Constitution, the general confiscation of property and the erection of a Democratic Republic founded on the ruins of all religion and of all political and civil society, and framed after the model of France.[12]

This was perhaps scaremongering: the radicals wanted the constitution to remain but in a fairer and more democratic model, with the unique status of the Church of England abolished. Both these things would eventually happen in 1828 with the abolition of the Test and Corporation Acts and with the Reform Act of 1832 which started the long journey to democracy in this county. Only those who directly benefitted from the oppression of others objected to making society a fairer place. Earl Fitzwilliam once more: 'it is not the red-hot balls of her [France] cannon that are to be dreaded, but the red-hot principles with which she charges them. An invasion from these is what you and I dread.'[13] The Crown embarked on a new wave of repression.

114

Magistrate Beckett wrote from Leeds on 27 January 1798 to the Home Office about radical activity in the town, noting that:

> There are about five societies . . . established in this town (Leeds) and many others about Dewsbury and the other populous villages in our Neighbourhood. These societies consist of 10 members and whenever anyone society exceeds 10 in number two or more of the old members separate and become the root of a fresh society. We cannot find the least trace of any of them having arms.[14]

Beckett noted that the new factories were prime recruiting grounds for new members and 'inflammatory papers' were distributed in the area. He laid the blame on the emergence of the United Englishmen and the London Corresponding Society. He urged the government to take immediate action fearing that if not, 'It will not be in our power in so populous a place as this to repress that revolutionary spirit which most probably is to be our Ruin'. Beckett was a scared man.[15]

His fears, and those of the government, were not groundless. A spy reported to the Home Office that the United Englishmen were starting to arm themselves, and were readying themselves to act with the United Irishmen led by Wolfe Tone, and would rise in support of a French invasion. The spy noted furthermore that a well-known Jacobin 'John Astle' – John Ashley, secretary of the London Corresponding Society, we assume – amongst others, was in France as a delegate from the United movement.[16] The spy was perfectly correct: Ashley had travelled to France at the end of February 1798, and reported to Talleyrand in April 1798 that 30,000 'active and decided men . . . ready to co-operate against the government when opportunity shall present itself' were in London, and nationwide 100,000 were willing to rise to overthrow the government.[17] He was joined in Paris in October by the president of the London Corresponding Society Dr Robert Watson. An informer, Catholic priest John Waring, in a letter dated 15 February 1798 stated that he had been informed by one Bernard Kerr:

> There are here said at [illegible] twenty thousand of this society in Manchester ready to join the French in case of an invasion – their plan is to overturn the Constitution of England and to have an equal representation of the people in Parliament . . . they have delegates at Paris whom they change from time to time as circumstances may allow.[18]

When asked by Waring how Kerr dared show him the rules of the United Englishmen, Kerr replied that he trusted a Holy Father to keep a confidence but did not want his name publicised in case of attack by 'those infernal assassins'. Kerr also reported that printers in Birmingham, Manchester and Sheffield had printed the rules of the United Englishmen and distributed them in those towns.[19] Informants for the Manchester bench reported to the Home Office that for the past 18 months emissaries from the Irish rebels had been recruiting in London, Birmingham, Manchester and Sheffield preparatory to an insurrection.[20] From Nottingham came reports that two shopkeepers had stated that, if there was an invasion by the French, they would support them.[21]

It is now yet another spy appears: Samuel Turner was a Belfast businessman and a member of the United Irish mission in Manchester and later Hamburg, the centre of British Intelligence in Europe. He operated under the name Richardson. He never seems to have been found out. It was on Turner's evidence on 28 February 1798 that the authorities arrested the known ringleaders: James O'Coigly, John Binns, Arthur O'Connor, his servant O'Leary and John Gale Jones. They were arrested at Margate with a letter from the 'Secret Committee of England' to the French Directory, inviting Napoleon Bonaparte to invade Britain. The address, written by Dr Crossfield, read 'With the Tyranny of England, that of all Europe must fall. Haste then, Great Nation! Pour forth thy gigantic force! We now only wait with Impatience to see the Hero of Italy [General Bonaparte], and the brave veterans of the Great Nation. Myriads will hail their arrival with shouts of joy!' Crossfield, from Spennithorne in Yorkshire, was well known to the authorities: he along with Paul Thomas LeMaitre, John Smith and George Higgins, all from the London Corresponding Society, were arrested for plotting to assassinate King George III by means of a poison dart fired from an airgun in 1794 and acquitted in May 1796.[22]

In Paris, Tone expressed amazement; he had little sympathy for O'Coigly, but dreaded to think of a man of O'Connor's talents being caught in such extraordinary circumstances. Fortunately for them, O'Leary with great foresight disposed of the most significant documents in the privy of the King's Head. The primary target of the prosecution was Arthur O'Connor: yet when he was put on trial, a parade of progressive Whigs mounted the stand to vouch for him, amongst whom were Charles James Fox, Richard Sheridan and the Duke of Norfolk, who was stripped of his position as Lord Lieutenant of the West Riding for doing so. William Dowdall travelled from Ireland to defend O'Connor, but was later arrested and sent to Newgate prison in Dublin some weeks later. William Pitt was enraged when O'Connor and the Binns brothers were acquitted, along with John Allen and

Jeremiah Leary. The Crown wanted to make an example, and Father O'Coigly became the victim.[23]

Further arrests of leading members took place. On 19 April 1798 'The Central Committee of Delegates' was raided at a pub in Drury Lane, London. Together with parallel raids on corresponding societies in Birmingham and Manchester, a total of twenty-eight persons were arrested, among them Thomas Evans, Edward Despard, John Bone, Benjamin Binns, Paul LeMaitre, Richard Hodgson and Alexander Galloway. The next day, Pitt renewed the suspension of habeas corpus absolving the Government of the need to present evidence prior to imprisonment. The prisoners were held without charge until hostilities with France were (temporarily) halted with the Treaty of Amiens in 1801. One informant, a former member of the Society for Constitutional Information, reported the United Irishmen in London had plans to undertake 'some great design', and to that end had ordered that 'pikes were to be manufactured by Cook and Shirley at a forge at No 20 Pancras Place, London.[24] The Crown had uncovered links between Ireland, France and reformist societies, and with the arrests hoped that the threat from the United Englishmen had been eradicated. Across the Pennines, with support from the Home Office, arrests were made in Leeds in mid-April. Magistrate William Cookson requested from the Home Office that letters to Leeds be intercepted as he was of the 'opinion that some links of connexion may turn up which will bring to view some of the fraternity here' and requested copies of any information the Home Office had on Leeds Jacobin clubs, especially if the villages of Bramley and Morley were mentioned, Cookson also mentions other men, some of whom are members of the Leeds Constitutional Society: Luke Broughton – who had been arrested in 1794 – was arrested again, and was described as 'the focus of Correspondence'. Cookson urged the arrest of 'citizens Highly, Stead, Greaves, Talbot, Ainsley, Fenton, Pickles, Alderson, Brumfitt and Wright – some of these are members of the Corresponding Society and hold their secret meetings here'. One or more Cookson believed to be *the Charges d'Affairs* in contact with the Manchester radicals, whose arrest would 'bring home the connexion with any of the Manchester Culprits – to any of the fraternity here . . . they have some very abominable wretches here ready to disseminate & act upon the worst principles'.[25]

As anti-Jacobin hysteria once more reached fever-pitch. Unitarians and other Dissenters became targets for community anger. Colonel Cockell wrote to Earl Fitzwilliam in April 1798 expressing his concerns about:

the increase of disaffected people in this town & neighbourhood, which of late years had most rapidly spread amongst the lower orders, that have become Dissenters & from the indefatigable attention of the sect to make new converts, it was thought necessary to fall upon some means of checking the spirit of Disloyalty.[26]

The West Riding was dominated religiously by the Unitarian congregations in Halifax, Leeds (Call Lane and Mill Hill), Sheffield, Wakefield, York and to an extent Holmfirth, Rotherham, Selby and Bradford. It was here in Leeds and Wakefield that the 'wealthiest merchants in the county' worshipped.[27] Non-attendance at the parish church made you a traitor. For the authorities, thanks to the wave of arrests, the threat from the United Englishmen had been eradicated, but ideas and secret organisations are hard to eliminate.

The trials climaxed with the execution of O'Coigly: caught with the address to the French Directory in his pocket, he was found guilty of treason. Despite considerable inducements to turn king's evidence' O'Coigly went to his death on 7 July, keeping his secrets.[28]

In order to increase the number of troops at home to guard against insurrection and invasion, the Defence Act of 1798 empowered the formation of Armed Associations, to bolster the Militia and other Volunteer units. The Armed Associations were not expected to serve beyond a few miles from the towns in which they were raised, and undertook to serve without pay and provide their own uniforms. They were not subject to military discipline, except their own rules and regulations, and the officers were not to take rank in the army.

Already reeling from the shock of the near-revolution and French invasion of Ireland, to make matters worse for the Crown the military situation had gone from bad to much worse. Britain was losing the war with France. The coalition funded by Pitt collapsed, the Flanders campaign was a dismal failure, and General Bonaparte had dictated terms to Austria with the Treaty of Campo Formio. The national debt had trebled for no purpose. Now Britain found herself alone and faced the direct threat of invasion in the shape of the menacingly named 'Armée d'Angleterre' massing on the coast of northern France. Harsh reprisals in Ireland meant that hatred of the British Crown was intensified. The direct response to the failed revolution was the Act of Union. The Crown redoubled its efforts to crush dreams of Irish home rule, and also any hint of political reform in England. But they failed. In November news was sent to the Home Office that pikes were being made in Liverpool and taken to Irish rebels and toasts were drunk to the 'success to the rebels in Ireland'.[29] On 5 December at the Three

The Rev. Dr Richard Price FRS (1723–91) was a Welsh moral philosopher, Unitarian minister and mathematician. His political writings in favour of the American Revolution and his explicit support for people to overthrow their government and for the French Revolution placed him at odds with men like Edmund Burke, William Pitt and the British Crown.

Charles Watson Wentworth, 2nd Marquis of Rockingham (1730–82), British Whig statesman, most notable for his two terms as Prime Minister of Great Britain. Opposed to the actions of the British Crown over America in the 1770s, he set political reform 'four-square' in Whig politics.

The Rev. Christopher Wyvill (1740–1822), an English cleric and landowner, was a political reformer who inspired the formation of the Yorkshire Association movement in 1779. He championed reform throughout his adult life.

Major John Cartwright (1740–1824) was an English naval officer, Nottinghamshire Militia major and prominent campaigner for parliamentary reform. He subsequently became known as the Father of Reform.

The Rev. Dr Joseph Priestley (1733–1804) was a British natural philosopher, Unitarian clergyman, political theorist, theologian, and educator. His political works called for the people to over throw an unjust government. Prominent supporter of the French Revolution, his clash of ideology with Edmund Burke led to Priestley becoming the victim of mob violence in 1791.

Thomas Paine (1737–1809), the English-born American political activist, philosopher, political theorist, and revolutionary. His support for ideals of the French Revolution and democracy made him an 'enemy of the state' and he found sanctuary in France in 1792, from where he helped plan an invasion of England and Ireland.

Edmund Burke (1729–97): British and Irish statesman, economist, and philosopher. Born in Dublin, Burke served as an MP between 1766 and 1794. An outspoken critic of democracy and political reform, his ideals of social conservatism founded the modern Conservative Party.

William Pitt (1759–1806). A prominent Tory statesman of the late eighteenth and early nineteenth centuries, he became the youngest prime minister of Great Britain in 1783 at the age of 24 and the first prime minister of the United Kingdom of Great Britain and Ireland as of January 1801. A critic of democracy and freedom of speech, his vision of 'Britishness' shaped the values of the country for over half a century.

Charles James Fox (1749–1806), styled 'The Honourable' from 1762, was a prominent Whig statesman whose parliamentary career spanned 38 years of the late eighteenth and early nineteenth centuries. His open support for democratic ideals and political reform placed him at odds to his own party and the Crown.

William Wentworth-Fitzwilliam, 4th Earl Fitzwilliam (1756–1833). Whig statesmen and grandee, he split with Charles James Fox and the ideals of political reform. Edmund Burke sat as MP for Malton, a pocket borough in North Yorkshire which he controlled. He led the campaign in Yorkshire against political reform and democratic ideals.

Henry Redhead Yorke (1772–1813). His mother was a slave whose freedom was purchased by Yorke's father, though they never married. Of African/British descent, Yorke raised in a slave society on Barbuda until sent to England to be educated as a gentleman aged 6. He then had engaged in extra-parliamentary politics in Britain and after a trip to Paris in 1792 became a revolutionary radical. He was imprisoned for his politics in 1794 and on his release changed political direction and became a loyalist, supporting the government in the face of a potential invasion in the Napoleonic Wars with France.

The Rev. Thomas Johnstone (1769–1856) was a Unitarian minister, educator and political activist. Gaoled in 1793 for denouncing the Sedition Acts and the resulting impact on freedom of speech and conscience, he remained active in radical politics into his dotage. He was minister at Westgate Chapel, Wakefield, 1792–1834.

Edward Marcus Despard (1751–1803), an Irish officer in the service of the British Crown, gained notoriety as a colonial administrator for refusing to recognise racial distinctions in law and, following his recall to London, became a republican conspirator seeking the independence of Ireland along with political reform.

Thomas Walker (1749–1817), an English cotton merchant and political radical. His support for the French Revolution led him to France, where he spoke to the Jacobin Club in Paris. His outspoken support for democratic change resulted in his home, factory and newspaper business being destroyed by mob violence.

The Rev. William Robert Hay (1761–1839), a British barrister, cleric and magistrate. One of the Manchester group associated with the Peterloo Massacre, his outspoken hatred for religious dissent and political reform, led him to lead a campaign against both for over 30 years.

Robert Athorpe (1748–1806), JP for the East and West Ridings of Yorkshire and Colonel of the Loyal Independent Sheffield Volunteers. Along with Earl Fitzwilliam and the Rev. Wilkinson, vicar of Sheffield, he led the campaign in the West Riding against political reform.

Towns public house, in Holborn, London, one drinker was reported to have declared to be in favour of 'a Republican government to be established in the country the same as in France!' adding that the 'King is a mere Cosher! . . . he ought to be put aside and put out of the way and if there was no King it would save the nation'.[30] In January a report was received by the Home Office that toasts were being drunk in London 'that there ought to be no King in the country' and that 'if the French are to invade this country I would not fight for him [the King] no more than for a wooden peg'.[31] The Unitarian minister Gilbert Wakefield declared, in a 1798 pamphlet for which he was imprisoned, that the common people were so distressed that any change seemed desirable, and that if the French could land 70,000 or 80,000 men they would conquer the country. The actions of Pitt, coupled by famine in Ireland – snow fell in April 1799 – kept the flame of revolution burning.

Chapter 12

# ANNUS HORRIBILIS

As the eighteenth century ended and the nineteenth century began, the government faced an unprecedented wave of opposition not only to its repression of free speech and the suspension of habeas corpus, but also to the war. The Foxite Whigs, the anti-war liberals and the radicals believed that corrupt government ministers were using the war as an excuse to suppress the civil liberties of the British people, claiming the government was engaging in a reign of terror akin to that in France and dubbing Pitt the 'English Robespierre'.[1] In spring 1799, one James Greene, in a rather grovelling letter to the Home Office to secure employment, mentions that he had uncovered links between the United Irishmen and cells in Scotland and England, and had found a letter from Dublin dated 31 March 1799 in Leeds. This referred to similar meetings being held across Britain, and that returns were to be made to Dublin and London on 29 May 1799. Greene offered his services to the Home Office to be a spy, and suggested he travel to Paisley where radicals were planning to meet to 'nip the evil in the bud'.[2]

Parson and magistrate Thomas Bancroft informed the Home Office of the activities of a notorious Irish Jacobin, Hugh Hamilton. Whilst frequenting a public house in Bolton, Hamilton was overheard by the publican to have cursed the King. He was arrested for sedition.[3] On 14 April 1799, Bancroft reported to the Home Office that he had arrested a Jacobin called Fallows for seditious words and favouring revolution, universal suffrage, and freedom of religion and conscience.[4] To modern eyes, these demands are not seen as revolutionary, but in 1799 these words were treasonous. At the end of the month Bancroft submitted a bill to the Home Office to cover the cost of prosecuting two men for sedition: James Douglas for saying he did not care a damn for 'old George' and Thomas Simpson for saying 'Damn King George the Third

120

and those that will take his part' whilst in The Horseshoe public house owned by Richard Wilkinson.[5] John Nicholls was at a meeting on 19 April 1799 of the United Englishmen at the Green Dragon, London. He fled and a warrant for his arrest was made out by the Home Office, and he was gaoled on 31 May.[6] Based on a growing groundswell of discontent, the government began a new round of repression. The London Corresponding Society was declared illegal by Parliament along with all reform societies, including the United Irishmen and United Englishmen, on 12 July. The next target of the Crown was trade unions, which were seen as a hotbed of Jacobinism.

## Luddism

The same day that reformist societies were made illegal, Parliament passed an Act that made trade unionism illegal. But the Crown's plans backfired spectacularly! In August 1799 a government spy reported:

> A general spirit of dissatisfaction created in every class of artisan and mechanic by the late bill against Combinations and which I am afraid has caused more to combine than would have thought of such a measure but for the bill itself . . . it is a measure the democrats rejoice in most extravagantly will most assuredly strain every nerve to profit by it. I have found within these last 14 days . . . proof of a connected and desperate opposition being in preparation.[7]

With the economic problems caused by the advance of machinery, with its resultant deskilling of the artisan and imposition of factory discipline, if not the loss of livelihood entirely, combined with the political repression of the croppers' organisation and the obstruction of any route of legal redress, the merchants and the government actually shaped the conditions out of which Luddism arose, and led clothiers and croppers to join organisations such as the Black Lamp.

The legislation drove labour organisations underground and into the arms of the radicals. The same month, another government spy reported that 'The members of the new society are exceedingly numerous. It originated in Sheffield in the Republican society there – is connected with the principal manufacturing towns of Yorkshire.'[8] At the same time, the Home Office received alarming reports from across the North of England: the republican society in Sheffield had established like-minded groups in Leeds, Bolton, Manchester, Stockport and Bury.[9] Many of the members were reported to have enlisted in the Volunteers to learn how to handle a musket and gain access to firearms. The Home Office recorded that in Lancashire 60,000 were ready to rise, 50,000 in Yorkshire and 30,000 in Derbyshire: their grievance was the repeal of the Combination Act as it made 'masters Tyrants and servants' slaves'.[10]

Later in the month, information was received from a spy that the workmen were preparing to use whatever force was necessary to overturn the Combination Act, and the United Englishmen were using resentment of the act of further their own political ends. The spy reported 'there has been more persons turned Jacobins within the little time elapsed since the Bill was passed than for a year before'.[11] By September the spy had infiltrated the group in Sheffield, and noted that Timothy Gales – who we encountered earlier – was at the epicentre of the movement. Gales disclosed to the spy that a 'business meeting' had been held in Castleton with delegates attending from Sheffield, Manchester and Derby.[12] The spy could not prove such links, but reported that Sheffield maintained a Jacobin and Republican general committee, which was fuelled by a rise in atheism and attendance at lending and subscription libraries, one of which was at Upper Chapel on Norfolk Street which provided access to the works of William Godwin and Voltaire.[13] When news of Napoleon's return to France reached Sheffield, the spy in alarmed tones wrote of large crowds parading through the streets wearing French cockades, singing *Ça ira* and the *Marseillaise*, noting the slogan was 'Death or Liberty'.[14] Barlow's reports were taken 'with a pinch of salt' by the Home Office, and furthermore a former United Irishmen George Orr reported that 'I do not find any attempts are making in this country at a reorganisation of the United Irish or of the disaffected'.[15] Barlow may have exaggerated the situation in Sheffield but Magistrate Bayley darkly warned in November that a new tide of disaffection was on the increase in the form of agitation against the combination acts. The cotton weavers of Manchester demanded that they 'must either have positive laws to protect them from imposition' or else they would be 'reduced to a state of slavery and subject to the capricious dispositions of those who employ them', he reported.[16] Discontent in Lancashire was due to a rise in the price of bread, unemployment due to mechanisation and grievances with the Combination Act.[17] Bayley was perfectly correct: a bad harvest in 1799 saw food prices increase massively. Wheat for making bread had been 53s a quarter in 1789, by 1795 it was 79s, and by 1800 120s. By May 1800 it was estimated that no more than seven days of corn existed anywhere in Yorkshire. The other staple foodstuff, oats, was selling at 70s a quarter. Unable to afford bread or make a pottage, the poor were starving once more.[18]

The spy Barlow's reports from Sheffield may have been part fact and part fiction, but he was right to be worried. Long-harboured grudges against rich mill owners forcibly changing the nature of the West Riding and with the adoption of machines, increasing unemployment as the economy shrank, rapidly rising food prices lead to a new wave of radical activism. One handbill nailed up in Huddersfield declared that the first steps for the workers to redress their grievances was that they would 'pull down all machinery and return the manufacturing business to its old ways'.[19] This was no idle threat.

Machine-breaking erupted in the West Country.[20] Local agitation ensured the illegal gig-mills used to finish cloth in Huddersfield stopped.[21] As famine bit hard in winter 1799, the gig-mills belonging to Messrs Johnson of Holbeck were smashed and his mill burned to the ground.[22] In 1806 merchant and magistrate William Cookson reported that

> many hundreds were present and some disguised, ... and though a considerable reward was offered from the government and from the magistrates, and the parties were summoned up who were known to be there, and who could not prove an alibi, no argument or entreaty could prevail upon anyone to confess who were active parties in the business.[23]

This was the beginning of a struggle that would erupt in winter 1811 in an unprecedented wave of violence. For the business owners the Luddite campaign of 1799 to 1800 was mercifully short, but it was a portent of what was to come. Economic repression coupled with political repression led naturally enough to resistance and there is overwhelming evidence of the continuity of the struggle against machinery and the erosion of the domestic system, community and tradition, from 1799 to 1812 and beyond. Luddism was part of a broader working-class republican movement that sought to bring about change. In a deposition made to Magistrate Radcliffe, a cell of the Black Lamp reported that the committee's first move was 'that they should pull down all the machinery, which would return the manufacturing business to the old channel'.[24] For more on Luddism see the author's volume on the subject, also available from Frontline.

## Food and Famine
As the famine worsened a loaf of bread was now costing 1s 9d: for a labourer earning 9s a week, and paying out on average 6s in rent, a working man could afford just two loaves a week to feed himself and his family. In March 1800 a special public subscription was raised in

Wakefield, bringing in £162 14s in Wrengate and Kirkgate, £364 3s in Westgate and £132 11s from Northgate to provide food and 'necessaries to the deserving poor'. General Sir Anthony Loftus Tottenham headed the list, donating £25 25s.[25] Huddersfield was the scene of a riot by women in November 1799. The protestors were led by Martha Bray. She and her fellow women seized a great quantity of grain, the intention being not to steal it but to sell it at what they considered was a fair price. Martha organised the sale of the bushel sacks at 6s to women in the crowd. One of those who bought a sack of grain was Emma Holland, the wife of an unemployed cloth dresser from Deighton. Incensed by 'the riotous proceedings', the local magistrate Joseph Radcliffe called out the Huddersfield Volunteers. Radcliffe read the Riot Act. Volunteer soldiers, drawn largely from the middle class, were not trained in crowd control: an angry crowd of people protesting and shouting was no doubt intimidating. Both sides antagonised each other: in this situation a few hotheads lost their tempers: protest became riot when Abraham Broadbent kicked Radcliffe's horse. This was the excuse Radcliffe wanted to come down hard on the rioters and he let loose the Volunteers to disperse the mob and seize the ringleaders. Broadbent was arrested, so too Emma Holland and Martha Bray: the former were sentenced to three months' imprisonment. Emma Holland was gaoled for being in receipt of stolen goods: it was either buy 'knocked-off goods' or starve. Martha Bray, as the instigator of the riot, was made an example of and was gaoled for a year.[26] It later emerged that the Huddersfield Fusiliers had held a ballot about attending the riot; those that obeyed were called 'the Scum of Country' by their colleagues.[27] Recruited from the working class, the Volunteers' class loyalty could it seems override orders from their officers. The Huddersfield mob were lucky: by September 1800 a conviction for rioting carried a death sentence as the Crown escalated its war against the people.[28]

A bad harvest was a harbinger of social disorder. Fearing a repeat of 1795, the government attempted to address the problems caused by dealers allegedly profiting from high grain prices – mainly they were pushed into action by popular clamour. However, the Earl of Portland admitted that 'the experience of the year 1795 so fully confirms the policy of Government's abstaining from all manner of interference in providing the Public with any of the articles of daily consumption'.[29] Laws were passed or existing rules revived against 'Forestalling and Regrating' (i.e., buying up and hoarding produce in order to sell it later when prices were higher), granting subsidies to merchants who imported oats and rye, and also allowing beer to be made from sugar to free up grain for bread-making. Imported grain had a fixed price.

York Corporation took out a loan for £600 to buy corn, importing 100 quarters from Hull; 2,000 quarters of imported grain was sent to Malton. The scarcity of corn is exemplified by that fact that Hull was to hold 15,000 quarters,[30] but by September 1800, the warehouses held just 100. The harvest of 1800 was as poor as in 1799. By September 1800 wheat was fetching 90s a bushel in Hull, and 100s in Leeds, peaking at 145s in December.[31] In Pontefract the magistrates recorded 'indictments for seditious libel re favouring invasion by France by Bonapart'.[32] As the famine continued, from his home at Ledston Hall, West Yorkshire, Michael Angelo Taylor informed Fitzwilliam that hundreds had assembled at Baguley outside Tickhill. He had called out the Rotherham troop of Yeomanry in case of riot and stationed them in Tickhill.[33] The meeting was held on the 19th to discuss the high price of provisions, to bring about a lowering of the price of bread and to 'guard against . . . Oppressive & Tyrannical Designs' of the farmers and landowners.[34] A handbill declared William Pitt to be guilty of murdering fellow citizens in England and France in a war which had no end other than to place a king back on the throne of France, further stating 'My Belief in Religion – I believe in the equality of man; and I believe that religious duties consist of doing justice, loving mercy, and endeavouring to make our fellow creatures happy' and continued:

> Fellow Citizens, I hope the day is at length arrived when fanaticism and superstition will be deprived of their tinsel trappings, and exposed in their native ugliness to the view of mankind . . . I trust my countrymen are sick of religious and political imposture and that their decisive and manly conduct will command in an imperious tone . . . a melioration of those common abuses . . . to demand the annihilation of corruption and restoration of the originals rights of human nature . . . our country will be enlightened and the Sun of Reason shall shine in the fullest meridian.[35]

The Sheffield radicals demanded an end to the war, immediate political reform, an end to the Test and Corporation Acts, and fixed prices for bread. The same demands had been made in 1792, 1793 and 1794. Radicalism in Sheffield and the country as a whole had burst back into life. Almost simultaneously riots protesting the scarcity of corn and the high price of provisions took place in Birmingham, Oxford, Nottingham, Coventry, Norwich, Stamford, Portsmouth, Worcester, and a number of other areas. Rioting broke out in Sheffield from 27 August to 8 September.[36] Hull erupted between 19 to 22 September 1800 with the protestors calling for 'bread, a quartern load for 8d, down with the monopolisers'.[37] Fitzwilliam told his patron Lord Portland that he was facing insurrection and rioting over corn prices.[38] In Rotherham the Volunteers were kept mobilised to guard the corn mill.[39] William Dawson wrote to Earl Fitzwilliam that the rioting in Dewsbury over bread prices could have easily been contained if the local citizenry had not supported the mob, and had thus necessitated the presence of the Volunteers to disperse the crowd.[40]

## Volunteer Corps Mutiny

During the food riots of 1795, the political element was almost non-existent but the experience of rioting provided a working-class audience that by 1800 was willing to listen to revolutionary political ideas.[41] As rioting over food gripped the Midlands and Yorkshire, the only force the magistrates had to hand were the Volunteers, yet when the call came for them to go into action, it was quickly realised that the authorities had lost control.

In Sheffield, the Loyal Sheffield Volunteers, who had opened fire in 1795, were physically assaulted on the streets and in September 1800 backed the mob in their demands for fair prices and refused to be called out.[42] The corps, 'infected with Jacobinism', held a democratic ballot, and from this three-quarters of the Loyal Independent Sheffield Volunteers agreed that they would not support the magistrates if called out: yet the same unit of Volunteers had opened fire on a peaceful protest only five years earlier.[43] Indeed Lord Effingham, colonel of the regiment, had told the Sheffield magistrates that they should first call on the Volunteers if military assistance was required. The principal gentlemen of the town and some of the regiment's officers thought that the private soldiers would be reluctant to act against their own neighbours, and that considerable numbers of the Volunteers had left town to avoid being called out. The preferred option among the magistrates was to deploy the 16th Light Dragoons, two troops of which were stationed in the barracks. Despite this warning, Lord Effingham 'beat to arms' but only around fifty men joined the colours and three were seriously injured by the mob who pelted them with bricks and stones as they made their way to the muster. Fitzwilliam concluded that the main reason for the 'thinness of the muster' was the Volunteers' disinclination to disperse a mob composed of their friends and messmates, even their own families, calling for bread. He was confident that they could still be relied upon to act against Jacobinical or similar risings. He also reported that one of the Volunteers who had reported for duty was subsequently set upon by other workmen when he went to his workshop, with 'his head in a tub of water till he was almost drown'd'. Three workmen had been committed for trial for this outrage.[44] Leeds was gripped by rioting from 16 to 25 September.[45] Benjamin Gott wrote to the Home Office reporting that on the last market day a riot was suppressed except for a corn cart being overturned and two sacks of grain being cut open. He further noted that anonymous letters and handbills had been posted on walls in Leeds, urging the poor to destroy the corn mills and to assemble at the next market day. Gott requested a military force to be at the magistrates' disposal over the coming winter and, appreciative of the cooperation of Colonel Edward Goate of the East Suffolk Militia, hoped that the same regiment might remain in Leeds. The Leeds Volunteers had proved unreliable when it came to taking action against their friends and neighbours.[46] Lieutenant-Colonel Teesdale Cockell of the Pontefract Volunteer Infantry commented to Earl Fitzwilliam that the Volunteers were unlikely to open fire and oppose crowds containing 'their particular friends & messmates, perhaps even of their wives & Children'.[47] Mutiny was not just a West Riding phenomenon: in North Shields the Volunteers also refused to act against their friends and neighbours. Lord Clifford complained in 1801 that the Volunteers felt they had a right to withhold their service from the magistrates in the execution of duties which they disproved of.[48] In the West Country, the Volunteers were divided over obeying their officers' orders to disperse food rioters. Some of them participated in breaking open shops and selling flour and other goods at the previous lower prices. When challenged, the Volunteers stressed their continuing allegiance to king and country, but they asked the magistrates to compel the local farmers to sell their wheat in Sidmouth at lower prices. The magistrates ordered all refusers to give up their uniforms and they resolved to act decisively to prevent disaffection from spreading to neighbouring towns. Over half of the men refused to continue their service and gave up their arms and uniforms, leaving a compliant and willing core of men ready to do the magistrates' bidding against 'their kith and kin'.[49]

The magistrates and oligarchy had lost control of the very instruments which they had created to carry out internal policing duties. The country was facing its most dangerous threat since the '45 or the Monmouth Rising in 1685.

## Pestilence
The Four Horsemen of the Apocalypse are said to be War, Death, Famine and Pestilence: all four arrived at the start of the nineteenth century! Starving people are less resistant to disease, and the polluted, overcrowded squalor of late eighteenth-century towns and cities

made them breeding grounds for disease. Where records have been preserved, in Manchester in 1799 747 persons were admitted to the House of Recovery with typhoid fever, 1800 747, 1801 1,070 of whom 84 died, and 1802 601 with 53 deaths dropping back to 184 in 1804 with 34 deaths. In Newcastle the death rate jumped from 67 to 425, and London from 1,547 to 2,908 of recorded deaths from 'fever'. Indeed, one commentator noted 'in the years 1801 and 1802 an alarming epidemic fever spread in Leeds and the neighbourhood. The contagion extended so rapidly and proved to fatal that several hundreds were affected at the same time.' They added that 'in 1802 whole streets were infected house by house: in one court of crowded population typhus raged for four months'.[50]

The slum housing conditions of this era are graphically brought to life by Frederick Engels and archaeological excavations in Manchester and Salford.[51] So significant were famine and disease on the health of common folk of the West Riding that burial rates increased in Halifax 5 per cent and Leeds 41 per cent. In Malton, North Yorkshire, the death rate rocketed by 69 per cent, and in nearby villages like Norton-on-Derwent by 24 per cent. The available data shows that every time the economy shrank and food prices increased, death rates increased. In Manchester we see the rate of admissions to the House of Recovery for those with typhoid increase from 184 in 1805, to 311 in 1807, 208 in 1808, 260 in 1809 and 278 in 1810, dropping back to 172 in 1811. In Leeds the rates increased from 66 cases in 1805, to 75 in 1806, rising to a peak of 93 in 1809, 137 in 1813, 146 in 1815 and 254 in 1818. We see the same trend in Glasgow. The years 1807 to 1808 were marked by outbreaks of dysentery.[52]

## The Black Lamp

The working class and urban poor in the new towns of the industrialising North and Midlands had suffered the most from the famine. On average 8 per cent of an artisan's wage was spent on accommodation, the remainder went on food: cheese, mutton, beef and pork cost 4d a pound, bacon 7d a pound, butter 8d a pound, milk 1d a pint and oat bread 1d, or wheat bread 4d. On an average weekly pay of 9s, 90 per cent was spent on food, and as we have said 8–10 per cent on housing. A room measuring 2m by 3m cost 4d a week: it had no access to running water – that came from a pump on the end of the street; sanitation was a bucket tipped into a drain; cooking was on the open fire. An entire family would live and be raised in such conditions. A room measuring 5m square carried a rental of 9d a week, and often housed a family of five according to a report by the Leeds

Street Commissioners conducted in 1790. Low wages left no savings for illness and unemployment, or for price increases of bread and other essentials. No work meant destitution. Price rises meant starvation and homelessness. Imagine living in a cellar, lit only by a candle, washing in a bucket of stagnant water, cooking over a smoky coal fire, and having to defecate in a bucket kept in the corner of the single room which served as bedroom, kitchen and parlour! Little wonder that the working class had grievances against their social superiors! Struggling families, making the choice between paying the rent or eating, seeing loved ones die from disease, flocked to the banner of the radical cause and were bound by a test that promised to 'Remove the diadem and take off the Crown . . . [and to] exalt him that is low and abuse him that is high'? The link between the famine and radicalism was prove when Lord Eldon was informed that that due to the high price of food many thousands were taking the United Englishmen's oath in the counties of Cheshire, Derbyshire and Lancashire, particularly in Saddleworth. The informant noted that there would be widespread revolution if the farmers were not forced to bring their produce to market at lower prices instead of hoarding it.[53] In the North of England, the underground movement put out street lights: hence the sobriquet the Black Lamp.[54]

In response to the famine, the goals of Irish republicans, English radicals and the war aims of France coalesced. We have to turn to France to gain some understanding of what was being planned. A French spy who had toured London and the South Coast reported that 'the indignation of a great number' against Pitt made 'the majority cry for Revolution'.[55] On 10 July 1799, Dr Robert Watson – a former member of the London Corresponding Society who had fled to France – outlined to the French Directory a plan for using the disaffection at the Combination Act and desire for political reform to the aid of France. Watson wrote to Minister Reinhard with a length memorandum on fermenting a rebellion in London, to seize the Bank of England and the Tower of London, comparing it to the Hôtel des Invalides in Paris. He reported that the Tower held 120,000 muskets and 200 field guns which were guarded by a garrison of 500 troops which could be easily overcome. Watson reported that he had begun clandestine operations by sending circular letters addressed to all the radical societies affiliated to the rump of the London Corresponding Society, ostensibly purporting to be reviving parliamentary reform and peace with France. Once the French had landed, the radical groups in London and the provinces would be summoned to rise on the same day and stage rebellions and disturbances in the major provincial and manufacturing towns. Watson argued that these demonstrations against the British

Crown, would compel the dispersal of Crown forces to the provinces from London, where the radicals could stage a coup against the Bank of England and the Tower, and the landing sites exposed to the invading French army.[56] In this plan we see the genesis of the plot that would bear the name of Despard. A French spy, Irish émigré Charles Cavan, corresponded with radical groups in London and Portsmouth.[57] He was arrested in September.[58] Whatever was being planned by the radical groups in England, the French were taking a keen interest in what appeared to be a revolution in the making.

By the end of summer 1800 the Lord Lieutenant of Gloucester informed the Home Office that correspondence was being exchanged between the manufacturing people of Gloucestershire 'with Birmingham, Nottingham, Manchester, Liverpool &c . . . regularly, as to the mode & method they intend to pursue to lower the price of wheat & flour'.[59] A letter from a manufacturer in Birmingham sent to the Government neatly summed up the suffering of the working man. The writer informed the Crown that the very high price of all kinds of provisions made it impossible for working people to exist much longer. He noted that he employed 'about 40 men, most of whom are so close to death that they cannot work'. None of them earned, he noted, more than 16 or 17 shillings per week which, 'as many have a family of six or seven children, does not provide them with bread'. The writer noted that there was scarcely one street corner on which 'Dam Pit and the King' was not written on the walls. The writer concluded that, in short, the lower classes of people were in such a state of starvation they did not care what they did. He hoped that the Home Secretary would take some effectual means to redress the grievance as the 'poor will not be able to hold out much longer'.[60] History tells us the Crown was deaf to the pleadings of the starving masses.

Thus, it comes as no surprised that in October a handbill and publication proclaiming 'Vive le Republique' was sent to several public houses where workmen met in Birmingham and its environs. It encouraged the men to rebel, saying that they would be joined by men from Staffordshire who were waiting for a signal from Birmingham to rise.[61] Another handbill appeared in the Midlands addressed 'To the farmers of the County of Warwick' from 'thirteen hundred and seven men' stating that they would join with the men of Worcestershire and Staffordshire threatening that, if food was not cheaper within a month, they would burn every farmer's property in all three counties. The handbill stated that working men's families were starving because the farmers wished to make £40 an acre. Another handbill posted in

Birmingham stated that soldiers' pay had been augmented to secure their attachment to a 'Tyrannical, but trembling power, which governs by force of arms instead of Justice and Virtue'. The writers encouraged the poor to strike against the privileged and advised those expecting help from Parliament to give up any hopes and instead join the 'Army of Redress' at the head of which would be found, it was promised, the veteran reformer the Duke of Bedford and Earl Stanhope 'and others equally great and noble who are determined to set you free or meet a glorious death'.[62] The handbill stated that sixty similar notices had been delivered to all principal clubs across the Midlands and the toast and watchword was to be 'Down with Tyranny and Oppression that Liberty and Plenty may Reign'. Real anger was rising.[63]

In Lancashire a week later Magistrate Bancroft received a letter from the Bolton Volunteers and townsfolk saying that they would destroy all buildings housing corn, flour, meal or any other kind of provisions unless action was taken to relieve starvation in the locality.[64] A week later, he told the Home Office that he had not succeeded in discovering traces of an intended insurrection but that the 'spirit of dissatisfaction' was very great, due to 'the coalition between Jacobinism and Distress'.[65] Bancroft was perfectly correct. His spy network was busy hunting for Jacobins. One spy, assisted by a man identified as 'Robinson', had obtained details of George Hearmer, George Harmatage, John Cross, Turner and William Lee who were involved in seditious activity.[66] In early December, he told the Home Office that the signal for the rising would be given in London, and in order to arm the rebellion, Volunteer Corps members were to be seized and disarmed, adding 'the Duke of Portland would soon be knocked off'. Bancroft's spy network further reported that a man called Moorhouse from Stockport, posing as a travelling salesmen hawking pamphlets and books, was supposed to be a correspondent between the fraternities. There were said to be 6,000 determined men in Manchester alone, Bancroft noted.[67]

Rev. John Lowe, parson of Wentworth and also a Sheffield magistrate, reported to Earl Fitzwilliam that 'there is a system of organisation going on in secret committees and preparation of hostile weapons'.[68] Furthermore, he reported to Earl Fitzwilliam and the Home Office, that men were drilling at night in Sheffield, armed with daggers, but he felt sufficient troops were in the barracks and town to contain any rioting.[69] In addition, Lowe informed the Earl that Captain Warris of the Sheffield Volunteers had infiltrated the Sheffield radical group.[70] Warris informed Lowe that the Sheffield society had 2,000 members, and that they proposed that the 'master manufacturers should buy corn and hand mills and sell it out to the workmen at prime cost' and if the manufacturers did not assent to this, then the 'root of the Evil' was to be cut out, notably the government, and:

> That Mr Pitt and all his measures were execrable to Human nature and nothing could prosper in the present hands, he would starve them all to death, that nothing could relieve them but a change of ministers exterminating Mr Pitt and putting Charles Fox in his place.[71]

An informer told Fitzwilliam that Sheffield was ready to rise in rebellion.[72] In late November 1800 the Home Office pressed for investigations when rumours circulated that pike-heads were being transported from Birmingham to Manchester.[73] Sheffield was the scene of food riots at the end of November. Earl Fitzwilliam and magistrate Hugh Parker informed the Home Office that they were sure that there were secret committees discussing plans and preparing weapons. Fitzwilliam added that if something effectual was 'not soon done to relieve the distress of the lower orders of people', no efforts of the magistrates or military in the country would prevent the most serious disturbances.[74] In the Midlands, handbills were pasted up in Kidderminster inciting the British people to rise up against 'Tyrants & Monopolizers' who caused the lack of bread while enriching themselves and called 'Bishops Vicars Curates Parliament and Kings' as being 'Evils' and 'worthless Things'.[75]

A broadsheet appeared in Wakefield on 8 December 1800 which read 'Take care of your life, damn King George and Billy Pitt – may Hell be their portion'. A second handbill was nailed to the door of Wakefield Parish Church on 15 December and in part read 'we have now waited a long time in vain, in hopes that Parliament would have done something for us'.[76] The threat was unmistakable.

In December a spy, Thomas Amsden, was interrogated by Sir Richard Ford at Bow Street in London. Amsden reported he had become acquainted with seditious and disaffected people in Nottingham. He reported that the persons openly damned the King, the government and the church, and praised the French for shaking off their king, government and church, and expressed a desire to emulate France with a Revolution in England. He added that he had learned that 'Citizen Hoare the Chief Jacobin, Citizen Hardy, Mr Ferguson and Charles James Fox all desired a change in government'.[77] Lord Gower, Lord Lieutenant of Staffordshire was a worried man, telling the Home Office that:

the word revolution is in almost every mouth as if already entered into . . . five sixths of the labouring people would join these plans, their tempers having been soured by real distress . . . the Jacobins are taking advantage by instilling such base ideas amongst them as nothing but poverty and slavery remains their lot.[78]

A handbill appeared in London declaring 'NO KING! Buonoparte for Ever!' and urged the masses 'to maintain the noble cause of Liberty . . . Death or Liberty must be our Souls Desire!' In Wolverhampton a poster read 'Damn all the Kings men and damn the King to Hell'.[79] Revolution was in the air.

# Chapter 13

# ANTI-WAR LIBERALISM

As tensions rose between the haves and the have-nots, the property-owning class became more and more concerned at the prospect of the embers of rebellion flaring up into full-scale revolution backed by France. In the words of a report on the opposition movement written by a spy working for Colonel Fletcher in Nottingham, 'The poor are for a general rising for a revolution. The gentlemen are not, but are for obtaining redress by very strong petitions (worded alike) from every town in the Kingdom.'[1]

The solution to the prospect of revolution, famine and a faltering economy was an immediate cessation of hostilities with France. Yet, as Richard Slater Milnes, the MP for York, wrote to his mentor, Wyvill, on 7 December 1800, 'The war is now unpopular, but the opposition is more so'. He feared that little could be done to bring about peace and reform, and, further, that even the Foxite Whigs were viewed through the prism of loyalist propaganda as traitors and Jacobins:

> The real friends to liberty in this country are very few . . . From repeated trials we know them well; and from the experience we have had, it does not appear to me a judicious proceeding to persist in the objects that rather revolt than conciliate the public mind.[2]

Yet, much though they believed in the need for peace at any price, neither Wyvill nor Cartwright – the established middle-class reformist leaders – could agree on a unified plan of action. Out of the vacuum caused by the established leadership's crippling paralysis, a new, largely middle-class grouping emerged: led in the most part by Unitarians, this might be termed anti-war liberalism much though loyalists portrayed it as Jacobin. The Unitarian clergy and Yorkshire Association reformists took the lead: prominent amongst them was the Milnes family.

## Leeds

In Leeds, Samuel Hamer Oates of Mill Hill Chapel took the lead along with the minister William Wood, the latter declaring that 'war is in all cases displeasing to God and hurtful to man; in the end, destructive alike to the victor and the vanquished; pleasing to none, but harpies who fatten on human blood'.[3]

Oates had been directly involved in the two Yorkshire Association petitions of 1780 and 1783.[4] He was foremost amongst the anti-war liberals in Leeds, and, as a leading cloth merchant, had huge influence over those who supplied them with cloth.[5] However, he was not the only one, the firm of Thursby, Hainsworth and Dunn alone bringing together three chapel trustees.[6] Indeed, Oates claimed in a letter to Fox that the anti-war movement in the West Riding was supported almost to a man by the manufacturers.[7] Oates was appealing not just to the 'Merchant Princes' of Leeds, the cloth merchants like Cookson or Gott, but to the artisans who actually produced the cloth and, in particular, their more prosperous elements (until well into the nineteenth century, weaving and spinning were rural-based cottage industries, whereas the more highly skilled and most remunerative processes tended to be concentrated in urban centres: Wakefield, for example, handled the finishing and dyeing of a large proportion of the cloth produced in the valleys of the Calder and Aire alike). It was to these same groups that the 1780 and 1783 Yorkshire Association petitions had been distributed, and they were again the target in 1800. By appealing to such people Oates was building a broad base of support, which gave him a numerical advantage over the Tory merchant oligarchy that governed the town via the parish-church vestry meeting to the exclusion of the Unitarians and other Dissenters.

Oates, therefore, was deliberately seeking to overcome the powerful 'Church and King' interest of the vestry meeting and appealed to the surrounding towns and villages and importantly, the growing Nonconformist community in Leeds and its environs: by appealing to the rural population, he sought to negate the Tory monopoly of the Leeds civic leaders influence.

The meeting to discuss a petition for peace was held in the Mixed Cloth Hall, called by the trustees and was attended by the merchants and manufacturers of the town. The meeting was picked up by the *York Herald* which reported that it had been called due to the economic distress and famine caused by the war, and that Oates had both claimed that the latter, like the American War, would lead to total ruin of the manufacturers, and stated his delight that 'the time was come when the friends of peace, whom he considered as the best friends of the country, dared assemble to petition their sovereign without the dread appellation of Jacobins'.[8] The meeting unanimously resolved

> that the great number of laborious and industrious families, who have hitherto supported themselves by the manufactories of this neighbourhood, are now reduced to great distress; that many of the more wealthy manufacturers wanting sales for their goods, have been under the necessity of diminishing a great proportion of their workmen, who in consequence thereof have been obliged to apply for parochial relief, thereby adding to the numbers already dependent upon the parishes for their subsistence, which has advanced our poor rate beyond all example; that our taxes have advanced to a great or greater proportion; that in addition to those evils, every kind of provision and particularly corn, has risen to a most exorbitant price considering that the want of employment to the present extent, the excessive demands upon us for poor rate and enormous taxes and the high price of provision which were unknown in this country before this unfortunate war in which we are engaged; that the war is the principal cause of these complicated evils; that, if it be continued, the absolute ruin of a very great numbers of us is inevitable; and that it is a duty we owe to our country, our families and our posterity, to petition the king to stop such measures as His Majesty in His Wisdom may see fit for the purpose of obtaining a speedy peace.[9]

As might be expected, with loyalists excluded from the debate, a counter-declaration was put forward, this being the work of the town's mayor, six aldermen and a number of members of the Anglican clergy.[10] Colonel John Dixon noted that Benjamin Gott headed one of the lists in favour of peace. He also noted that the Presbyterian congregations at Mill Hill and Call Lane had been attacked in print by vocal Anglican clergy who were opposed to peace and, no doubt, to their religion. Dixon noted furthermore that petitions for peace seemed likely to be taken up across the country, especially the West of England, and that Charles James Fox was to be approached to head the peace movement.[11] In a letter to the Rev. Wyvill, Wood remarked that the petition had done the reform movement and his congregation great harm in that 'Church-and-King' crowds had renewed their attacks on his congregation, breaking windows at Mill Hill and nearby Call Lane, and defaming the congregations as 'republicans and traitors'.[12]

A counter-petition also appeared in Leeds, this objecting not to peace *per se*, but that the press and mass meetings' stress on the economic problems the country was facing was tantamount to treason as it could not but encourage the French to think they were on the brink of victory.

Also obnoxious, meanwhile, was the notion that the people had the right to petition the king. The petition against the peace petition was headed by John Brooke, Lord Mayor of Leeds; the aldermen, John Backet, John Calverley, William Cookson, Richard Bramley, William Hey and Henry Hall; and the commander of the Leeds Volunteers, Colonel Thomas Lloyd.[13] No doubt the Leeds Tories felt that as their petition as backed by the 'right sort of people', it was a legitimate act, whereas the 'wrong sort of people' had no say in governance.

## Bradford

In Bradford, the meeting was called in the Piece Hall on 29 January 1801. The chairman was Benjamin Kaye, aided by George Walker, a Unitarian associated with Mill Hill.[14] The meeting resolved:

> I. From the alarming and unprecedented decay of the trade of this town and neighbourhood; from the great and rapid increase of our POOR RATES and of our TAXES, from the lamentable circumstances of great numbers of the work people, who were lately engaged in our various branches of manufacture, being now totally destitute of Employment; and from the high price of every sort of grain and other necessaries of Life, that this part of the Kingdom is reduced to a situation most seriously distressful and which imperiously calls for prompt and effectual relief.
> II. That the WAR is a principal cause of these evils.
> III. That we are convinced that an immediate PEACE is the only event which can effectually remove these general and increasing calamities: that peace can alone give activity to our stagnant commerce by opening to us the shores of the Continental markets from which we are excluded; that peace can alone restore the confidence at home and abroad which is so essential to the existence and advancement of our commercial prosperity.
> IV. That impressed with a conviction of these truths, we humbly petition his majesty to make every possible exertion to restore PEACE to our suffering country.[15]

An addendum noted that 'In our present exhausted state, deserted by almost all our Allies, Half of Europe confederating to our ruin ... we see no probability of obtaining that success ... which can compensate the nation for the additional Evils which the prosecution of the war will inevitably occasion'. The war was being fought and lost for no good reason, the good people of Bradford felt, who continued

> we are oppressed with burdens which reduce wealth to mediocraty, mediocraty to poverty and which leaves the poor man destitute: Our

manufacturers are daily declining; Great numbers of our Artisans are without Employment . . . These evils combined with an enormously high price of grain and all other necessaries of Life, which if continued threaten famine and dearth, form indeed an awful group of calamities, which justify the most melancholy apprehensions.[16]

Opposition was led by the Rev. Miles Atkinson of Leeds, a well-known politically active pro-war Anglican clergyman.[17] Despite this vocal opposition, 20,000 signed![18]

## Wakefield

In Wakefield, the Whig leadership was to the fore. As in Leeds, the town was governed by a cartel of Tory Anglicans via the Vestry and Street Commissioners, which excluded Unitarians and other Dissenters. Despite strong opposition, Magistrate Dawson reported to Earl Fitzwilliam that 'a very considerable number' attended the meeting, perhaps 700 persons or so, and further remarked that the meeting was opposed by the Tories, clergy and 'leading merchants of the town'.[19] Despite huge opposition, the Wakefield meeting resolved:

I. That most of the industrious and laborious families in this town and neighbourhood, who have hitherto supported themselves by their labour in the Woollen Manufactory, are now reduced to extreme distress.
II. That many of the lesser manufacturers are daily sinking into a state of insolvency.
III. That most of the ports upon the continent of Europe, being now closed against us, our more wealthy manufacturers are thereby deprived of a market for their goods, and are under the necessity of dismissing a greater proportion of their workmen, who in consequence thereof, have been obliged to apply for Parochial Relief.
IV. That our Poor Rates, have, in the last few years increased beyond all former example.
V. That our Taxes have increased in as great, or great proportion, and in addition to these evils, every kind of provisions, but particularly corn, hath risen to a most extravagant prince.
VI. That the loss of our trade, and the want of employment to the present extent, the heavy demands upon us for Poor Rates and Taxes, and the high prices of corn and other necessaries of Life, were unknown in this country before the UNFORTUNATE WAR in which we are engaged.
VII. That the WAR is one great cause of these complicated distresses; that if it be continued, the destruction of our TRADE and the absolute RUIN of very great numbers of us, appears inevitable; and that it is a duty we owe to our King, our Country and our Families, humbly to lay our deplorable situation before his Majesty, and petition him to adopt such

measures as he in his wisdom may see fit for the purpose of obtaining a SPEEDY PEACE.[20]

Colonel John Dixon of the 1st West Riding Militia reported that due to the fervour of those present, the meeting 'bore down every opposition that could be made'.[21] Disgusted at 'the Jacobins in their midst' wanting to seek peace with France, the Tory pro-war faction lodged their own protest in the press:

Wakefield January 30th 1801.
    We the undersigned Clergy, Landowners, Merchants, Woolstaplers and Tradesmen in Wakefield, do openly protest against a meeting being held this day in the Moot Hall, in consequence of a requisition of certain Merchants, Woolstaplers, Manufacturers and others concerned with the woollen manufactory, because we conceive that the said meeting was very unreasonably, partially, and prematurely called.
    Unreasonably called with respects to the day.
    Partially, as excluding the Clergy, Landowners and General Commercial and Trading Interests of the Town:
    Prematurely, as being convened before the substance of His Majesty's Gracious Speech to the Imperial Parliament which was daily to be expected, and the subsequent declarations thereon, could possibly be known.[22]

The protest was signed by General Loftus; Anthony Tottenham and his son, John, the latter being the commander of the Royal Wakefield Volunteers; the slave owner Edward Dyrne Briscoe; cloth merchants John and Jeremiah Naylor; the Rev. Dr Munkhouse, vicar of St Johns; the vicar of Wakefield, Rev. Dr Bacon, and over 100 others.[23] What this group wanted was a general meeting of the town to discuss the matter at hand.[24] However, in this they met with fierce resistance. To quote a remonstrance published by the *York Herald* that was probably written by someone such as James Milnes:

The number of protestors . . . amounts to 118 . . . several that I cannot find out at all . . . several had their names affixed without their knowledge or consent . . . to this motley crew, we count ten or perhaps dozen respectable merchants and tradesmen, in the woollen business.
    Having thus seen who the protestors are, let us examine the composition, which they chose to call their open protest, containing their reasons why in their wise judgements, upwards of THREE THOUSAND Merchants, Mill Owners and Manufacturers should not lay, the state of their distressed and ruined condition at his Majesty's feet and humbly implore him as the father of his people, to relieve them,

by putting an end to the War, and restoring his starving people the blessings of peace.[25]

Clearly, the outraged Tories had forged signatures on their counter-petition to make up the numbers, and beyond a shadow of a doubt their views were distinctly in a minority: their privilege counted for naught when challenged and defeated by the unprivileged majority. Bakewell and Lumb were no doubt 'cock a hoop'. From being despised Jacobins and traitors who had been gaoled in 1793, they now represented the 'will of the people'. The tide was starting to turn against the elite and the privileged classes. The working man had found strength through unity both in the workplace and now in politics.

In spite of opposition, a total of 3,023 names were collected by the Wakefield petition, and it was handed to Parliament by Wilberforce.[26] The editor of the *York Herald*, Alexander Bartholoman, made much of the fact that the 'High Sherriff of Yorkshire' James Milnes, and Richard Slater Milnes as MP for York had signed the Wakefield petition, the latter of course being a Unitarian and member of Westgate Chapel, where he was buried in 1814. Through the pages of his newspaper the editor called for a national plebiscite on peace or war. He reported that Dewsbury had also petitioned for peace, and remarked that, if the war went on, most of the manufacturing towns in the West Riding would be driven to the necessity of increasing their poor rates.[27]

Ultimately, over 42,000 freeholders of Yorkshire signed the petition. It was the largest mass participatory political act since the Yorkshire Association petition of 1783. Yet it achieved nothing. The despised war continued; food prices did not drop. The government, it seems, literally took no notice at all to the voice of the people. As the famine continued, the anger from the working class got louder. The peace petitions may not have brought peace, but it empowered an entire generation of the working class into collective action. Disillusioned by legitimate lines of protest, direct action was for many the only way to get their voice heard.

> Is not petitioning parliament to redress these grievances like petitioning a corrupt agent to remove himself? – Yes – And will you still suffer yourselves to be thus imposed upon by a Majority of unnecessary hirlings, government pimps – Corner dealers – place men- petitioners – parasites & C and yourselves starving for bread! No, let them exist not one day longer, we are the sovereignty: rise then from your lethargy and attend at the place appointed – drag the constitution from its hidden place – and lay it open to public inspection – shake the earth to its centre – and make the authors of an unjust war the victims of its Fury![28]

Chapter 14

# PLANNING REVOLUTION

As might be expected, in the wake of the failure of the peace petitions, political activity surged when the Seditious Meetings Act and the Habeas Corpus Suspension Act expired in March 1801. In Somerset a handbill was nailed up which implored the reader to 'tread oppression down', to 'pull down the tyrant from his throne' and to avoid starvation 'by Pitt's decree'. That same day, a food riot was brutally put down by the Queen's Bays at Taunton.[1] An informant to the Crown reported 'a most alarming state of disaffection among the lower orders especially in Yorkshire and Nottinghamshire, stimulated in places by Methodist preachers'.[2] No doubt 'Thom Paine' Methodists as opposed to Wesleyans!

With the ending of the Suspension of Habeas Corpus Act, on 10 March 1801 a group of recently-released state prisoners met at the Green Dragon Inn in Fore Street, London. Thomas Evans – arrested in 1798 alongside James O'Coigly – upbraided the assembled members of the United Britons for the lack of activity during his imprisonment. Evans was not being totally fair: men like William Curry, Thomas Pemberton, Joseph Bacon, Richard Oliphant had worked hard at keeping the United Briton movement alive whilst he, along with Colonel Marcus Edward Despard and William Cheetham, were imprisoned. Within days, Evans, Galloway, and the radical hatter, Richard Hodgson, along with Cheetham and John Nicholls, were part of a shadowy United Britons national committee working towards the overthrow of the government.[3] Despard had not yet been released from prison.

No sooner had a committee been assembled, than the authorities struck: on 20 April seventeen members of the United Britons were arrested at the Green Dragon in London, and packed off to Newgate Gaol, including John Heron, Charles Pendrell, Wallis Eastburne,

141

John Blythe, Joseph Patten, Jasper Moore, John and Benjamin Binns and Michael Doyle. These men would all play leading parts in what was to follow. On 31 May John Nicholls was arrested 'on a vague and undefined charge of treasonable practices' and conveyed to Tothill Fields prison. He was transferred to Gloucester gaol, where he languished for seven months.[4] Key players were 'John Macnamara' and Patrick Finney.

Despite these arrests, the planning for the revolution continued unabated. In Plymouth, Earl Fortescue reported to the Home Office that a 'Jacobin conspiracy' had taken hold of the dockyards.[5] The centre of operations, it seems from extant paperwork, was once more Manchester and Leeds.

## Lancashire

Rev. Thomas Bancroft with fellow magistrate Colonel Ralph Fletcher began using their spy network to infiltrate Jacobin groups. They were endeavouring to uncover the activities of locally disaffected persons following reports of seditious words being uttered in local public houses. They told the Home Office that they had placed informants into the company of the Jacobins who were known to have been transmitting intelligence between London, Manchester and Sheffield.[6]

On 23 February 1801, a mass meeting was held in Stockport, to discuss grievances and about planning a petition in Lancashire in support of peace and reform. The delegates could not agree if petitioning was the best way of getting their grievances heard. In response, the meeting was adjourned to the 'German Hussar' on 9 March. The meeting was to discuss the lowering of prices of food and ending the war, as well as political reform. The chairman of the meeting was overt Jacobin 'Citizen Bent', a shoemaker of 4 Foundry Street, Manchester and a government spy or if you prefer secret agent. Bent was arrested, on evidence received from another government spy at the meeting, Edward Hilton, who noted that Bent had goaded the meeting and had sought to politicise the famine: Hilton had no clue that Bent was an *agent provocateur*. In the background of the organisation which called the meeting was William Cheetham who had been recently released from Cold Bath Fields Prison, Clerkenwell, where he had been gaoled with Marcus Edward Despard for his part in the United Englishman Plot in 1798. The next meeting of the Manchester group was held at the Britannia Inn on 16 March, which was raided by the Manchester Constables, when five men, including Bent, were arrested for attending an unlawful meeting. During the raid, copies of the United Englishmen's oath of 1798 was discovered.[7]

On 27 March, a mass meeting was held at Newton Heath. In response to the meeting, a handbill reported that 18,028 people had signed their names to a petition handed out at the meeting to fight for cheaper food. The handbill darkly warned that 'the people would give the gentry time to consider their case' before they would 'take what comes'.[8]

Later the same month, five men were arrested for administering illegal oaths and attempting to 'debauch the minds' of employees of a large factory and of the Little Lever Volunteers.[9] The same month, Bancroft uncovered a plan for a mass meeting at Preston with 400 said to be attending, organised by a United Irishman called Callaghan. Bancroft reported that partisans wished to overthrow the constitution and destroy the king and stated that within a 20-mile radius of Bolton, '9/10 of the people are sworn to overthrow the present constitution' and laid much of the blame on the high proportion of Irishmen in the population.[10] That same month, John Singleton wrote to the Home Office to say that a seditious society had been formed in Wigan, which transmitted its membership returns and minutes of their meetings to a society in Manchester, which passed on the information to a central committee in London. The London committee, he alleged, was planning an uprising, believed to be on 1 May, with the Volunteers to be disarmed and banks raided.[11]

The spy network trapped William Gallant, 'a committed Jacobin' who had damned the King and had stated that the Uniteds intended to capture the 200 cannons at Sheffield as well as swords, pikes and staves in Birmingham, and he was tried and gaoled at the Lancashire Assizes.[12] Bancroft's spies also provided evidence against others in Bolton, and brought to trial for seditious activities men identified as Maudsley, Moore, Williams and Chadwick. Bancroft reported to the Home Office that about 200 persons, some of whom had travelled in the night and a few in women's clothing, taking precautions against discovery by the authorities, had attended a seditious meeting in Bolton and that it appeared according to his spies, that the leaders in London had been obliged to restrain the Ashton people from rising prematurely. He concluded his report by noting that a certain Scholfield, a schoolmaster at Delph, Saddleworth, had written a book, printed by Cowdrey at Manchester, which he hoped to obtain.[13] A copy of this book was later found in Yorkshire. We have no clue as to its content other than it dealt with the five books of Moses in the Old Testament, and was presumably apocalyptic cum millenarian in the mould of Joanna Southcott.

It is now that the third Jacobin-hunter of Lancashire emerges, the Rev. William Robert Hay. Ideologically opposed to political reform, he sat at the bench that was to say 'OK' to the Peterloo massacre. Hay and Fletcher's hatred of non-Anglicans and of political reform knew no bounds. Hey reported that on 2 May thirty delegates had met at Buckton Castle to support a petition for reform. In his letter to the Home Office, Hay noted that the meeting had originally been planned to take place at Tandle Hill near Rochdale and that having arrived early in the morning he had found large number of people assembling, and in consequence had read a proclamation referring to the law recently passed in the House of Lords. Having read this, he ordered the dragoons to use whatever force was necessary to disperse the assembled crowd and spectators from the surrounding hills. Some arrests were made, including men from Manchester and Stockport.[14] Ralph Fletcher opined that those who had assembled had not broken the law, the Riot Act was of no use, and if apprehended that they could be impressed for the Navy as idle and disorderly persons. He appreciated that they would hardly be ideal recruits but that even the threat of a short term in the Navy would effectively discourage further meetings.[15]

Seditious meetings were rumoured to be taking place at Thornham, Royton and Oldham. Magistrate John Entwistle set out with a party of the 17th Light Dragoons and two pieces of horse artillery. He remarked to the Home Office, that the population should be made to understand that as prices were falling and trade was reviving, they should not listen and act on the advice of 'seditious wicked persons'.[16]

On the 18th a spy for Rev. Hay reported that meeting had been held at the house of one John Stott or James Stott at Heyside in Crompton. Thomas Cooper of Heyside was the Treasurer and Stott the Secretary. Caleb Taylor, from one of the Royton districts, better known as Caleb o' Calebs, proposed a plan for getting arms by disarming the military, particularly the Volunteers, in the Manchester area. He noted worryingly that some members had already armed themselves with pikes. A factory called Wood in the Crompton Division had turned out en masse to become attested. In London, the spy reported, planning for a new form of government was in hand and that John Horne Tooke was expected to present a petition to the House of Commons for a redress of grievances. If the petition was rejected by Parliament, it was to be the signal a general rising in London. The spy added that a meeting to be held at Heights Chapel, also known as Friar Mere, near Saddleworth had been cancelled. Magistrate Hay felt that this may have been a deliberate attempt to harass the military and the magistrates by announcing meetings that were never intended to take place. He added that his spy informed him that funds 'are devoted to defending those being tried for administering oaths' and that he 'expects to seize any printing presses that the revolutionaries may obtain'. He concluded that members are warned to eat any papers they were carrying should they be arrested, and very little is committed to writing.[17]

Two days later, John Singleton of Wigan informed the Home Office, that a seditious meeting had been broken up at Horwich Moor on 20 May, and described those who attended as 'vile'. He condemned the Whig press in Manchester for 'corrupting the minds of the lower orders'.[18]

The same day that Singleton was writing to the Home Office, Magistrate Bancroft also told the Home Office how he and Ralph Fletcher had broken up a seditious meeting on Rivington Pike on 24 May. He notes in his letter that the meeting had been confidently talked about in the neighbourhood of Wigan, Chorley and Bolton with the time of the meeting given as 3am. He notes that Ralph Fletcher and Major Gore of the 17th Light Dragoons, had issued orders to troops stationed in these towns to meet at Rivington Pike at 3am. Fletcher and other gentlemen, says Bancroft, went earlier to examine the ground with members of the Little Lever Volunteer Force on foot 'in ordinary clothes' with their bayonets concealed. Two troops of the 17th Dragoons under the command of Major Gore and Lieutenant Smelt and two small detachments of the 4th Dragoons from Wigan and Chorley arrived to assist. Bancroft reported that about 200 persons attended the meeting, many having stayed away when they had heard of the military preparations he supposed. Fletcher read the Proclamation against Riots and many people dispersed, twenty-one being taken into custody after being chased by the soldiers. One of those arrested was William Wronskley or Rauksley, and Joseph Flitcroft on the charge of bigamy, suspicious and bad conduct. Bancroft observed that these 'violations of Sunday' would tend to destroy all religion of the lower classes.[19] Was this William Wronskley the same man who would appear in Sheffield a year later?

Hay triumphantly reported to the Home Office that 'the delegates' were in low spirits because their plan to meet on Rivington Pike had been frustrated. Regretfully he noted that a spy had informed him that a meeting of the delegates from Bolton, Bury, Ashton, Saddleworth, Rochdale and Failsworth would take place on Kersal Moor, the Manchester Race Ground. One estimate had had received was that the number sworn to the society in at Bury, Bolton, Oldham, Glodwick Hamlet, Rochdale and one division of Manchester, totalled some 1,531 men. He added that the disaffected of Oldham were so intent on having a printing press that they had got a United Irishman, who had been in

145

gaol in Birmingham and had left Ireland with a £500 reward on his head, to set it up for them in the town.[20] Henceforth, detachments of cavalry accompanied by horse artillery patrolled Bolton, Oldham, and Rochdale, the idea being to teach 'the inhabitants of this very populous country . . . *a lesson* . . .'.[21] Slave owner and colliery proprietor Jonathan Blundell reported to the magistrates that many men in in his employ were 'United's' and had warned off his men from attending the Rivington Pike meeting and from taking any further part in seditious activity on pain of dismissal. The breaking-up of the Rivington Pike meeting considerably depressed the spirits of the United Britons in Lancashire.[22]

By the early summer, on the advice of Bancroft and Fletcher, local cotton spinners began to examine their employees' politics and to dismiss any with Jacobin leanings. Freedom of opinion was a thing of the past as 'the thought police' in the guise of an Anglican vicar clamped down on anti-government speech and thought. The spy network that he and Colonel Fletcher sat at the heart of reported that the Jacobin leaders were deeply concerned about lack of secrecy and infiltration by spies, who now risked assassination. Bancroft suggested to the Home Office the Jacobins were convinced that the French would invade Great Britain whereupon on a signal, reaching Edinburgh from London in four hours, there would be a universal rising. He also told the Home Office that he was still arresting local Jacobins and traitors as he understood the men to be: James Taylor for saying 'Damn the King and Constitution' and 'Damn the King and Country'. Bancroft added that Taylor had further damned the magistrates and Volunteers whilst drinking at the White Lion public house in Bolton, and had thanked Taylor's drinking companion, Thomas Simpson, for denouncing his friend to the authorities.[23]

## Yorkshire

Across the Pennines, by late March 1801, radical groups had emerged in Leeds, Sheffield and Huddersfield, where magistrates reported to the government that they feared 'an insurrection was in contemplation by the lower orders'. That month Magistrate Radcliffe in Huddersfield, who was becoming one of the most hated men in the West Riding for his heavy-handed treatment of food protests, received a letter threatening to behead the overseers of the poor, corn dealers and magistrates for being in league in setting high prices and 'making mothers destitute of their sons and daughters . . . 50,000 are redey boys & stedy boys' poised to rise in armed revolt.[24] This was perhaps no exaggeration. The stated aims of the Black Lamp, like the United

Englishmen before them, was 'The independence of Great Britain and Ireland, An Equalisation of Civil, Political and religious rights . . . a liberal reward for distinguished merit'.[25]

Magistrate Busfield wrote to Earl Fitzwilliam to inform him of a letter he had received which reported that a mass meeting was to be held at the bottom of Bradford Moor on 26 March 1801 for the people of Pudsey, Calverley, Idle, Windhill, Shipley, Heaton, Bradford, Bowling, Rose [Wrose], Leeds and its adjacent villages. The meeting was called to address the calamity of rising rents and food prices with an 20,000 expected to attend the meeting.[26] As the protests increased, the magistrates received more reports about underground radical groups. One of these met in Huddersfield, whose

> proceedings are very secret and no person is informed of the particulars of the plan until he has sworn to support it and not on any account to divulge it. They people are told that they will be supported not only by numbers in all parts of the Kingdom but by great folks and that the numbers will be such so suddenly called together so as to withstand any military force.[27]

The Anglican Rev. Thomas Bancroft informed the Home Office that his spy network had informed him that 'Lancashire was not so forward as the other counties – that delegates from Birmingham, Sheffield, Hull, Leeds & every other considerable town meet once a week, that these delegates communicate with provincial meetings & these with one in London'. He added that printed rules of the meetings were 'delivered from London'.[28] Nationwide anger was building.

As well as relying on spies, the Crown received information from 'members of the public'. One such informant was the Rev. Dr Thomas Coke, a Wesleyan Methodist and long considered the successor to John Wesley. Coke is today revered as the founding father of the Wesleyan denomination across the globe, and his activities as a spy are largely unknown. As a nominal Dissenter, he would have been viewed with considerable suspicion by some in society: yet both Wesley brothers, like Coke, were Loyalists and ardent 'Church and King' men. Coke was seemingly happy to turn spy, and raise his concerns over the rise of what he no doubt considered to be dangerous working-class rights consciousness.

As a man of wealth and status in society, he had a lot to lose from an expansion of human rights and democracy. Coke informed the Secret Committee at the Home Office that a linen draper of Hull called Middleton, who lodged in the same house where he himself had, had spoken seditious words and said that a 'grand association is forming in Lancashire and the North of England similar to that carried on by the United Irishmen'. Middleton – is this the same man as arrested later by William Dawson? – under the influence of alcohol, on a business trip to Bolton bragged aloud that 1,000 oaths had been taken in the town. This no doubt confirmed to the Home Office the validity of the Rev. Bancroft's report about seditious activity in Hull and Lancashire. The Rev. Dr Coke would provide evidence that placed Leeds and Sheffield centre stage in the upsurge of radicalism.

The good Rev. Coke, it seems, established his own spy network amongst congregations in the North of England. One of Coke's informants was Mr Wild, the choirmaster of Sheffield Wesleyan Chapel on Norfolk Street. Wild, said Dr Coke, had informed him that he had uncovered evidence that a seditious 'plan was on foot' in Sheffield and further afield. One can only assume Mr Wild infiltrated the Sheffield group or 'eves dropped' on conversations in public houses. Clearly, under Coke's direction Wesleyan Methodists were now spying for the state on their fellow townsmen in Sheffield, Hull and no doubt further afield. Alarmed by what he had learned, Coke set about 'Jacobin-hunting' and informed that Home Office that in Bolton and Manchester that:

> There is a very dangerous association forming in this County [Lancashire] at least, against the Government. One of our preachers ... informed me this morning that he had many reasons to believe that there were numbers of people of the lower rank who had been sworn in some way or another ... I shall be in Bolton the beginning of next week, when, through the assistance of a friend ... I shall obtain some solid information on this subject; and shall continue, from time to time to impart to your Grace everything.[29]

A month later he reported to the Home Office that seditious meetings of 'the Rebels' were being held at Ryton in Oldham, Lancashire, who he alleged, communicated via the ringing of church bells. He added:

> I indulged sanguine hopes that Leeds which contains a numerous Body of Loyalists would be preserved from this plague: but I am greatly afraid that it is not the case. I have been informed that there are many small parties of five or six who meet by night in particular houses in the town to learn the military exercises. I shall soon see one of the Magistrates, with whom I am in habits of intimacy, to whom I shall impart my fears.[30]

Coke, like his Anglican colleagues, had a very narrow and particular world view. He understood the struggle facing the nation was of good versus evil. The term 'plague' sums up his views about working-class rights consciousness and political reform. Methodists, far from being supportive of 'the Rights of Man', were loyalists, and the spread of evangelical Christianity via the Wesleyan Connexion – once the 'Thom Paine' Methodists had been expelled and had formed their own Methodist New Connexion in 1797 – contributed to the suppression of radicalism with a message of 'sufferings in this life will be rewarded in the next' to draw the working class into apathetic stoicism to accept their place in the world and not to question their betters. Such a world view kept the poor in their place, and the rich elites in theirs. As an Anglican priest once explained to me, 'It was not for man to change the world, but the coming of Christ to bring about justice and a new world order'.[31] Coke was no supporter of democracy: when Alexander Kihlman was expelled by the Methodist Conference in 1796, Coke described this schism as the 'expulsion of 5000 democrats from our society' in a letter to Henry Dundas, Secretary of State for War, dated 8 November 1798. The term 'democrats' being used in a highly derogatory sense, seeing such supporters of Thomas Paine as 'dangerous' for their desire for political change. Democracy had no place in the Wesleyan denomination or in Wesleyan society. Coke created a network of itinerant ministers to report on local matters, and used the Connexional network to gather information which was passed to the Home Office.[32] He was desperate for his new denomination to be seen to be 'respectable' and to be of 'no concern to the authorities': by spying on radicals, and by distancing the denomination from the charismatic groups like the Swedenborgians and Ezekielites, Coke was saying 'We are loyalists, nothing to see here'. Methodists had been considered 'dangerous' to society in the 1760s, and now presented themselves as anti-democratic and supporters of repression, and quite literally 'got the mob off their backs' to show religious dissent did not mean political dissent. The persecuted became the persecutor. Wesleyan Superintendents threatened with 'excommunication' any Wesleyan who signed the 1808 peace petition, condemning any who signed as 'Jacobins'.[33] Working-class conservative politics owes a great deal to Coke and a later Methodist leader, the Rev. Jabez Bunting.

In 1801 Coke informed the Duke of Portland that 'I was not a little alarmed two or three days ago in hearing that three Methodists were taken up on suspicion or proof of being engaged in this rebellion business. But on the strictest scrutiny and fullest satisfaction, I was happy enough to find that these three men had been expelled [from] the late Mr Wesley's society about five years ago solely for their democratic sentiments.'[34] For Coke, being a loyalist and being seen to be loyal was far great than religious inclusivity: in the crisis years of 1817–19, the Wesleyans by and large backed the atrocities at Peterloo and were seen as 'the bitterest foes to freedom in England'. In support of such anti-democratic actions, a modern-day Methodist historian states that 'alleged Methodist connections to subversive groups would have raised concerns similar to the infiltration and radicalization of a 21st century mosque'.[35]

Returning to the events of 1801, magistrate Bacon Frank, writing from Wakefield to Earl Fitzwilliam, noted that at the time of national distress that:

> you may depend upon the enemies to the country internal and external: the Jacobins do not fail to avail themselves these times particularly of working upon the feelings of the lower classes and that there are persons most actively employed in going about the country tendering an oath to the deluded people.[36]

Frank concluded in a postscript that Jacobinism was at almost epidemic level in Huddersfield and its environs. To prove his point, he informed the Earl that suspected Jacobins and traitors had been arrested in Pontefract, adding 'that Mr Garforth, had interrogated the prisoners in Pontefract Courthouse and gained much valuable information about a meeting' which he had promptly transmitted to the other magistrates.[37]

This may have been the planned meeting at Steeton Moor near Keighley, which was to be held on 20 April 1801 to 'consider the exorbitant price of provisions' as well as 'to obtain a fair and impartial representation in Parliament'. Panicked, magistrate J.A. Busfield suggested that the Craven troops of Yeomanry be called out in case of riot, backed by the Militia.[38] Earl Fitzwilliam agreed, and lookouts were placed on the roads to Steeton Moor to pass on any reports of people travelling to the moor to the officers of the 18th Light Dragoons which had been ordered out from the barracks in Bradford.[39] Earl Fitzwilliam also informed the Home Office that:

> I have devised that the two Craven troops of West Riding Yeomanry Cavalry, to assemble on the day pointed out by the paper . . . in order that they may be ready, should occasion require, to proceed to the spot. I have likewise desir'd Mr Busfield who is himself LtCol Com' of the Bradford Volunteers to have his corps parade at Bradford on that morning.[40]

The leaders of the proposed meeting on Steeton Moor cancelled the event once news reached the convenor of the actions Fitzwilliam had taken. Magistrate Thomas Garforth reported to the Home Office that he:

> had some constables on the Moor . . . not a single person . . . have been seen, not even a spectator from curiosity – and though the alarm had become general . . . I am included to believe the report was altogether discredited. Lord Ribblesdale is with his troop at Skipton, Major Ferrand's troops at Keighley and Bingley.[41]

The meeting may have been 'fake news' to draw the authorities away from discovering the location of the actual meeting. Certainly anti-government agitation in Saddleworth was high. The minister of St Thomas Parish Church, Heights, the Rev. Buckley had his life threatened on 10 April and a mob gathered outside the church calling him 'a hell-rake, a villain, a ruffian and a scoundrel' for his preaching in support of the Government while 'his neighbours were starving'.[42]

The Rev. Thomas Bancroft informed the Home Office with much alarm that a released felon named Robinson '*a very dangerous busy man*' who had been in prison in both Wakefield and York and planned to travel through Yorkshire, Nottinghamshire and Derbyshire in the guise of a Quaker. Robinson was believed to be involved in seditious activities and Bancroft hope to arrest him.[43] Radical groups on both sides of the Pennines were clearly in contact to organise action, and this lead to the use of Saddleworth Moor as a meeting place. Magistrate Radcliffe reported that meetings were taking place at Hartshead Moor, informing Earl Fitzwilliam that 'I think there are but few of the disaffected United Englishmen in this Neighbourhood. Saddleworth produces more being so near to the general body of them in Lancashire and the eastern part of Cheshire.'[44]

Working on information from spies, the Crown began to make arrests. The Commons Secret Committee reported on 15 May that delegates from London, York, Birmingham, Bristol and Sheffield as well as other towns were in communication, and were linked to the United Irishmen and the French Government. Revolution was planned to occur in London, Ireland and principal towns on the same day, and that the King and House of Commons would be seized and private property protected. The Tory press redoubled its efforts, in a general spirit of repression, to crush the renovated ardour of Jacobinism.[45]

151

Chapter 15

# PREVENTING REVOLUTION: THE LOYALIST RESPONSE

The first blow against the Black Lamp outside London was struck at Clew Wells, near Saddleworth. A mass meeting was planned around Saddleworth on Sunday 24 May 1801: Rev. Hay, the Jacobin-catching parson of Pontefract, in his capacity as magistrate dispatched 40 regulars and 250 cavalry from the Huddersfield troop of Yeomanry 'to show the disaffected a ready and formidable appearance of the military . . . by way of intimidation'.[1] For Hay, the poor and starving had no right to protest – a stance that is seemingly becoming very popular again with right-wing politicians – about the cost of living and the lack of democratic representation. By the time the cavalry had arrived at Saddleworth, the moor was deserted. Hay did note however that there were few disaffected people in the vicinity of Huddersfield but in Saddleworth, parts of which bordered on Lancashire and Cheshire, he noted there were people of a 'more turbulent disposition' and in Lancashire and East Cheshire there were large numbers of disaffected people. Radcliffe stated to the Home Office that he would be ready at a moment's notice should his help be needed to police the county borders.[2] So keen on supressing anti-government propaganda was Radcliffe, that he sought to seize printing presses in Sheffield owned by John Crome, who was suspected of printing seditious material and being a 'key player' in the seditious plot then developing in the West Riding.[3]

In June, the Rev. William Robert Hay wrote to the Home Office from Lancashire, passing on news from his spy network:

we are informed that agents from York, Sheffield, Birmingham, Bristol and London have been lately in the neighbourhood, and they have laboured successfully to convince the people of the strength of their party and the certain success which would attend an insurrection. They are said uniformly to have held out that they can rely on the support of a considerable part of the Volunteers and other military – We are further informed that two persons are daily employed in the adjoining Parish of Saddleworth in administering Oaths and collecting signatures.[4]

Before the oath was taken, Hay noted, the person to be sworn in read the 25th verse of Ezekiel 21 'O though profane Prince of Israel whose time has come'. The spy network run by Ralph Fletcher had identified a house in Saddleworth where class tickets, books and other seditious materials were held. In reply, the Home Office gave permission on 17 June for the house in Saddleworth to be searched.[5]

By the end of the month, Major Gore in Bolton informed the Home Office of 'seditious' meetings in the West Riding. He was transmitting information from one of his spies. The spy was undertaking an intelligence-gathering exercise about the disaffected societies across the North of England. Gore noted that the man was on a tour with a delegate who resided near Manchester, and had visited groups in Sheffield and Wakefield. The informant reported that the delegates were 'more active than ever' and that he had seen letters from Lord Stanhope and Major Cartwright. The spy furthermore told Gore that he had procured letters of introduction to 'Citizen [Thomas] Hardy'.[6] The same day as Major Gore wrote to the Home Office, Jacobin-hunting parson the Rev. Thomas Bancroft reported information from his spy and the released felon Robinson. He reported that Robinson had gone with a person in the confidence of the United Britons to visit different districts across the country. He noted that the spy's communications had so far been entirely from Yorkshire, where he was employed to collect money from persons appointed to sell a publication by Schofield of Delf [Delph] called 'The analytical investigation of the five books of Moses'. The spy and Robinson initially travelled to Saddleworth, where membership was reported to be 30,000 and had met with men called George Savage and that 'the better sort of people had ceased meeting or subscribing'. The pair travelled on to Huddersfield, Ripon, Elland, Halifax, Bradford and Leeds. The 'principal man' at Elland was identified as Robert Burnelly and the society had lost the support of 500 members. In Bradford, Job Jennings was the leader, who also acknowledged the loss of support locally. The same was true in Huddersfield where the delegate complained that 'many respectable people had abandoned them'. The spy reported that 'a certain Phineas Lumb' could muster 10,000 men from the surrounding area at any

153

given time. The pair were referred to other leaders in Beeston, Holbeck and Pudsey Hill, notably Luke Brafton aka Luke Broughton who was already well known to the Home Office. The Leeds Committee stated that with three days' notice they could muster 30,000 men from 10 miles around Leeds and seize the cannon from foundries and march across the country to the powder mills before the Government could react. At Beeston the pair made contact with James Lumb, William Walker and Benjamin Wood, the latter being identified as the secretary of the committee. From Leeds, the pair were ordered to call on three houses in Wakefield identified as belonging to the Garnett,[7] Longbottom and White families. The spy added that 'the United frequently met on Heath Green' – presumably this is Heath Common. Heath Green is overlooked by houses, one of which in 1801 was the home of John Smyth MP and his son John Henry Smyth. The common, on the other hand, is and has always been a vast expanse of open moorland bisected by the Weeland turnpike, and would have made an ideal meeting point. From Wakefield, the pair travelled to Sheffield where they called on Crome, the printer.

From Crome they obtained a copy of the rules and orders of the society together with some songs and printed books. The spy, reported Bancroft, was told that the Sheffield Society were armed and that society secretary William Camage had letters from Lord Stanhope, Citizen Hardy and Major Cartwright. In addition, it was reported that the Jacobin group had a meeting on 18 June near Justice Parker's house, at Woodthorpe Hall, Handsworth. The meeting was no doubt held on Woodthorpe Common rather than the grounds of the Hall. The spy, Bancroft reported, believed that two sorts of pikes were buried in gardens near Sheffield.[8]

A few days later Bancroft wrote to the Home Office that he had received a package of 'papers of a generally blasphemous or seditious nature relating to various areas of Yorkshire' that had been printed by Crome. Sadly, these papers have not survived so we cannot judge their content. However, Bancroft did record in his covering letter that not one of the papers was recent, most being two or three years old in his estimation. Bancroft also noted that the spy had obtained two models of pikes and that 24,000 had been issued in Sheffield. Bancroft cast doubt on the agent's effectiveness as the spy was 'so easily admitted into their confidence & is ever likely to penetrate the designs of the disaffected fraternities' and wondered if 'they have suspended their operations'. Questions we cannot answer. Were the magistrates being fed false information so that the spy would get paid? Quite possibly, as Bancroft wondered if the books and papers had been so easily obtained because the society in Sheffield had 'privately sold them away' and openly challenged the credibility of the evidence and also the actions and motivation of Ralph Fletcher – who we come to shortly.[9] Certainly Crome, Camage and Broughton were well known to the authorities. Was the evidence part of a 'fit-up'? Was the spy feeding in old material to sensationalise and inflate the threat of the plot? Or were the radicals using old stocks of handbills out of necessity? Three questions it is impossible to answer. Bancroft clearly felt something was not quite right about what he was being told by the spy network. Was the entire plot a government-organised conspiracy to once and for all discredit the radicals and to support a harsh clampdown on sedition? It is perfectly possible, but unlikely. For 200 years the seriousness of the events that took place leading to the arrest of Despard have been downplayed: if the evidence sent to the Home Office was genuine, then the Crown faced imminent danger. On the other hand, if one or two persons in London were feeding spy networks false information, then there was nothing to fear and it was a deliberate trap, aimed at capturing radicals. Both hypotheses are perfectly possible, as is that 'Citizen Bent' was a double agent passing information to both the radicals and the Crown. We cannot be certain, but it is doubtful if Bent was alone in these activities.

Back across the Pennines, magistrate Bertie Markland estimated that '225,000 unemployed and disaffected would rise in Revolution' in Manchester. A spy who worked for him added that there were partisans in every town and village in the kingdom and many soldiers and Volunteers had taken the oath to be faithful to the party, adding that when the revolution took place the National Debt would be expunged, the powers of the Crown would be narrowed, and the laws of the nation would stay as they were. If the King refused to sanction the changes, then he would be banished or lose his life. The spy also reported the production of weapons in Sheffield, and insinuated that members of the Whig club were synonymous with the 'New Party', i.e., the Jacobin threat.[10] The Crown appears to have been endeavouring to link the London Corresponding Society, the Foxite Whigs and Major Cartwright to the unfolding conspiracy. Was this likely? Possibly, as we shall see later.

A key person in the events that followed was Colonel Ralph Fletcher. He was a 'spymaster' in the pay of Whitehall, having established 'The Society for Information and Correspondence', which was essentially a network of local paid spies, most of whom were out-of-work men willing to betray their fellow sufferers for money. In this role, Fletcher was required to report almost daily to the Home Office on any so-called 'seditious activity'. He was named JP in 1797 and colonel of the Bolton Volunteer Infantry, and through his indefatigable hatred of all those who opposed the state and policies of William Pitt earned himself a reputation for ruthlessness against workers' collectives and reformers. Fletcher took a leading role in the Peterloo Massacre: he never showed any contrition for his actions and was awarded a silver gilt trophy in recognition of the violent suppression of the open-air meeting. Indeed, Fletcher was seen beating some of the demonstrators with a club. Such was the man who, with his network of spies, sought to crush working-class radicalism in Yorkshire.

Using his spy network and released criminal and double agent Robinson – we met him earlier being arrested by the Rev. Thomas Bancroft for sedition while travelling through Yorkshire – Fletcher infiltrated the radical group in Sheffield. Reports were received by the Home Office in June, that in Sheffield, a group of around 300 were meeting to drill amongst whom was Crome. Another of the spies working for Fletcher reported that arms were being produced in Sheffield, including cannon and pikes as well as ammunition. Fletcher also noted that he had learned that a weekly subscription of 6d a week was collected from members, which went to a central committee for the expenses of delegates and their families; money was also raised from fines and punishments of members and was used to take action against informers and spies.[11]

Robinson reported that Sheffield had 15,000 sworn men ready to act, and stated that, whilst the evidence that pikes were being made and concealed in the area was strong, as yet no evidence had been found that men were actually being trained in their use. Fletcher in his report notes that his spy had met with some of the committee when they claimed to have many thousands of pikes buried. The spy asked to purchase a few on the pretext of financing a further 100. Shaw introduced him to a recently-sworn man who would make them for 3s 6d each, and in consequence the spy now had two different types in his possession. The spy reported that he had been introduced to a committee of ten persons by the aforementioned Robinson, and had obtained the names and details of eight members:[12]

Francis Moody, shoemaker of 45 Fargate, Barker's Pool
Matthew Shaw, silversmith of 27 White Croft
Thomas Trouth, silversmith of Bolton Brigg Field
Timothy Gales – nephew of the radical Joseph Gales no less – pressman at Montgomery's Printing Office
J Crome, printer of Waingate

William Camage, leather ink stand maker of Tipper Lane
William Wilkinson, tailor (meal man for a society), of Shambles
Allcock (a Quaker), leather inkstand maker of Church Lane.

Fletcher's spy noted that Crome was printing material for the radicals: this makes a mockery of earlier reports about the printed materials being several years old! The spy noted that Crome was so worried about being discovered to be printing the material and arrested again that he kept two loaded blunderbusses in his attic office, and furthermore had set a mantrap on the top of the stairs to his rooms. Fletcher himself commented that the West Riding of Yorkshire was more infected with Jacobin principles than Lancashire, and was he noted, centred in Sheffield and Huddersfield according to the reports of Mr Radcliffe.[13]

Fearing that the Sheffield plot was the 'tip of the iceberg', in response magistrate William Dawson began a campaign of infiltration of the Black Lamp across the West Riding. He was right to be worried. Dawson wrote to Fitzwilliam on 27 July about meetings in Ossett and at Staincliffe common near Dewsbury and of the precautions which he had taken in case of further gatherings. At Ossett over 700 had attended and he reported that the assembly was 'clearly . . . composed of two different descriptions of person, Viz. Parties to the business and lookers on' and noted that the former made a ring and admitted nobody without a ticket. Furthermore, he reported that over 1,000 had attended a meeting at Hatchett Moor, the leading haranguing the crowd whilst wearing a mask. Dawson added that section leaders from Leeds, Huddersfield, Dewsbury, Ardsley, Birstall and others places were present. Thanks to Dawson's spy – a servant to Mr Michel Angelo Taylor – a merchant of Gomersal called Gill was identified as the committee man for Birstall. The chairman of the meeting, a spy told Dawson, a certain Safford had come from Sheffield, and was a journeyman heading to Scotland.[14]

Dawson began a campaign of suppressing meetings: a planned meeting at Dewsbury on 26 July came to his attention. On the appointed day, he set out from Wakefield with a troop from the 11th Light Dragoons, but by the time he arrived at Ossett, his spy told him the meeting, having been informed of the advancing troops, had dispersed. Dawson hoped to catch some of the attendees and continued to Dewsbury where he found the 'town was quiet'.[15] At Ossett, Dawson estimated that about 700 had attended a nocturnal meeting held on the 30th. He believed that the Black Lamp gathered every night in the open fields to plot sedition in groups of up to

1,000 people. His spies followed the leaders home from Ossett hoping to discover their names and places of residence. With such information Dawson hoped he could then obtain a warrant to seize papers and other evidence from the leaders' houses. Dawson believed he had sufficient evidence concerning Josiah Walker, Gill and Charles Middleton, the committee man from Cleckheaton, to request from the Home Office the permission to arrest either Gill or Middleton.[16]

Meantime, Earl Fitzwilliam reported to the Earl of Portland on 30 July that meetings of the Black Lamp had been held near Batley, and on Hatchett Moor near Halifax. Fitzwilliam informed the Home Office, that the meeting, based on Dawson's report, had no specified agenda but the impression was given that it was about the price of food and the falling-off of trade. Fitzwilliam felt that the local Volunteer infantry and Yeomanry would be adequate support for the local officials to contain any threat the Black Lamp posed, especially 'if one or two regiments of dragoons could be stationed at Leeds'. Fitzwilliam noted that the regulars were essential 'as they could be mobilised more quickly than the militia, speed and secrecy being paramount if the leaders of these meetings were to be surprised and arrests made'. He concluded his letter reporting to the Home Office that a lot of information was being passed to the magistrates that was 'obscure, and may not been wholly reliable, by the various informants'.[17]

A day after Fitzwilliam had sent word to the Home Office, he wrote again. He said that Dawson would do nothing about Middleton or Gill until he had heard from the Home Secretary and requested a warrant issued to arrest Richard Brooke. Brooke had attended a meeting which advocated the ending of all taxes and pensions and proposed lowering the price of provisions, all of which, Dawson thought, amounted to high treason.[18]

At the close of August, the Home Office authorised Dawson to arrest those he considered a danger. Armed with a warrant under the Seditious Meetings Act, Dawson made arrests:[19]

> In Gomersal the aforementioned Gill was arrested and his house was raided.
> Richard Brooke of Honley was arrested because he 'had plotted to put an end to all taxes . . . to lower the price of provisions'.
> Also from Honley 'a man called Carver' was arrested with no specific charge.

Dawson admitted to Fitzwilliam that the Crown should not rely on the current fall in food prices and increasing levels of employment as the panacea to stave off rebellion, and believed that the conspiracy would continue whilst ever the Crown ignored the reasons for disaffection.[20] In order to get to 'the bottom of things' Fitzwilliam requested 'a spy or someone who is familiar with persons suspected by government' be sent to Yorkshire 'to attempt identification of the leader of the meetings as they were not local men'.[21] Clearly, the local network of spies and informers was not considered 'up to the job' and a 'man from the ministry', i.e., a professional spy, was needed.

Concerned by the increasing insurrectionary threat facing the West Riding, John Brooke, magistrate and Lord Mayor of Leeds, requested a troop of cavalry be posted to Leeds to aid the magistrates to quell the meetings.[22] He further warned the Home Office that open-air nocturnal meetings were taking place around Leeds, urging the people to rise up in armed insurrection. He added that the time of the meetings and the matters discussed were known only to a select circle 'separate from the surrounding multitude' and noted that the magistrates were inclined to think that the arrest and detention of some of the leaders would act as a strong check and deterrent to the meetings. Brooke confided to the Home Office that he and the magistrates were aware of the names of some of the delegates from the neighbouring townships that met in Leeds. He added that the bulk of the evidence that the magistrates had gathered related 'to a person resident in Leeds who is greatly disaffected by the government, has been accused of persuading someone to take the United Englishmen's oath, and has attended a nocturnal meeting on Hartshead Moor'. Alas, Brooke does not give us a name! He concluded his letter to the Home Office by noting that he and his fellow magistrates believed that four delegates from Leeds and its environs were in London, attending an important meeting relating to the uprising, but did not know where, where or with whom they were meeting.[23]

The Rev. Dr Thomas Coke wrote from the Wesleyan Methodist Manse on West Parade, Wakefield in the middle of August with information he had gathered about seditious activities in the West Riding. He noted in his letter that 10 days earlier, an estimated 1,800 people had assembled on Grange Moor near Huddersfield to attend a seditious meeting. He was concerned that, if the French could evade the Royal Navy and invade, the people who assembled at the meetings might become a danger to the country in its hour of need by diverting the army to contain them. He wondered 'is it possible the government is not sufficiently alarmed' by the threat posed by the Black Lamp and United Britons. Coke was clearly a very worried man. He left Wakefield shortly after for Dublin to minister to Methodists in

Ireland and to act as a spy at his own request, noting 'I was travelling through the province of Ulster, when the rebellious uniting business was going on [1798] . . . and did myself the honour of writing to Mr. Pelham, then Secretary of State for Ireland on the subject'.[24] We know nothing more of his career as a spy, but given his avowed hatred of the United Britons, it seems reasonable that he continued his activities in Ireland against the United Irishmen.

By September the reports of clandestine meetings ended: seemingly the threat of revolution was over. The Leeds magistrate John Beckett told Earl Fitzwilliam that his spy network informed him 'that there would now be no occasion for any further meetings till the French Landed'.[25] The Black Lamp refused to rise without a French landing. The French invasion force had been ready to set sail at the end of July.[26] But instead the invasion fleet set sail for Saint Domingo. The preliminaries for the signing of the treaty of Amiens meant that for France any invasion attempt was 'off the cards'.[27]

At the same time, food prices were starting to drop thanks to a good harvest. This does not mean that the Black Lamp had given up hopes of reform, however. Unitarian Whig Edward Baines, editor of the *Leeds Mercury*, accepted that the grievances of the working man existed, and argued that with peace coming, now was the time to oppose the government with 'constitutional boldness and not shrink into lurking holes like a *lawless banditii*'.[28] To try and keep one step ahead of the revolutionaries, the Crown formed an aptly-names 'Committee of Secrecy', which reviewed alarming reports produced by provincial spies. The committee concluded in August that a renewal of the Seditious Meetings Act and the Habeas Corpus Suspension Act was necessary to preserve peace.[29]

Chapter 16

# THE DESPARD COUP

What happened next was largely driven by Irish affairs. The conspiracy that the Black Lamp and United Britons served was not of their making, nor of the man whose name it bears. As in 1796–8, Ireland wanted home rule, and if the French would not help, then with the help of the Black Lamp in England, the Irish would rise themselves. The plot, which ever since has carried the name of Colonel Marcus Edward Despard, had little to do with the colonel and precious little to do with England or London either: it had everything to do with Irish hatred of the Act of Union and the betrayal of the Catholics by William Pitt.

In order to ensure the Act of Union was passed in England and Ireland and for the Irish Parliament to vote to dissolve itself, as a concession to the Protestant Ascendancy in Ireland Pitt quietly dropped his plan for Catholic emancipation. Perhaps Pitt, who had sought Catholic emancipation in 1793, had hoped that he could introduce legislation through the new Parliament of the United Kingdom once the Union was a 'done deal'. It did not come to pass until 1829. Disappointment and anger led to the United Irishmen seeking aid from France once more. The plan had been developed since summer 1799: Despard was neither the originator of the plot nor its leader. The real leaders were the heirs to Wolfe Tone: William Dowdell, Thomas Russell, the Emmet brothers and William Putnam McCabe. McCabe was in Paris in summer 1799, and so too were Arthur MacMahon and eleven other senior United Irishmen like Colonel O'Neale, who had fled the events of 1798.[1] What was discussed and planned is lost to history. English revolution became harnessed to dreams of Irish independence. Senior members of the United Irishmen, who had held field commands in the Army of Wexford in 1798 during the aborted revolution of that year which had been backed by the French 'putting boots on the ground', had emigrated to Lancashire, mostly around Liverpool. A spy reported

161

that the Irish leaders were holding secret meetings with John Thelwall and other radicals.[2]

Amid such heightened tensions, a spy reported that the United Irishmen said they could call on 30,000 armed men from various districts of London in three-quarters of an hour, summoned by a horn. The spy added that these men were known to each other by secret signs, and were the same group who had broken lamps the previous year.[3] The 'lamp breakers' are almost certainly the Black Lamp. A national underground network of Jacobins and radicals was on the move once more.

The extensive spy network in the North of England reported that a major underground revolutionary plot to overturn the government was being planned. Informants confirmed the government's worst fears.[4] Almost simultaneously, the English Revolutionary Committee met emissaries from the United Irishmen, John MacNamara and Charles Pendrill – the former would go onto to figure in the Despard plot – at the Queen's Head public house near St Martin-Le-Grand, London. The United Irish sought to harness the disaffection in England and provide leadership.[5] The Rev. Ralph Fletcher told the Home Office that a man called Smith, a resident of Ashby de la Zouch, had left Manchester for Sheffield on 9 October, where he was reported to have ordered 2,000 pikes to be made.[6] In Heywood near Rochdale, Richard Clough 'was found in the act of administering an unlawful oath to John Pollitt'[7] and had been before magistrates three years earlier for saying the nation was 'governed by a lunatic king, ruined prince and a runaway duke'.[8]

Real anger at the Crown's inept handling of the famine, the economic slump, increasing mechanisation and the resulting unemployment meant that England's revolutionary moment was approaching. Peace was still seen as the panacea for society's ills, yet for the radicals in London it would bring a new wave of supporters. As one commented, 'when the sailors come to be paid off and the soldiers disembodied, there will be no employment for them, that wou'd be the time if anything was to be done'.[9] In February 1802, a riot among Irishmen occurred at the Goat public house on Stafford Street, Manchester: the press reported that 'the quarrel arose from a dispute on the subject of the Union'.[10] It was that dispute over the Act of Union that fomented revolution in London.

## Enter Despard

We have mentioned Despard before. He was an Irishman who had joined the army in 1766 and attained the rank of colonel. After serving in Jamaica, he was sent to Central America in 1781; there he was made governor of Roatán Island, off the Honduras coast, and soon afterward of the British Mosquito Coast and Gulf of Honduras. In 1784 he took over the administration of Belize. There he supported the land claims of recent immigrants from the Mosquito Coast against those of earlier settlers, whose complaints meant he was recalled in 1790. Charges against him were dismissed in 1792, but the British government refused to employ him further. From then on, he campaigned to have his name cleared and he became involved with the United Irishmen as we noted in earlier chapters. In January 1802, Despard was in Ireland with William Dowdall, who had been released from Fort George with the ending of the Suspension of Habeus Corpus Act. He was back in England by the end of February and was now actively involved in the plot that forever bears his name.[11]

In April 1802, the Jacobin-hunting Ralph Fletcher reported that seditious activity was on the increase. His spy network informed him that Manchester Committee had sent William Cheetham as a delegate to the National Committee which met in London in order to obtain orders. The spy noted that the committees in Leeds, Wakefield and Sheffield had contributed to his expenses. Fletcher further noted that a delegate by the name of Winn had travelled to London from Stockport and had been eventually accepted and sent back with instructions. Also involved, the spy network told him, was a schoolmaster by the name of Clegg who taught arithmetic and navigation and gave lectures on the British Constitution. More worryingly, Fletcher reported that a delegate from Ireland called Maginnis had attended the London Committee and had told the assembled delegates that there were 36,000 supporters in Dublin who were waiting for the disbandment of the army before they would act. Fletcher also noted that the Sheffield committee gave one member a pike and an instrument called a cat – a caltrop – intended to lame horses. The aim of the Committee, Fletcher noted, was to secure a government based on the will of the people, the independence of England and Ireland, freedom of religion, to wipe out the National Debt and 'to disburden the people of taxes'.[12] An agent called Benson reported that John Nicholls and Farrell were in London in March where they met a delegate from Leeds, who met other United Irish leaders and also disaffected soldiers.[13] The plan seems to have been to overthrow Addington's government and install the Whigs who would grant universal suffrage and lower food prices. The Tower of London was a key objective to be taken to obtain arms and powder. However, the enthusiasm of the soldiers for the planned revolution was already proving to be an issue: soldiers and sailors were being sworn into the movement by a carpenter called John Woods and a shoemaker called

John Francis, as well as a journeyman leather breeches-maker John Hayes.[14] Whatever was being planned, it was centred on Ireland. The United Irishmen's plans rested on Despard containing the anger until Ireland was ready to rise in rebellion and the French could land. It was useless if England rose, and no French forces landed in Ireland. The two events had to be co-ordinated, and Despard was key in 'tempering' the spirit of revolution in England.[15]

## The Black Lamp Ablaze Once More

In this regard, Despard had an almost impossible task. English radicals were angry and wanted to act regardless of co-ordination with the United Irishmen or France. The 'explosion' of English radical activity from spring 1802 showed the very real level of anger in the country among the working class at the lack of political reform and taxation. Anger is a very powerful force, but without being harnessed, contained and directed towards a specific goal, they would be little more than an angry mob. The mob had to be turned into an army, its anger tempered and checked till the time was right to act. History tells us the Irish revolution was planned for some time in summer 1803. Despard had to keep control for 18 months.

On 18 May 1802 radicalism burst back into life in the West Riding – or at least made itself visible again – when Fred Flower wrote to Henry Addington to report secret nocturnal meetings were taking place near Wakefield, Dewsbury and Leeds. Earl Fitzwilliam was asked to report on what he knew by the Home Office, and commented that, yes, meetings had taken place in April, but said there was no cause for alarm.[16] He was wrong. This was the beginning of a fresh round of agitation by the working classes seeking to obtain the vote, and overturn the government. Trade unionism and radical politics collided across the country in the most serious attempt at armed revolution since 1745.

A week or so later, on 27 May 1802, William Dawson reported to Earl Fitzwilliam, frequent 'meetings of the lower order . . .' were taking place at night in fields around Leeds, Morley, Batley, Ossett and Wakefield. In Huddersfield, Justice Walker reported to Fitzwilliam that seditious meetings were taking place amongst the working class 'to assert and regain their natural rights'.[17] Garrisons in Sheffield, York, Leeds, Bradford, Pontefract and Doncaster were strengthened: Earl Fitzwilliam believed that a 'true Jacobinical sort of conspiracy . . . does exist . . . and I trust, the real secret is in very few hands, that the rest are dupes . . .'.[18] In June Magistrate Richard Walker noted to Earl Fitzwilliam 'I ought not to have forgotten the despondency and distress that pervades this district from the rapid decline of the woollen manufacture'.[19] Despite peace and the economy starting to recover, many thousands lacked work: desperate times lead desperate people to desperate acts.

At the beginning of July, Ralph Fletcher from Manchester reported that delegates from Manchester and Leeds had attended a meeting of the Directory in London. The Manchester delegate was William Cheetham and from Leeds a Mr Pawson, the meeting having taken place on 27 May. Pawson met with local leaders at Marsden on 27 June. One of the local leaders was one of Fletcher's spies, known as 'B'. The spy reported that Pawson had left Manchester on Wednesday 26 May, and had met other known 'United Englishmen' on the 27th at the White Horse, Fetter Lane. One of those Pawson met was called Nicholls. Pawson met with the Directory on 30 May, one of whom was a man called John MacCloud or MacCleod, a delegate from Ireland, at the Pewter Platter, near Holborn in London to discuss the proposed insurrection. The spy reported that two soldiers from the Guards and one from the Light Dragoons also attended and carried with them a paper stating that all soldiers involved should be paid one guinea per week and, if the point be carried, they should be permitted to retire and receive ten acres of land and money to cultivate them. The discussion centred on the plan of operations which stated that:

1. The Tower of London to seized and used as a base of operations
2. The bank of England to be seized
3. Woolwich Arsenal to be seized
4. 'It was the opinion of the army that both houses of parliament should be seized when sitting.'
5. 'That the army should do all in their power to bring over horsemen if possible.'

The spy reported that the Directory felt that nothing should happen till Parliament was dissolved, and that the towns concerned in the business were to be given notice so as to have their Flag of Liberty ready. Private property was not to be meddled with, reported the spy, who also noted that MacCloud claimed he could bring more than 7,000 Irishmen in half an hour to join the rebellion. The spy added furthermore that the Directory believed 15,000 Irish had joined in the cause in London and 57,000 English, and that in Ireland 160,000 were ready to take up arms. In the North, the Directory noted that they had a Legion 574 strong in Stockport, 330 men in Buxton, 95 at Leek, Courbridge had 207 men ready to act, at Burslem 290, Hardy Green 200, Newcastle under

Lyme 241 and Wilmslow 133, some 2,070 men in total. Manchester and Liverpool delegates were, it was reported, in direct and constant contact with Ireland. The Directory agreed that when England began the revolution, the Irish would do the same. Fletcher commented that the figures given were perhaps exaggerated to encourage the Leeds delegate, but there is no doubt that the conspirators were industrious and were collecting large sums of money.[20]

On 15 July, a group of West Riding Magistrates chaired by J.A. Busfield, and including Joseph Radcliffe and Richard Walker, resolved to petition the government to garrison the West Riding because:

> nightly meetings of numerous bodies of disaffected persons are frequently held for the mischievous purposes of sedition and insurrection, and in such numbers, that the civil powers & [illegible] totally inadequate to suppress those meetings or to bring any such persons to justice. That the Volunteer Corps being long disbanded and there being no troops quartered in this district, it appears to us, that the impunity with which these meetings are held, may give rise to serious insurrections.[21]

The magistrates were worried, yet Fitzwilliam was sanguine, feeling that they were 'tilting at windmills' and were exaggerating the threat, particularly Walker. Fitzwilliam commented about handbills being posted: 'it is possible that they are sent merely to play upon Mr W alarm's; for he seems to have rather a tendency that way which his neighbours have discovered: Being sent by the post gives ground for the suspicion.'[22]

On his part, Walker felt the handbills 'maybe of little consequence' and that at least one had come from Stockport: others he noted were from the same stock of handbills taken in Birstall 'a few years ago', when a printer's shop was raided and the printer gaoled at York for three months. We should recall that Bancroft in Manchester had only found material that was three years old, and had uncovered no new printed material. Either the material was being planted for the magistrates and spies to find, or old handbills were still in circulation. Both hypotheses, as we noted earlier, are possible: we cannot say for sure what was going on. By 1802 the famine had largely passed, peace was at hand and the economy was slowly recovering: the 'engine' that drove the Black Lamp and United Englishmen had 'powered down'. What was left was real anger in Ireland about the events of 1796–8 and the brutal repression of the English Crown. It is hard to judge where the demands over political reform now lay. When we look at the documents Walker sent Fitzwilliam, they comprise an 'Address to the United Britons' dating from 1799 and also a copy of 'Rights of Swine', printed as far back as 1794.[23] Certainly, Fitzwilliam's belief that Walker was over-reacting seems to be grounded in some basis of truth, and perhaps also for the other magistrates in the West Riding. The use of old printed material by the Black Lamp may have been out of necessity: John Crome had been gaoled, Joseph Gales was in exile and John Hurst had become a loyalist. With no press and printer in their ranks, it is highly likely that the Black Lamp had no means at all of producing new material, and were using whatever they had to hand. This scenario does not seem to have been contemplated by Fitzwilliam but it does fit the known facts!

In getting back to the events of spring 1802, Magistrate Walker felt that total press censorship would be for the greater good. He noted discontent locally had been worsened by newspaper coverage of 'extravagant feasts and expensive entertainments . . . especially calculated to feed the discontent' and argued that the food riots of 1795, and 1799–1801 were made worse by the press.[24] For Walker, it was fine for the great and good to eat lavish meals with displays of conspicuous consumption at times of famine, but the press had no right to report this and therefore enrage the starving majority.

More worrying for Fitzwilliam was the news that members of disbanded Volunteer and Militia corps were active amongst the Black Lamp. Nevison Scatcherd of Morley reported 'It appears that there are frequently nightly meetings of considerable numbers of people on which occasions they are marshalled in military order' and added that they 'have manifested a person taking command and are appointing inferior officers to drill by squads . . .'.[25] In a letter to Fitzwilliam, magistrate and colonel of Militia John Dixon was convinced that ex-soldiers or serving Volunteers or militiamen were in charge of the ad hoc forces, estimated at least 1,000 persons in Morley. Dixon also sent news that amongst the men drilling could be found wealthy merchants, owning £2,000 in property, who had formerly been in the Horse Guards. Alas we do not have a name of this 'father and Son'. Dixon expressed a desire have regular troops deployed in the West Riding, particularly the manufacturing districts, and noted that:

Leeds contains the full proportion of the disaffected – at the meeting I understand they proposed [illegible] all grievances, particularly the new malt tax, the window tax &c & they also talk of a reform of Parliament, but I believe their real objectives is levelling & plunder. Mr Buck laid before us also an account of a meeting that was held the other night in his Park at New Grange – my great fear arises from the civil powers having no force to call unto their aid should these disaffected Gentry break out in open acts of violence.[26]

A week later came news of seditious meetings taking place in public houses in Halifax for 'The grand business of the Revolution' and added that the radicals 'Publicly boast that 100,000 of the military have promised to join them – alluding more particularly to the disbanded Volunteers and the disbanded Militia'. He concluded his letter fearing 'that everything is perfectly rife for a rebellion in Leeds, Halifax and Wakefield'.[27]

Concerned about an uprising in Leeds, Fitzwilliam felt that the 1,000 stands of arms housed in Leeds would be an obvious target. The arms were kept without a guard, and had been withdrawn from the stood-down 1st West Yorkshire Militia, which in its disembodied state mustered 27 corporals, 12 drummers and 107 men. He sought permission from the Home Office to call the 'men to' in case of emergency.[28] This power was granted by Downing Street and regulars were dispatched to garrison Halifax, Huddersfield and Wakefield[29] in addition to the two troops of the 4th Dragoons in Sheffield, principally seven troops from the 18th Light Dragoons.[30]

Magistrate Radcliffe reported from his Milnsbridge home about 'frequent seditious nocturnal meetings' taking place in Huddersfield. He noted 'a large meeting was held here not two miles from this place one night last week, & an other it is reported will be held on Ledston Common near Honley'.[31] A handbill sent to Earl Fitzwilliam on 27 July 1802 proclaimed the aims of the Black Lamp rebellion as follows:

1. Protect every member of the community equally, in the fullest enjoyment of his natural rights, from the force and injustice of any of his fellow subjects.
2. Protect the whole nation in all her rights, industry & commerce of any other nation or society on earth.
3. Instruct the community in those branches of education which are essential to form the useful citizen.
   You yourselves are the only men with whom the Deity has deposited the unalienable power of righting all your own wrongs; and it certainly is the highest of all high treason tamely to resign it, no, you have resolved to obtain, 1st An equality of Civil, Political and Religious Rights; this must effectually cut off oppressors from power – 2nd An equal representation in the legislature of your country. This is perfect liberty, with the power of preserving it.
   Tyrants Tremble, the People are awake.[32]

These words could have been written by Marat or Thomas Paine. To us today, the sentiments are not shocking, as we take it for granted that we all have the vote, that no one is excluded from society on grounds of religion, and that every child in the country has access to free education: in 1802 this was treason! The modern world owes much to the Black Lamp and the home-grown Jacobins. Religious, economic and political grievances coalesced as had been feared by Magistrate Busfield. Joseph Radcliffe forwarded a second packet of seized 'seditious material' from Huddersfield to Earl Fitzwilliam on 27 July, which entreated people to join the Black Lamp and take the secret oath of allegiance.[33] The same day a letter arrived from the Home Office informing the Earl that:

> there are three houses at Leeds and three at Wakefield where the committees met – that one of them was expected to be searched some time since, and that their papers were hid under a trapdoor in the floor of the house and amongst the coals; that each member paid 1d. per week to the fund; that there were many committee men made, and that each committee man got ten more ... that they carry their weekly pennies to Leeds; that there would be a rising all over the country on the same night, and everything overturned the next morning.[34]

Furthermore, from the spy network managed by Magistrate Cookson, Fitzwilliam had become increasingly aware of reports of a rising tide of successful trade unionism beyond the woollen trade.[35] Earl Fitzwilliam was a worried man for two reasons: with the Peace of Amiens, the Volunteer force had largely been disbanded; it had been reported to him that a meeting of 4,000 to 5,000 had gathered near Leeds on 17 July 1802, and was warned that 100,000 were ready to rise up. He now believed that a major plot was under way and he had insufficient troops to contain any rebellion. He explained his situation:

> It is necessary that I shall here state to your Lordship, what Volunteer Establishments will be forthcoming within the district in question, in aid of the Magistrates upon emergency. There are two viz: 1st the Leeds Volunteer Cavalry, an excellent troop, but officers included, is consist of 38 only – & 2ndly the Skirac Troop of West Riding Yeomanry, which I expect will continue its service, if its numbers can be made up to 40, but as yet I have no heard that they are so ... I fear none but Regulars will answer and effectually. I feel it therefore my duty in transmitting the inclos'd memorial to your Lordship, to add my request to the opinion of the magistrates, that Troops be quartered in the large manufacturing districts.[36]

Fitzwilliam noted as that the Skyrac Yeomanry was scattered across the Wapentake, it was unrealistic to expect that the troop could muster in times of emergency. The Leeds Cavalry, being based in the town, could be expected to muster in a shorter time, but overall, both troops of cavalry were of little use as they were not immediately to hand: here Fitzwilliam identified the Achilles heel of these part-time soldiers. More worrying for Fitzwilliam was the news that members of disbanded Volunteer and Militia corps were active amongst the Black Lamp. Fitzwilliam called for the West Riding to be garrisoned by regular troops. Without a shadow of a doubt revolution was brewing, driven by Irish freedom fighters.

In July, William Putnam McCabe, returning to Paris from a visit to Dublin, brought news to Manchester that the United Irishmen were ready to rise again as soon as the continental war was renewed. In this expectation, preparations in England were intensified.[37] A spy working for Ralph Fletcher, identified as D, reported that McCabe had visited James Napper Tandy in Hamburg. The spy also noted that McCabe was dismissive of the need for French assistance and encouraged his interlocutors to be ready to act on their own initiative. McCabe argued that the London Directory had been slow in seizing the initiative.[38] What is certain, is that whatever plan was taking shape in England it was happening almost in a vacuum as nothing yet was 'on the radar' in Ireland or France.

Despite turmoil in the London leadership of the United Britons, as July turned to August, Fitzwilliam's panic had abated a great deal. He now felt there was no real underground plotting for revolution. On 9 August, ever the pragmatist, Fitzwilliam wrote to the Home Office, noting that none of the panicked magistrates or private persons passing information on to himself had actually observed first-hand the nighttime meetings themselves. He was concerned that the magistrates were being fed 'fake news', or that the fear of revolution was so strong, the slightest hint of anti-government sentiment sent these men into 'meltdown'. When endeavouring to find the eyewitnesses who informed the magistrates of the events taking place, Fitzwilliam admitted no one could find out who the informer was, and that the numbers present at the meetings were likely to be excessively exaggerated. He noted that:

> All who are parties to this confederacy, on admission subscribe a certain oath written in a book: & that each of them receives a ticket for admission to future meetings . . . both the ticket and the oath . . . is of several years standing as well as the declaration of the objects for which they are to connect.[39]

Fitzwilliam concluded saying he had spoken to Mr Radcliffe, 'but I was unable to collect from him <u>anything like evidence</u> of any kind'. One of Radcliffe's spies noted that a hawker had attempted to coerce two labourers into joining the disaffected, telling them that great men were involved in their cause including Mr Ingham, a considerable merchant in either Halifax or Huddersfield. Upon examination, reported Fitzwilliam, Mr Ingham had no knowledge of such an association. He added that General Bernard had interviewed a discharged soldier who reported alarming language throughout the public houses of Lancashire, and he had been sent to London with a letter of introduction to Lord Hobart. Fitzwilliam remarked:

> I have now reported to your Lordship everything I have been able to collect at York. The Gentlemen whose names I have mention'd, all seem deeply impress'd with an opinion of the disturb'd & disaffected state of the lower orders, & that mischief is brewing: nevertheless, they seem tolerably [illegible] that through the surveillance of the magistrates backed by the strength of the military . . . what ever it may be, it will be discomfitted.[40]

He concluded his letter by noting that the majority of the bench felt that there were no grounds for alarm, and that whatever was occurring in the West Riding was related to industrial discontent and not revolution.[41] William Cookson noted in a letter of 19 August to Fitzwilliam that meetings of the Black Lamp had been held close to Birstall and an informant told him 'That by Christmas they should be able to carry these parts and one night the rise was to take place in every quarter'.[42] John Dixon informed Fitzwilliam that members of the Black Lamp paid 1d a week, which was banked in Leeds. He reported furthermore that he had taken part in a raid on the homes of persons suspected of being 'home-grown terrorists'. Dixon also noted from information he had received from a spy and the contents of the documents he had found that he had uncovered evidence that there was to be a rising 'all over the country on the same night and everything overturned the next morning'.[43] Dixon included one of the papers recovered in his letter to Fitzwilliam, in which the Anglican Apostles creed was adapted to read 'I believe in one Billy Pitt, Chancellor of the Exchequer, Mighty maker of the Lords and Commons . . . and in Henry Dundas beloved of Pitt . . . was incarnate by the Devil . . . was three days burnt in effigy the third day he came again according to the newspapers and now sitteth at the right hand of Bill Pitt . . .'.[44]

General Bernard of Heaton Lodge, Huddersfield, received a threatening letter, warning him if he did not deliver up in 'the dearest interest posterity and general happiness of the universe' 1,000 muskets and bayonets by the evening of 24 August, then his 'house will be blown down before 8 in the morning'. adding 'may the great god of heaven smile on the United company of Great Britain and Ireland and crown them with success. The Tirants Tremble. The people are awake!'[45] In response Bernard blamed the disaffection in his area on religious Dissenters: 'I am of the opinion, as with many other gentlemen in this neighbourhood NOT Presbyterians, that there is a great reason for Alarm, and the country is merely deterred from rising by the great number of troops in it'.[46] Fitzwilliam responded to Bernard, thanking him for sending him a copy of the threatening letter and a spearhead that had been recovered.[47]

From Milnsbridge, Magistrate Radcliffe, who was rapidly becoming one of the most hated men in the West Riding, wrote to the Home Office with his own appraisal of the events taking place. He had been informed by Mark Haigh, a yeoman farmer, of seditious meetings taking place at the home of David Midgley in Almondbury and of Samuel Buckley for '5 or 6 Sundays past, eight or ten people who are strangers in Almondbury have come . . . during the whole of the afternoon service of those days . . . books or accounts of seditious society are kept in the house of the said Midgley . . .'. Radcliffe added that a second informer, Edward Hasling or Harling, added that meetings also took place at night in the same houses. Radcliffe had arrested Robert Lodge of Almondbury for being a suspected member of the society. Lodge reported that Sykes was a member of the society and had given him a membership card in exchange for 1d. Radcliffe sought permission to enter the men's houses under a warrant and to seize evidence. Radcliffe was utterly convinced of the danger to society from the 'secret meetings' of the Black Lamp.[48] Magistrate Cookson noted that 'the Black Lamp' assembled 2 miles from Birstall, and that scouts were placed some distance from the meeting, who communicated with whistles to warn of approaching constables and soldiers. Cookson added that a 'gentleman' was the leader, and 200 or more had gathered to petition for an abolition of taxes, the 'full enjoyment of natural rights' and to raise wages.[49]

It was now that a government agent became involved in hunting out the radicals. Thomas Hirst had been employed as a spy in July, reporting to General Bernard and Magistrate Radcliffe, but we know very little of his activities till August. Hirst is a very shadowy figure: he had been a trooper with the 20th Light Dragoons serving in Ireland, but had been discharged for bad conduct, and was a perhaps unlikely honest candidate for this task, but his history may have made him more credible to the plotters. Magistrate Beckett informed Fitzwilliam on 6 September that he had interviewed Hirst and noted he was 'a very quick intelligent fellow very hearty to the cause he has undertaken'. Hirst informed Beckett that he hoped to be sent to the committee meeting of the Black Lamp that was to be held in York and that once he had gained the trust of the movement he would be sent as a delegate from Leeds to London where he would identify the ringleaders. Hirst considered the London meeting of delegates to be of great importance and convinced Cookson that a 'number of persons are industriously at work for carrying into execution an organised system of mischief & that it is highly necessary they should be prevented . . .'. Hirst was indeed dispatched to York and then travelled onto London with three guineas to obtain information. He added that Leeds was the centre of operations.[50] Two days later, Beckett had received intelligence from Hirst who had sent him intercepted letters from the United Britons.[51] Alas these documents are not preserved, so we do not know what Hirst had uncovered, or perhaps even invented! In a deposition sent to the Home Office, Hirst added that the aims of the United Britons were the independence of Great Britain and Ireland, the introduction of old age pensions, freedom of religion i.e., to legalise Catholic and Unitarian worship and remove the Test and Corporation Acts, and universal male suffrage. Samuel Sykes was named as conductor, and Joshua Kaye secretary on an oath card of the United Englishman that was handed over.[52] Earl Fitzwilliam reported to Lord Pelham that he felt that the oath-taking was illegal, and hoped action would be taken to stop the practice.[53] Pelham felt that on evidence sent to him by Fitzwilliam and Beckett – i.e., from Hirst – that the illegal oath-taking and disaffection in the West Riding were all linked to an attempt to overturn the constitution.[54]

However, Hirst had not uncovered new evidence: he had delivered exactly the same material to Magistrate Radcliffe a month earlier! Radcliffe reported to Lord Pelham that Hirst had made contact with members of the Black Lamp in Almondbury and obtained oath cards signed by Thomas Sykes, David Midgley, Josh Kaye and Samuel Buckley, the superintendent of the committee there. All four men were clothiers, thus demonstrating the link between the Black Lamp and embryonic Luddites. Hirst added that women met in groups, and talked in hushed voices: he observed that the women knew something was being planned, but none of them would 'let the cat out of the bag'.[55] Radcliffe had not passed this news onto Fitzwilliam, so when Hirst made a deposition to Magistrate Beckett, this was the first the Leeds bench and the Lord Lieutenant knew about activities in Almondbury. Hirst was clearly feeding 'old news' to Beckett in exchange for money. We assume that Hirst had obtained more than one membership card, and passed on both to different paymasters. Exploiting the lack of communication between the interested parties could led us to question everything that Hirst came to report to the Home Office.

Lord Pelham knew far more than he told Fitzwilliam. John Moody, a spy working for Richard Ford, magistrate of Bow Street and head of the 'Bow Street Runners', had infiltrated the London Directorate. He was tasked by Ford on 21 September to 'Sniff the matter out'. Moody, who worked for the radical Sir Francis Burdett, reported that Despard, Wallis Eastburn, John Heron, Thomas Pemberton, John Heron, Charles Pendrill, Blythe, Nicholls and a man known as 'Farrell' along with a Dr Crossfield were behind the plot, and all were former members of the London Corresponding Society and United Englishmen. Moody also reported that Despard was under great pressure to act rather than wait for Ireland and France. A key liaison between republicans in England and Ireland during 1802–3, Dowdall travelled to London on United Irish business in July 1802, posing as a clerk in the firm of the Dublin merchant Philip Long.[56]

## The French Connection?
In a full deposition to John King at the Home Office, Thomas Hirst reported that he had infiltrated the plotters in Yorkshire and further afield, and implicated Sir Francis Burdett, the Duke of Norfolk and Charles James Fox in a plot to the seize the Tower of London and take the King and House of Commons hostage. To fund these activities, Hirst said £1,000 had been received from Paris to fund the United Englishmen, and had been administered by 'General Painite' who had travelled to Yorkshire from Portsmouth. On meeting the 'general' Hirst was shown letters from Francis DeCastle and Thomas Paine, sent from Paris. He added that the 'conductor' from Yorkshire was to meet with two conductors from London, one from Portsmouth and one from Ireland to plan the seizure of the House of Commons. Who was the 'general'? We have two candidates for the French agent.

A French spy was in London that summer, and Despard had reportedly negotiated with him,[57] who has been traditionally identified as Colonel Beauvoisin.[58] However, can we prove it was him? A spy named Fiévée was in London May to June 1802, his brief to identify the motivation behind English political acts, and report on the political mood of England and also France to war or peace.[59] He also compiled a lengthy document reflecting on the trade and commerce of England and the advantages that France would derive from a commercial treaty with England. He noted that it was especially important for France to regain its past glory, to restore its greatness and restrict the power of England. The first move to this he noted was that France 'must start by killing Anglomania at home'.[60] In the middle of June Fiévée reported on the national debt and the difficult fiscal situation the Bank of England faced.[61]

Aware of the building sense of tension in England, once more the former Bishop of Autun steps into the picture. In the last days of September, Talleyrand requested Pierre Claude de Poterat to establish the means by which the French could help the Irish but to ensure that he kept his plans hidden so as not to raise any accusations that they were conducting a subversive secret war against England at a time of peace.[62] Poterat was in contact with Dr William James MacNeven, an émigré in Hamburg since 1797, as delegate to the United Irish Committee in Paris, and over the intervening months submitted various schemes for the invasion of Ireland in order to exploit discontent in England. Ireland was very much 'the poor relation' in Franco-Irish discussions at this stage. MacNeven told Poterat that the Irish would no longer be 'mischief makers'. Indeed, MacNeven told Poterat – and ultimately Talleyrand – that as France had failed Ireland since 1798, unless France made a firm commitment to land troops in Ireland 'that it would be difficult to bring the people out again'.[63] How much of this was already in hand before September we cannot say, nor how much of it Despard knew.

Beauvoisin – a colleague of Bernard MacSheehy in Egypt – had been sent to London to replace Fiévée and reported to Consul Bonaparte on 15 October concerning the public mood, following his secret mission to England and Scotland in a letter written from Calais.[64] We have no idea if he met Despard. Scarcely had Beauvoisin reported to Bonaparte than he was sent back to London to investigate the activities of French royalists seeking to cause disturbances in France as well as to collect anti-French and anti-Bonaparte newspapers and publications. Napoleon in effect 'weaponised' the émigrés and their activities to undermine Windham and Addington. The newly-promoted colonel arrived in London on 20 October.[65] On the following day he wrote to Napoleon concerning the hatred of the English newspapers to France.[66] In a letter written at the end of November, he warned of 'the evils which would overwhelm England in the event of war'.[67] If the French were involved, it was only liminally as the French ambassador General Andréossy would tell Talleyrand that the plot was of little value.[68]

In getting back to the motivation of Despard's group. Hirst reported that its key aims were the redistribution of land, to end enclosure, abolish taxes, and that every man would have the vote, and that parliament was to be elected annually. Furthermore, he said that the 'Uniteds' in Manchester were in contact with 'Uniteds' in Yorkshire and London, as well as communicating with Ireland via Liverpool. Indeed, he admitted he travelled to Manchester and Liverpool, Warrington, Knutsford, Stafford and Leeds where he passed letters to the secretaries of the 'Uniteds'.[69]

Chapter 17

# THE REVOLUTION THAT NEVER WAS

As summer started to turn to autumn, the Crown's spy network uncovered what they believed to be 'hard facts' about what was considered to be a very real and very present danger. In the West Country, the disbanded Militia formed a majority of the disaffected, it was reported, and the magistrates feared that such disaffection 'could become very dangerous if not stopped'.[1]

Undeniable links between the Black Lamp and Ireland were uncovered in September. The Honourable Henry Legge wrote from the Irish Office to the Home Office reporting that David Midgley, Superintendent Samuel Buckley, Secretary Joshua Kaye and Thomas Sykes, who were leaders of the United Britons cell in Almondbury, West Riding, had signed a handbill circulating in Ireland. This called for the independence of Great Britain and Ireland; an equalisation of civic, political and religious rights; ample provision for the families of Heroes who might fall in the contest; and a liberal reward for distinguished merits.[2] The report was corroborated when a spy, Edward Hasling – we met him earlier – who reported directly to George Armitage, magistrate of Huddersfield, sent the same information to the Home Office.[3]

Confirming the Crown's worst fears, another spy reported that 'schemes for attacking the Tower, the Bank & St James' were being planned and that the Duke of York was to be assassinated. The plot, the spy reported, was led by Colonel Despard and would be carried out by 'the disaffected' aided by the 1st and 3rd Battalions of the Foot Guards who had taken illegal oaths.[4] What scared the Crown, with the Naval Mutiny of 1797 and '98 still very fresh in the memory, was the fear that the Army had 'been corrupted' and was likely to turn against its masters. We cannot judge the loyalty of the Army as a whole, though it transpired that as we shall see, the loyalty of troops in London, where they were more exposed to radicalism and radical ideas in alehouses and taverns, was not what the Crown would have hoped. Remembering this was an army where a soldier could be flogged 'till his back ran red with blood' for the slightest misdemeanour. Hatred of corporal punishment and draconian discipline, low pay and bad food, could, and clearly did, lead soldiers into the 'arms of the radicals'.

The same day that the Home Office had learned of the plot, Earl Fitzwilliam forwarded to the Home Office a report by his spy, Thomas Hirst. Hirst claims he had infiltrated a group in Wakefield, which met at the Rose & Crown public house: having met with the committee, he then left and walked with the group on the road to Newmillerdam, today the modern A61. On arriving at Sandal, the group turned left at the 'Three Houses', this would be along the modern B6312, whence he walked for about two miles to an isolated cottage, which would be somewhere on 'Chevet Lane'. The men he met in Sandal claimed they were members of the 'National Institute' and sworn members of the United Britons Institute. The men stated they were under orders from:

> Major General Despart [*sic*] who on account of his former prosecutions & by request of the Duke of Norfolk he should be the commander in chief of their union. I need not mention the Duke of N again by that you will know he has in Charles Fox Earl of Mix, Lord Delavel, Sir Francis Burdett, Mr Grey, and Mr Jones these are all men of very great names and Directors of the English Union and their correspondent with Ireland, Lieut General Tarleton & [illegible] with Scotland I have not learnt their names, from this place this man with delegation returns was to go to London to receive the orders from the directing messenger which is C Fox and order his something from him and from Paris.[5]

Hirst further noted that he had met in the cottage a delegate from Sheffield, who was a member of the London Directory, and that he had met others from Ireland, as well as a man from Harrogate. He concluded his letter by saying the 'English Union' would act at the opening of Parliament. Hirst noted he left the cottage and walked to Royston at break of day by crossing fields to catch the coach to Leeds. Fitzwilliam passed on the intelligence to Whitehall. Thomas Hirst confirmed that by summer 1802 Ireland and the North of England were set to rise in rebellion, coordinated by 'General Painite' who had come from France, paid for with French gold. However, Hirst cannot have visited a 'Rose & Crown Inn' in Wakefield. No such public house existed in Wakefield: George & Crown, yes, but not Rose & Crown. The closest Rose & Crown to Wakefield is either in Lofthouse, 4 miles north, or the Rose & Crown at Darton, near Barnsley, where Hirst got his coach to Leeds. The 'Three Houses' is still a public house in 2021. Was Hirst mistaken about the name of the pub or had he travelled to Lofthouse? We also wonder how much of what Hirst was reporting had he been in fact been fed to him by the Secret Committee at the Home Office, given his report confirmed what the Home Office already seems to have known? A question we cannot answer without more archive documents coming to light.

Was Fox involved? We cannot say. We could suggest a tacit link: in 1797 Thomas Pelham wrote to Lord Sheffield about the United Irishmen's activities. Pelham notes that Fox was a frequent correspondent with Arthur O'Connor. Roger O'Connor was reported as 'flying from one of my warrants (against him as a general to command in Munster). There has been some strange neglect about apprehending him, as but I understand that he is still in the country disguised as a sailor. I have no doubt that Fox's intelligence about the South came from him.'[6] This implies Fox knew very well what was being planned in Ireland in 1797 – he was related to Lord Edward Fitzgerald, the leader of the United Irishmen – and had passed on some information to the Crown. This may be as close as we can get to placing Fox with the United Irishmen.

Without shadow of a doubt Sir Francis Burdett was involved. The Home Office were so concerned about his involvement that they placed a spy in his office, John Moody, who in May 1802 had identified Horn Tooke, Burdett and Despard as being linked in the unfolding plot along with radicals like Dr Crossfield, Wallis Eastburn and John Nicholls. Burdett visited Despard in Coldbath Fields prison and knew the Duke of Norfolk as well as the exiled Arthur O'Connor in Paris.[7] Indeed, The National Archives in London preserve letters between Lord Henry Fitzgerald, Sir Francis Burdett, Arthur O'Connor.[8]

Another man of note implicated in the plot was Major Cartwright. At the trial a man named Heron was identified as a key person of interest: Heron worked for Cartwright. On hearing of Heron's involvement and imprisonment, Cartwright arranged his release. We cannot be sure what he knew of Despard or how involved Burdett was, but it does seem that Despard did have links to 'great men'.[9]

Chapter 18

# A SHOW TRIAL?

It is likely that by late October Despard and the United Irishmen had lost control of events in London. Despard was working tirelessly to keep the three-part plan alive, and walked 20 miles a day reassuring London radical groups and keeping the situation calm. The French had offered aid, but not in 1802, and the United Irish in Ireland were not ready to rise. Despard, it seems, was desperately trying to 'put the brakes on' the plot. He met radicals across London in Newington, Tower Hill, Hatton Garden, Whitechapel, Haymarket and Lambeth trying to calm tempers. A meeting was held on 12 November at the Flying Horse: anger at inaction boiled over. Spies informed the Home Office of the date of the London plot. On the evening of 16 November 1802 at the Oakley Arms, Lambeth, Despard met with section leaders in London in an effort to resist efforts to state a specific date for the rebellion. Informed of the meeting John King from the Home Office ordered arrests to be made. Despard, along with thirty others including serving soldiers in the Guards were taken. The following day other identified ringleaders were arrested, notably Macnamara.[1]

The Crown congratulated itself that revolution had been 'nipped in the bud'. What was needed now was convictions: with the stinging failure of the treason trials of 1794 still a cause for regret, Despard and his supports would be found guilty, and executed. The Crown needed to find Despard and others guilty of treason, no matter how shaky the evidence was. Despard probably knew this the moment he was arrested. The British Crown could not let him live: he was a symbol of everything it despised, and the Crown hoped his execution would cow the radicals into submission. Despard was probably never the national leader, but he was well known and popular and was significantly involved: that was sufficient for the Crown. He and other radicals had dared mount a challenge to the power of the elite and oligarchy and British imperialist intent in Ireland: they had to die for their crimes. This was a show trial, as the result was a foregone conclusion the moment they were arrested.

A week after Despard's arrest for treason, Earl Fitzwilliam warned Lord Pelham that based on evidence from Hirst, seditious nocturnal meetings had not ceased but if anything were more frequent and more members were being sworn. Hirst had warned the Earl that there was a general expectation of a great rebellion taking place.[2] He was quite right: the French and United Irish were planning to invade Ireland but not just yet.[3]

John Beckett of Leeds was certain that if Despard's plot had gone ahead, then a revolt would have followed in Yorkshire through an 'extensive conspiracy'.[4] In Sheffield, a plot to seize the barracks and to make arms was revealed. William Wronskley or Rouksley or Roukersley had ordered pikes to be made and was identified as a Conductor for the United Englishmen.[5] Wronksley and fellow conspirator were imprisoned at York: Lee for administering illegal oaths and Wronksley for his 'Diabolical intentions' and those of the United Englishmen to overturn Parliament and to seize the barracks and its arms in Sheffield when 'ordered by their directors'.[6] At their trial in March 1803, the *Newcastle Courrant* identified both men as being involved with Despard.[7] Wakefield radicals John Smaller and Benjamin Scholes, identified in March 1802 as being members of the 'Wakefield and Almondbury Committee', were arrested, as was William Wolstenholme in Sheffield: all would go onto lead radical politics in Wakefield and Sheffield and would be directly involved with conducting arms raids for Luddites in 1812.[8]

On 1 December 1802, Edward Marcus Despard, Charles Pendrill, James Sedgewick Wratten, William Lander, Arthur Graham, Samuel Smith, John Macnamara and Thomas Broughton were committed to Newgate for High Treason by warrant under the hand and seal of Lord Pelham; and on the same day John Wood, John Francis, Thomas Newman, Daniel Tyndale, John Doyle, John Conolly, Thomas Phillips alias Jackson and Thomas Winterbottham were committed to Surrey county gaol. The other twenty persons were discharged.[9]

Prior to the trial, the accused were all interrogated by the prosecution. Despard himself never seems to have been questioned, or at least nothing has survived from him. The interrogation allowed the Crown to build a case against Despard. In preparing evidence, two of the accused turned king's evidence. A key person in the case against Despard was his co-accused Thomas Windsor, a soldier serving in the

181

3rd Battalion 1st Foot Guards. Under interrogation, Windsor stated that John Francis of the 1st Battalion had made him take an illegal oath 'to overturn the present system of tyranny' and had also sworn William Bownas, Thomas Blades and a soldier called Meadows of the Coldstream Guards, who was very active in recruiting soldiers to take the oath. Windsor identified a former soldier known as Atkinson as a delegate from the 3rd Regiment of Foot Guards, and that 250 members of the regiment 'were united and had been sworn . . . that meetings of 15 or 16 at a time . . . had been held in different public houses'. Windsor also identified a man called Thomas Broughton – is this Thomas Broughton of Leeds we wonder? – who had met with Francis and that the United Englishmen had seven Divisions in the Borough of Southwark. He added that the United Englishmen hoped to join with the disaffected Irishmen who had served in the Navy and had taken part in the Naval Mutiny of 1797. Broughton was further identified, along with 'two strangers . . . one of whom who had been in the Horse Guards' who were engaged in raising funds to send delegates to link with societies in the North, as well to print and distribute material. Windsor stated that he, along with Wrather, Broughton, McGrae and Wood, had met Despard at the Flying Horse at Walworth, along with 'Smith a Master Hatter', and noted that Despard planned to seize arms held at the Tower and could call on 40,000 men to bring about his plans. John May, a constable, who was present at the arrests, stated he seized seditious material from one Thomas Jackson alias Philips, and other papers were found on Dennis McGrae. These papers were never presented at the trial or even described in the evidence against Despard.

The Guards' involvement with a plot was proved by interrogation of those arrested, who included many from the regiments. Arrested from the 1st Foot Guards was John Pike, who under interrogation admitted he was a member of the United Englishmen and had attended meetings at the Ham and Windmill with fourteen or fifteen other soldiers in a society based on Jacobinical principles. Thomas Blades, who had been denounced by Windsor, stated under oath that John Francis and Windsor had sought to form a society 'determined to sacrifice their lives and fortunes, as to establish a free and independent constitution and to encourage their comrades to do the same' which met at the Ham and Windmill. Here, Irishmen Mack and Conolly 'exhorted the company to persevere, to get men together as possible, and to arm themselves so as to be able to make head against government, and threatened that if any man should divulge the secret, he should have a dagger in his breast'. Blades also identified a man named Broughton as distributing printed materials, and had introduced him to Colonel Despard. He reported that he overheard that a party of the United Englishmen would seize the King travelling between St James's and Buckingham House, as the King would not be guarded, adding he heard Broughton address the meeting saying that Parliament was to be seized, and as soon as the Houses of Parliament had been taken, the Tower was the next target.

One of the men implicated in the plot, William Francis, was a serving member of the 1st Battalion 1st Foot Guards. Under examination, he admitted that he had been sworn by Wood into a society 'against the King and Government and to Overturn the Parliament' and added that the society 'had met with great success, particularly in the Coldstream'. Francis had sought to leave the society, but had been reprimanded by Despard who reminded him of his oath. Francis implicated the aforementioned John Pike and a breeches maker known as Conolly from Oxford, and admitted that 'about 30 of the 1st Battalion' had taken the oath.

Sergeant James Humphreys of the 1st Foot Guards, also amongst those arrested, implicated Thomas Windsor as a leader in the 'society'. Thomas Winterbotham, of the 3rd Battalion 1st Foot, implicated Wood, Blades and Francis as leaders of companies 'of the society' who had forced him to take the oath. He further admitted that he believed 25,000 men had taken the oath, of which 'two or three thousands . . . were soldiers . . . had 500 stand of arms and that there was to be a general meeting throughout all England'. This surely is the meeting that Fletcher and other magistrates in the North had mentioned. He added to Serjeant at Law Abbott that he had been promised an increase in their wage to 3 shillings a day if he joined the Corresponding Society and took part in activities for *'overturning* the present government'. John Wood, it was stated, offered to post himself sentry with a cannon to fire at the King's carriage as it was going to what was then called Buckingham House.

Army Agent William Bownas, implicated by Windsor, was also one of the men arrested on the 16h. Under examination, he spoke of being recruited to join the United Englishmen by Windsor. John Francis was arrested but denied any involvement, so too Broughton and John Wood.[10] Under a separate interrogation, Thomas Winterbotham named Wood, Blades and Francis of the 1st Foot Guards as ringleaders, as well as Scott of Colonel Ashford's company, and Thomas Windsor and Joseph Dixon of Colonel Salisbury's company as being members of the United Englishmen and that when the King went to the Houses of Parliament on 23 August, he would be seized in the park.[11] Thomas Blades, in evidence used in Despard's trial, asserted that a man known as Pendle said he could 'bring 1000 men into the field at any time and that any man who should shew the least symptom of cowardice he would blow his brains out'. He also implicated a carpenter known as Tindall. William Francis, under further examination, stuck to his story about John Woods being a key personality in swearing soldiers 'into the society' whose aim was the independence of Great Britain and Ireland, and the equalisation of civil, political and religious rights.[12]

Fletcher's spy, Citizen Bent, informed the Home Office that the defence was confident that Francis would be proved to be a deserter and thief, two other soldiers would also be proven to be deserters and 'the watchmaker will be proven to have left the country and to have taken from different persons eight watches and to have defrauded another person of his watch. This man is a Methodist and knows a great deal.' He noted furthermore that the evidence that Despard met Thomas Windsor and others on 5 September 1802 at the Bleeding Hart, Hatton Garden, would be disproved by a letter from a Mr Adamson, in which Despard said 'he would have *nothing* to do with the business'.[13] The 'watchmaker' was a man called Cassel. If he had testified, he would have incriminated Francis for being an accessory to Cassel's theft and burglary charges, putting Francis's evidence in doubt. The charges were made in the trial about the theft of watches: Francis was exposed as an accessory to robbery and was therefore an unreliable witness, but his evidence stood.[14]

Another eyewitness, the spy reported, had Francis as the ringleader and not Despard, and it was Francis who proposed to '*seize the Tower and arm the citizens*', supported by 500 men from the Guards on either the 5th or 12th at night: when only one soldier came forward, the plot collapsed. John Macnamara, named by the spy, was a prosecution witness, but cautioned that his real name was Farrell, and he the same man who was tried in Dublin for the assignation attempt on Lord Carhampton but turned king's evidence. Fletcher also reported evidence from another of his spies known as 'D' who reported that a delegate from Hull, John Walker, had travelled through Nottingham and Birmingham to Bristol, and was in communication with delegates in Birmingham and French residents in Bristol and Hull. He added that according to 'D' the people of Nottingham were also subscribing to Despard's defence and were 'extremely depraved in their politics'.[15]

Despard was put on trial on 7 February 1803. The trial hinged on Thomas Windsor turning king's evidence and the testimony from a man called Emblin proved crucial in linking Despard with a nationwide conspiracy, and indeed he was the key witness in the case. Emblin reported that:

> Colonel Despard said, and I believe this to be the moment; the people, particularly in Leeds, in Sheffield, in Birmingham, and in every capital town in England, are ripe;' and he said, ' I have walked twenty miles to-day, and the people are everywhere ripe where I have been'. He said, 'the attack is to be made on the day his Majesty goes to the house, and his Majesty must be put to death'. He said, 'that the mail coaches were to be stopped, as a signal to the people in the country, that they had revolted in town'. That was principally what Colonel Despard said at that moment.[16]

Despard denied the witnesses' statements and told the court that they were not credible. The only evidence against him came from his co-accused.[17] Lord Nelson, the hero of the Battle of Nile, appeared as a character for Despard.

In the trial, the prosecution took several approaches to the case:

1. Despard was the ringleader in issuing illegal oaths.
2. Working for the Independence of Ireland was treason: certainly the Crown, since 1798, was terrified of more rebellion in Ireland backed by France. Any suggestion that Ireland could gain her independence had to be quashed.
3. Working for universal suffrage, and affording all the same protection under the law and religious freedom, was understood to be a direct attack on the constitution, Church and King and was therefore treason. Similar charges made in 1794 in the notorious treason trials had failed to get convictions based on hearsay evidence, and the Crown was determined to get convictions and subsequent executions.
4. To argue that the soldiers in the Guards had been influenced by external forces. Indeed, the Crown went out of its way to demonstrate the loyalty of the Army and to play down any suggestion that the it was in any way 'mutinous' as had been the Royal Navy in 1797. The Crown had to exonerate the armed forces, lest any evidence of mutiny reach France and cause panic in the wider population.

The public was enthralled and newspapers could not provide enough coverage on the Despard Plot. Evidence against the conspirators was weak with little physical proof, so the prosecutor focused primarily on the assassination attempt. Of the fifteen men indicted for treason on the grounds that they 'did conspire, compass, imagine, and intend' the King's death, eleven were found guilty. In passing sentence, Lord Ellenborough said:

> Such disclosures have been made as to prove, beyond the possibility of doubt, that the objects of your atrocious, abominable and traitorous conspiracy were to overthrow the government, and to seize upon and destroy the sacred person of our august and revered Sovereign, and the illustrious branches of his Royal house.[18]

## Execution

Although the jury recommended mercy, Despard, together with John Wood, 36, John Francis, 23, both privates in the army, Thomas Broughton, 26, a carpenter, James Sedgwick Wratten, 35, a shoemaker, Arthur Graham, 53, a slater, and John Macnamara, a labourer, were sentenced to be hanged, drawn and quartered on 21 February 1803.[19] Spencer Percival, the then Attorney General, noted that John Macnamara had been omitted from the list of men to be executed, and ordered he was to be.[20]

Lord Ellenborough, in a style of awful solemnity highly befitting the melancholy but just occasion, addressed the prisoners nearly to the following purport: 'You' (calling each prisoner separately by name):

> have been separately indicted for conspiring against his Majesty's person, his Crown, and Government, for the purposes of subverting the same, and changing the government of this realm. After a long, patient and, I hope, just and impartial trial, you have been all of you severally convicted, by a most respectable jury of your country, upon the several crimes laid to your charge. In the course of evidence upon your trial such disclosures have been made as to prove, beyond the possibility of doubt, that the objects of your atrocious and traitorous conspiracy were to overthrow the Government, and to seize upon and destroy the sacred persons of our august and revered Sovereign, and the illustrious branches of his Royal house, which some of you, by the most solemn bond of your oath of allegiance, were pledged, and all of you, as his Majesty's subjects, were indispensably bound, by your duty, to defend; to overthrow that constitution, its established freedom and boasted usages, which have so long maintained among us that just and rational equality of rights, and security of property, which have been for so many ages the envy and admiration of the world; and to erect upon its ruins a wild system of anarchy and bloodshed, having for its object the subversion of all property and the massacre of its proprietors; the annihilation of all legitimate authority and established order – for such must be the import of that promise held out by the

leaders of this atrocious conspiracy, of ample provision for the families of those heroes who should fall in the struggle. It has, however, pleased that Divine Providence, which has mercifully watched over the safety of this nation, to defeat your wicked and abominable purpose, by arresting your projects in their dark and dangerous progress, and thus averting that danger which your machinations had suspended over our heads; and by your timely detection, seizure and submittal to public justice, to afford time for the many thousands of his Majesty's innocent and loyal subjects, the intended victims of your atrocious and sanguinary purpose, to escape that danger which so recently menaced them, and which, I trust, is not yet become too formidable for utter defeat.

The only thing remaining for me is the painful task of pronouncing against you, and each of you, the awful sentence which the law denounces against your crime, which is, that you, and each of you (here his Lordship named the prisoners severally), be taken from the place from whence you came, and from thence you are to be drawn on hurdles to the place of execution, where you are to be hanged by the neck, but not until you are dead; for while you are still living your bodies are to be taken down, your bowels torn out and burned before your faces, your heads then cut off, and your bodies divided each into four quarters, and your heads and quarters to be then at the King's disposal; and may the Almighty God have mercy on your souls![21]

On Saturday 19 February, the warrant for execution, to take place on the following Monday, was made out, which contained a remission of part of the sentence – viz. the taking out and burning their bowels before their faces, and dividing their bodies. On Monday 21 February, at about 7.00am, Despard was asked to go to confess his sins and take the sacrament. He refused to do so. John Francis, John Wood, James Sedgewick Wrattan, Thomas Broughton, and Arthur Graham did so, and joined Macnamara and Despard about 8.00am when their shackles were taken off, and the men were bound by their arms and hands and taken to the scaffold. About half past eight, the prisoners were brought to the platform and:

as soon as the cord was fastened round the neck of one, the second was brought up, and so on till the cords were fastened round the necks of all the seven. . . . Despard was brought up the last, dressed in boots, a dark brown great coat, his hair unpowdered. He ascended the scaffold with great firmness. His countenance underwent not the slightest change during the fastening of the rope round his neck.[22]

When the noose had been placed around his neck, Despard adjusted the knot so it rested under his left ear to ensure instant death when

187

the platform dropped. Before their deaths, each prisoner had an opportunity to speak. Despard proclaimed:

> I come here, as you see, after having served my country, faithfully, honourably, and usefully served it, for thirty years and upwards, to suffer death upon a scaffold for a crime of which I protest I am not guilty. I solemnly declare that I am no more guilty of it than any of you who may be now hearing me.
>
> But, though his MAJESTY'S Ministers know as well as I do, that I am not guilty, yet they avail themselves of a legal pretext to destroy a man, because he has been a friend to truth, to liberty, and to justice. Because he has been a friend to the poor and oppressed. But, Citizens, I hope and trust, notwithstanding my fate, and the fate of those who no doubt will soon follow me, that the principles of freedom, of humanity, and of justice' will finally triumph over falsehood, tyranny, and delusion, and every principle inimical to the interests of the human race.[23]

The assembled crowd of about 20,000 broke out in spontaneous cheering at this point.[24] At this significant phrase – 'the human race' – the sheriff admonished him for using incendiary language. 'I have little more to add', Despard continued, 'except to wish you all health, happiness, and freedom, which I have endeavoured, as far as was in my power, to procure for you and for mankind in general.' As his fellow conspirator John MacNamara was brought up to the scaffold, he said to Despard, 'I am afraid, Colonel, we have got into a bad situation'. Despard's answer, the newspapers noted, was characteristic of the man: 'There are many better, and some worse'. His last words were, 'Tis very cold, I think we shall have some rain'.

The clergy then prayed with the five prisoners who had visited the chapel earlier. The Rev. Winkworth then shook hands with each prisoner, asking them to confess their sins and recite the Lord's Prayer. Despard had made no confession, nor did he recite the Lord's Prayer with the other accused: it is reasonable to suppose that, like Thomas Paine, he was a Deist. Despard shook hands with Rev. Winkworth, who had tried to convince him of 'the error of his denial of Revealed Religion of Christ' and then the 'most awful silence' prevailed reported the press. At seven minutes to nine the signal was given and simultaneously the platform under each man dropped.[25]

Newspapers reported on the deaths in gruesome detail, noting that Despard did not struggle, although 'he simultaneously opened his clenched fists twice and then stirred no more'. Macnamara, Graham, Wood, and Wratten 'struggled for a few moments, and then they too remained motionless'. However, Broughton and Francis 'violently struggled, and supposedly to end their misery, the executioner tugged on their legs, which immediately stopped their movements'.[26]

In the days before measured ropes and weighted drops, death by hanging was an uncertain business. It was 37 minutes before the executioner finally cut him down, and wrestled his corpse over the block. The press reported that Despard's dark coat flapped back in the breeze as his body hung limply from the scaffold to reveal a blue undercoat with gilt buttons, a cream waistcoat trimmed with gold lace, and a strip of scarlet flannel turned over the waist of his grey breeches.[27]

Despard had been condemned to hanged, drawn and quartered, but rather than being quartered he was to be decapitated in a final macabre ritual. The executioner stepped back to make way for a surgeon with a dissecting knife. This was the part of the ritual which had barely been seen within living memory and, as soon became clear, had never previously been attempted by anyone present. In endeavouring to cut off Despard's head, the surgeon aimed at a joint between two cervical vertebrae but missed it: out of desperation he was soon reduced to nervous hacking. In a scene reminiscent of a horror movie, the executioner barged the blood-spattered surgeon out of the way and began twisting Despard's neck 'this way and that' to 'snap off his head' in a spectacle which 'filled everyone present with horror'. When the head was eventually separated, the executioner picked it up by the hair, blood dripping from the stump of his neck, and carried it to the edge of the scaffold in his right hand and held it before the crowd and spoke the words which had for centuries marked the climax of the ceremony, but which were now ringing out for the first time in London for over a century: 'This is the head of a traitor: Edward Marcus Despard'.[28] Many called the execution 'murder'.[29]

Despard is buried somewhere close to the north door of St Paul's Cathedral London in an unmarked grave. A few days after his execution, an Irishman called John English was imprisoned for selling 'inflammatory handbills' that consisted of a word-for-word printing of Despard's speech on the scaffold. The Crown was keen to suppress Despard's words in case they triggered rebellion.[30]

Chapter 19

# AFTER DESPARD

Despard's arrest did not end the Black Lamp or other radical groups. On 30 January 1803, Earl Fitzwilliam sent a letter to the Home Office reporting that John Nicholls, 'the well-known revolutionary', was in Leeds and that the Rev. Dr Coulthurst had committed to York gaol a man called Robinson for sedition.[1] Ralph Fletcher submitted evidence to the Secret Committee of the Home Office regarding the accused. Fletcher's spy network noted that Nicholls was raising money for his defence, and had travelled to Manchester and Sheffield for this purpose. The defence rested on blackening the character of the witnesses.[2] Whitehall hoped that 'Nicholl's subscription would be totally defeated'.[3] A French secret agent, M. Middleton, was sent to England to report on the political and economic situation: basically, his remit was to assess if the country was still ripe for revolution. He replied that public mood was changing for war, and was against France in the newspapers.[4] The executions had clearly tempered the immediate spirit for insurrection – no doubt the aim of the Crown!

If the Crown felt Despard's death would end radical activism, they were wrong. At the start of February, William Iredale, who worked for Messrs Gott & Wormald as a cropper in Leeds, was arrested and charged with distributing seditious pamphlets.[5] In Huddersfield, Magistrate Joseph Radcliffe arrested Joseph Jubson, a clothier, for sedition.[6] Men of the 18th Light Dragoons billeted in the town in a sworn statement reported Jubson as saying 'Damn all superiors I like none of them . . . I wish the King and his friends were at the gallows . . . I'll stand to say what I say, I feel withing my own breast for I wish your master the King and all his ministers were in hell . . .'[7] Jubson had stated he had been involved in the Navy Mutiny of 1797 and was a support of Richard Parker who had led it. He was gaoled at York without trial.[8] William Hay, Lord Mayor of Leeds, informed the Home

Office that Nicholas O'Connor, a corporal in the 18th Light Dragoons, said that he was in the George and Dragon public house in Briggate, Leeds, and heard John Wilkinson, a servant to Mr Rayson the Druggist, say that he wished Colonel Despard's head was down the King's throat. John Skelton said that he heard Jonas Hartley, cordwainer, say that all kings were tyrants and that we were ruled by a military government.[9]

When war broke out again in May 1803, Charles James Fox blamed the Prime Minister Henry Addington for not standing up to the King. Fox was adamant that the British government had not left Napoleon 'any alternative but War or the most abject humiliation' and that the war 'is entirely the fault of our Ministers and not of Bonaparte'.[10] As in 1792, public opinion was divided: the Tories were for war, and the Whigs, as was ever the case, were against it, and more importantly the spectre of economic collapse and famine haunted the middle classes and urban poor.[11] The same month, the Home Office received reports that William Cheetham, the well-known radical Jacobin in Manchester, was sending 'seditious papers and handbills' to Leeds in a consignment of hats.[12] In the summer came alarming reports from Devon, where handbills were posted which declared:

> You are called upon with others of your country by an oppressive government to be sent on the continent to be butchered- will you tamely submit to this new act of Tyranny & leave your wives & Children to despair & ruin? NO! rouse yourselves, be United – its time to resist those cruel rulers & let them know that you will no longer submit to their will when it is cruel and unjust.[13]

In Portsmouth forty-two suspected United Irishmen were arrested at the end of March.[14] A month later, delegates from Dublin 'seems to have been sent with the view of enquiring into the reason of the backwardness of the Manchester Citizens which has . . . given great uneasiness to their friends'. Despard's execution seems to have dampened the ardour for revolution, just as the authorities hoped. Fletcher noted furthermore that his network of informers reported that three United English delegates had arrived from France, and that an Irish delegate had been in Manchester. Yet Fletcher noted that Patrick Finney was at large in the North of England and noted that he, according to a spy, 'spoke confidently of the French invading Ireland in case of war and should the dispute be patched up between their country and France, the Irish would shake off the yoke themselves'.[15] On the evening of 16 July 1803, one of the rebels in Dublin inadvertently sparked off an explosion of their stockpile of gunpowder kept in a warehouse on Patrick Street,

191

causing a massive explosion. Believing the authorities to be on their trail, Emmet and the other leaders decided that the plans must be accelerated, and they advanced the rising to the next week, 23 July. Without French aid or significant organisational unity across the country, and with poor coordination within the capital itself, the rising was limited to skirmishes in Dublin, which the British quickly suppressed. Yet the fear of an invasion of Ireland was real enough. Another writer, London resident Thomas Faulder, opined on 3 August that 'I HAVE heard . . . that if the French can land (in Ireland), with some troops, they will immediately be joined by 100,000 Irish . . . The fact is, that nothing can satisfy them but a separation from this country.'[16]

John Lumsden, writing from London on 3 August, reported to a friend 'Discontent may, it is true, manifest itself among the lower classes in London, as well as in our great towns; but I do not think that it can ever be of great consequence. My only fear is for Ireland, where the standard of rebellion has been hoisted a-new.' A few weeks later Francis Hartwell opined that 'ALL England is under arms; but I am sorry to have to inform you that the people of Uham (that is, the lower class) are not among the number of the loyal, they have refused to offer their services'. Real anger was building in London for revolution. In Bradford, Magistrate Busfield reported that if Bonaparte landed, it was undeniable that hundreds of thousands of the 'lower orders' would have risen in support of France, and the ideals of the French Revolution. A handbill posted in Bradford declared:

> We are to observe that our rulers seem to indicate that the Chief Consul in France is nothing better than a committee of Robberies, Murders & Rapes, and shou'd he succeed in his attempt upon this Island, he'd reduce it to a state of Beggardom. Pray my friends, wou'd he reduce it lower than it is? Where does beggardom originate? . . . To begin with, our supposed invader he has arisen from a very low and obscure rank and birth (yet no lower than Moses who released Legions of people from their Shackles), and according to his time of life, has perform'd wonders . . . Foolish Britons, don't think that your powerful armies you have so wrongfully amassed together from the sweat of the labourers brow can save you from the wickedness of being avenged . . . The great men seem to say this is a very alarming crisis. The poor who will be found to be the strength of the nation, don't seem to be alarmed, their general cry is Let BONAPARTE COME, how can we be worse.[17]

Busfield reported to Earl Fitzwilliam that the 'evil spirit of sedition is by no means laid in this neighbourhood', and was concerned that the opportunity to be issued a musket and have military training without any oversight was received 'avidly by many who are suspected of being disaffected'.[18]

Unsurprisingly, anti-Catholic, anti-French and anti-Irish sentiment reached hysterical levels in some quarters. The Rev. Thomas Robarts, Vicar of Tottenham, wrote to the Home Office about a French émigré living in London since 1792, who he considered to be a spy and had set up a Catholic chapel along with other French exiles where Irish émigrés worshipped. The good reverend wanted the men deported.[19] The same month Ralph Fletcher informed the Home Office that a French alien, Leonard Thomas de Manneville, who had resided in Bolton since his marriage to a Miss Crompton in April 1800, had been seen in the French encampment at Boulogne, and had also been observed travelling to Liverpool. De Manneville was, Fletcher noted, a friend of a Yorkshireman called Atkinson who was a:

> Yorkshire merchant who supplied the French with cloathing [sic] throughout the last war and who was said to have fallen under suspicion of government for his entertaining so many reported foreigners at their house. He is a Craftsman and capable of furnishing his majesty's enemies with plans & information which may be useful to them and dangerous to the country.[20]

This was without a shadow of a doubt Law Atkinson, a Unitarian merchant of Halifax, who hosted French businessmen in 1792.[21] Clearly once more Unitarians were considered 'Jacobins'. Furthermore, Fletcher's spy network indicated that the French would land at Boston, then travel through Cambridge to London as there would be few obstacles in their way and that the United Irish in Manchester would rise in support.[22] A worried Earl Fitzwilliam wrote to the Home Secretary on 29 August that illegal oaths were being taken by croppers, clothiers, merchants and others across the West Riding. He was agitated by that fact that it was the same oath as used for men involved in the Despard conspiracy. Fitzwilliam was also concerned by the 'vast number of pikes made' and the 'nightly drilling of rebels' who, he informed the Home Office, were in 'constant conversation both with Ireland and France. That their correspondence is never entrusted to the post, but carried by a special messenger, little is committed to paper, but what is, is destroyed as soon as communicated – so great is their evasion.'[23]

James Wood reported to the authorities on 27 October that a man identified as James Stewart was overheard in the Bull and Star public house of Putney that 'Mr Boyd is gone to France and made an officer in the French service and I am glad to hear it' adding that 'If the French make a landing in this country and with great force, one half of the English would join them. As for my part, I will be one of the first.'[24]

Arrested in Sheffield was Thomas Ramskar for 'receiving stolen files', all seemingly fairly mundane till we read the next statement by the magistrate '... I have no doubt of his being concerned of making weapons for the Sheffield Society'.[25] It seems very credible that arms were being prepared as part of a planned uprising. In London a former member of the London Corresponding Society turned informant, reported that bills and pikes were being made, under the direction of a man called Eastburn, 'who would stop at nothing to [illegible] or overturn the government of this country', who frequented the Green Dragon on Fore Street. The informant added that 'I conceive that they might cause great confusion in the metropolis with their endeavours and private machinations with events of an invasion of this country'.[26] From Newcastle came warnings that at the Crown and Thistle public house, an agent provocateur drank toasts to 'the Rights of Man' and boasted when intoxicated that he had been a member of the London Corresponding Society. He had been arrested for treason, but had been acquitted, with a £500 fine. Taken before the magistrates, he was placed in Durham gaol for wanting a reform in government and freedom of speech.[27]

A spy working for Ralph Fletcher reported that Patrick McCabe and John Finney were operating in the country, having escaped from Dublin along with another Irish rebel called Kavanagh.[28] In Plymouth, Colonel Paget informed the Home Office of a 'pernicious conspiracy which appears to be generating here'.[29] Groups of over fifty men were observed drilling at night and were considered to be a serious threat to the working of the dockyards.[30] Suspected United Irishmen were arrested in Plymouth suspected of 'of a plot to damage the dock yards or make mischief in the Navy'.[31]

When famine returned in winter 1803, which lasted into 1804, anger built against the Corn Laws in Scotland and the North of England, with handbills and pamphlets regarded as 'an emanation from the Jacobin School'.[32] In Leicester the Mayor informed the Home Office that if the French landed 'quarter of the population ... would join them in order to be fed'.[33] Yet violence did not break out: 'all was quiet' on the Home Front. The French had given up any thought of landing in Ireland, as impracticable given the collapse of July rebellion and the diaspora of the leadership.[34]

The public mood was shifting. French secret Agent Duverne reported on 29 September 1803 to Consul Bonaparte that the public in London was now in favour of war, and that Addington's administration had begun recruiting for the Army and also had mobilised thousands as Volunteers.[35] He was quite correct: the Crown had embarked on an ambitious propaganda drive, to rally the public mood to war through alarmist nationalist appeals. As in 1794, the government sought to harness hatred of reform, hatred of the French and love of 'King and Country' to raise a new force for national defence. By 1804, over 380,000 men were enrolled in the 'Volunteer' forces of the country through the 'Levy en masse' Act: The act required all men aged between 17 and 55 to be placed into four classes: those of the first class were invited to enrol in the Volunteer Corps if they were to escape the militia ballot.[36] As the public mood changed, Nicholls fled Yorkshire and began his exile in Paris where he requested a pension from Talleyrand in 1804 and 1806, but the French state considered him a prisoner of war.[37]

The change in public opinion was in part due to a recovering economy and as in 1791 with the Reeves Association, a highly successful propaganda war launched by Henry Addington and William Pitt. The success of 'Pittite' patriotism lay in its ability to focus the multiple identities and inclinations of the Whigs and non-Anglicans into acceptance of and active participation in the wars against Revolutionary and Napoleonic France, with radicals and loyalists coming together in what John E. Cookson has described as 'National Defence Patriotism'.[38] The propaganda machine of William Pitt and Addington stressed that the 'enemy' wanted to steal much-vaunted British liberty and carry out bloody repression which was projected with the propaganda by Gillray and others. This external threat was seen to be several times greater than that of the native 'old corruption' by the loyalist Tories. The remarkable Hannah Lindsey shifted her sympathy for the French Revolution to a deep suspicion of Bonaparte, coupled with fear of invasion, and supported the raising of Volunteer regiments for home defence. In this change of mood, along with many others, she embraced a patriotism which decried both overseas and domestic threats to liberty and which placed a higher priority upon the preservation of those liberties than upon a veneration for existing institutions. Yet at the same time she deplored the impact the war was having upon British public life and culture, noting in March 1805 'He [Bonaparte] has done by his threats, what never can be undone, changed the manners and views of this country from Commerce merely, to a Military cast'.[39] Ralph Fletcher in December 1805 noted that groups had ceased meeting but opined that the Jacobins had gone underground. He feared that a resurgence of Jacobinism would follow a military reverse.[40] The 'home front' did not remain quiet: events starting in 1807 climaxed with the execution of Luddites in 1813, which we explore in our companion volume, also available from Frontline.

# CONCLUSIONS

The French Revolutionary and Napoleonic Wars were matched on the home front with a war between contrasting ideals of 'Britishness' related to property, law, democracy, the rights of man and religious toleration. Ultimately it was about who had power: the people or a coterie of the elite. This battle of ideology, more than anything, defined the conflict.[1]

The exclusivity of 'Britishness' led to hundreds of radicals and moderates alike fleeing the country: the expatriate radicals who gathered in Paris felt that the political scene in Britain held little hope for the sort of change they desired, despite concerted efforts to bring it about through political engagement or satirical writing. Disillusionment with legitimate efforts to seek redress of political grievances through petition was another factor for the radicals to remove to Paris. There was a pervasive feeling among British radical groups in Paris, and at home, that their political views, the exercise of political power, the sense of justice and concept of society were at direct odds with mainstream opinion. The experience of marginalisation, albeit to differing degrees, was a unifying factor, linking members of the British Club in Paris to the Society for Constitutional Information and London Corresponding Society as well as the Catholic Committee. The war threw the gulf between the haves and have-nots into stark relief which was a reflection of Tory v Whig politics, and kings in the cause of despotism.[2] The French Republic declared that the 'natural and imprescriptible rights of man' were to be defined as 'liberty, property, security and resistance to oppression'. The republic demanded the destruction of aristocratic privileges by proclaiming an end to feudalism and exemptions from taxation. It also called for freedom and equal rights for all human beings (referred to as 'Men') and access to public office based on talent. The monarchy was restricted and all citizens had the right to take part in the legislative process. Freedom of speech and the press were declared and arbitrary arrests outlawed. The Declaration also asserted the principles of popular sovereignty, in contrast to the divine right of kings that characterised the French monarchy, and social equality among citizens, eliminating the special rights of the nobility and clergy. The 'one nation conservatism' of Edmund Burke witnessed a consolidation of a sense of 'Englishness' centred on Protestantism and the Established Church. This consolidation of what it meant to be English produced a growing sense of marginalisation for non-Anglicans – Catholics and Unitarians – and alienated radicals – both supporters of reformist agendas led Cartwright and Wyvill and revolutionary figure headed by Despard. In response, these two groups embraced cosmopolitan republicanism as expressed in America and France (before 1794) to assert their own sense of identity. The politics of identity were at the heart of the United movement.

Many in Ireland, Britain and Scotland felt the same, especially at times of famine, when the rich oligarchs dined at lavish banquets and the poor starved to death. For loyalists and radicals, it was a battle for the very soul of the nation, a battle the loyalists refused to lose. Earl Fitzwilliam noted that:

> with regard to peace with France, we could have no hopes of it under the present system, unless we were prepared to sacrifice everything that was dear to us. . . His Lordship contended that the safety of the country, the preservation of the constitution, of everything dear to Englishmen and to their posterity depended upon the preventing the introduction of French principles, and the new-fangled doctrine of the rights of man; and that this could only be effected by the establishment of some regular form of government in that country upon which some reliance might be placed.[3]

The aim of the war against France was to be nothing short of total annihilation of the French Republic and democratic or 'French' principles. Fitzwilliam refused to support Fox and reform because the 'wrong sort of people' desired to have their voice heard: 'I never will *act in party* with men who call in 4,000 weavers to dictate political measures to the government—nor with men whose opposition is laid against the constitution more than against the Ministers'.[4] For Fitzwilliam and his colleagues in government, the working man and the middle class could not have a say in how the country was governed, and in defence of privilege, Pitt moulded a large part of the population to support his actions. That most redoubtable of writers, Jane Austen, was part of the propaganda war against France and French ideas – i.e. democracy – through her novels *Pride and Prejudice*, *Mansfield Park* and also *Emma*.[5] The propaganda machine of William Pitt stressed that the 'enemy' wanted to steal the much-vaunted British liberty and carry out bloody repression which was projected in propaganda by Gillray, Rowlandson and others. This external threat was seen to be several times greater than that of the native 'old corruption' by the loyalist Tories.

Those excluded from 'British Liberty' on religious and economic grounds never shared this view, and government propaganda probably did not convert the most ardent radical into a diehard loyalist. The United Englishmen were perhaps the first overtly working-class political movement in the country, and like the Suffragettes a century later, were prepared to use violence to get the vote and political reform. The Despard affair suggests that at least a significant portion of radicals were ready for and even preparing an insurrection. But the depth of the plot and the support for it are impossible to know. Despard was part of a multi-national plan to free Ireland from English rule. In endeavouring to link English working-class anger with Irish freedom-fighting, lay both the strength and weakness of the plan. English anger was driven by famine and repressive legislation and wanted immediate 'vengeance'. Irish anger was levelled at the English: the latter could be far easier moulded and shaped to suit political aims, the former was 'mob like', intent on immediate acts of violence. In the end, harnessing two vastly different grievances to the same cause was 'never going to work'. Neither group were unified by a single point of action.

For loyalist and radical, the Napoleonic Wars on the home front was a battle for the very soul of the nation. The English Revolution remained a 'might have been' because the middle class felt no cause to assume the role of Jacobins. English *enragés* failed because they could not harness more people to the cause. This does not mean that the threat was not real. The actions of the Crown speak volumes on the reality of the threat working-class rights consciousness posed to the élite.

Limited electoral reform was conceded in 1832, universal suffrage not until 1928. This slow evolution might be attributed to the resilience of the British political elite, the weakness of political opposition, or the failures of the extra-Parliamentary reform movement. But the French Revolution was also a critical factor. British liberal and opposition writing up to 1789 concentrated almost entirely on the dangers of the excessive power of the Crown. In contrast, nineteenth-century conservatism and liberalism were united in seeing the people themselves as the principal threat to liberty. Haunted by the spectre of popular revolutionary violence, the political élite refused to trust the people to exercise democratic rights responsibly – while simultaneously understanding the importance of their loyalty. From 1793, propaganda, political ritual and the cultivation of a popular monarchy became key elements in a strategy that recognised the power of the people, but declined to accord them democratic rights.

The failure of the English Jacobins to bring about radical change set the scene for over a hundred years of working-class struggle: the Despard plotters never gave up their dream of universal suffrage. The ideals of Despard drove the explosion of radicalism that rocked the country from later 1811 into 1813. The Spa Field riots and the Cato Street Conspiracy also involved Despard plotters, and followed a very similar plan. In 1817 Wakefield militants John Smaller and Benjamin Scholes were arrested on charges of sedition. Arrested at the same time was William Wolstenholme, who told the authorities he was one of Despard's men and had been 28 years in the cause; so too Smaller and Scholes. Charles Pendle who was directly involved in the Despard Coup was also convicted for his involvement in the Pentrich rising. The Peterloo massacre was a direct result of the Crown and elites refusal to give the people the vote, so too the riots of 1830 over the Reform Act and the Chartist riots of the 1840s, led by the grandsons of the Despard plotters. Despard is important: he represents the beginning of the great struggle for freedom by the working man which culminated with Labour Party leader and Unitarian lay preacher Ramsey MacDonald becoming the first working-class prime minister in 1924.

# NOTES

## Introduction: A War of Ideas

1. For more on the philosophical origins of Jacobin thought, see Gregory Dart (1999), *Rousseau, Robespierre, and English Romanticism*. Cambridge and New York: Cambridge University Press, pp. 1–19.
2. Samuel Heywood (1789), *The right of protestant dissenters to a compleat toleration asserted*. London: J Johnson, p. 45.
3. John Seed (1985), 'Gentlemen Dissenters: The Social and Political Meanings of Rational Dissent in the 1770s and 1780s', *The Historical Journal* 28(2), pp. 299–325.
4. G.M. Ditchfield (2007), *The Letters of Theophilus Lindsey (1723-1808)* 2 vols. Woodbridge, United Kingdom: Church of England Record Society, Vol. 1, pp. 204–05.

## Chapter 1: The American Revolution

1. Ditchfield Vol. 1, pp. 208–09.
2. Sheffield City Archives (hereafter SCA), Wentworth Woodhouse Muniments (hereafter WWM) R81-22. See also ibid. R1-1974.
3. Ibid., R142-1, Rockingham to John Stephenson of Hull, (illegible) 1763.
4. Ibid., R9023, Rockingham to Portland, 5 December 1769.
5. Ibid., R1-1551, Rockingham to Pemberton Milnes, (illegible) February 1775
6. James E Bradley (1990), *Religion, Revolution and English Radicalism: Nonconformity in Eighteenth-Century Politics and Society*. Cambridge: Cambridge University Press, pp. 337–59.
7. Ditchfield Vol. 1, pp. 204–05.
8. SCA WWM R1-1553, Rockingham to Pemberton Milnes, (illegible) February 1775.
9. It would not be for a hundred years that constitutional amendments and federal laws would increasingly grant equal rights to African Americans, Native Americans, poor white men and women.
10. Richard Price, 'Observations on the Nature of Civil Liberty, the Principles of Government, and the Justice and Policy of the War with America', in *Political Writings*. Cambridge: Cambridge University Press pp. 28–9.
11. William Turner (1777), *The whole service as performed in the congregation of Protestant dissenters, at Wakefield, on Friday, December 13, 1776: Being the day appointed for a general fast. Printed at the request of the congregation. By William Turner*. Wakefield: Thomas Waller.
12. Ibid., p. 33.
13. SCA R1-1550, John Smyth to Rockingham, 6 February 1775.
14. Paul Lindsay Dawson (2019), *Lexington to Waterloo: Yorkshire Unitarians and National Politics*. Wakefield: Westgate Chapel, p. 53.

15. North Yorkshire Record Office (hereafter NYRO), Wyvill papers fol. 137-138.
16. SCA WWM R1-1868, Wyvill to Milnes, 5 December 1779.
17. York City Library (hereafter YCL), WYV/1/39/67, letter from John Milnes of Wakefield, 1 June 1780
18. Ibid., WYV/1/39/50, letter from John Milnes of Wakefield, 18 April 1780.
19. Ibid., WYV/1/39/70, letter from John Milnes of Wakefield, 10 July 1780.
20. NYRO Wyvill Papers fol. 155.
21. YCL, WYV/1/39/312, letter Henry Duncombe.
22. YCL, Yorkshire Association Papers. WYV/1/39/97, letter from James Milnes Jnr, 1 October 1780.
23. Ibid., WYV/1/39, uncatalogued letter Robert Lumb, 2 October 1780.
24. Ibid., WYV, Duncombe to Wyvill, un-catalogued letter, 19 May 1781.
25. Dawson (2019), p. 77.
26. Ibid, pp. 68–9.
27. YCL WYV/1/38/8, Letter from Pemberton Milnes, 12 January 1783.
28. Ibid., WYV/6, Pemberton Milnes to Holmes, 26 January 1783.
29. Ibid., WYV/6, Yorkshire Association Papers.
30. NRYO, Wyvill Papers Folio 270-271, Duncombe to Wyvill, 23 October 1783.
31. Dawson (2019), p. 94.
32. SCA WWM/F, John Pemberton Heywood to Earl Fitzwilliam, 28 February 1784.

## Chapter 2: Revolution in France

1. William Wood (1788), *Two Sermons preached in Mill-Hill Chapel, in Leeds*. Leeds: Thomas Wright, pp. 32–3.
2. Dawson (2019), p. 52.
3. William Turner (1792), *Sermons on various subjects published at the request of the congregation of Protestant Dissenters in Wakefield*. London: J. Johnson, p. 89.
4. Ibid., pp. 302–3.
5. Richard Price (1789), *Discourse delivered on the love of our country*. London: J. Johnson, pp. 49–50.
6. Archives parlementaires de 1787 à 1860; Assemblée nationale constituante, Du 12 novembre 1789 au 24 décembre 1789.
7. British Library Additional Manuscripts (hereafter BL Add MS). 64814
8. Michael Fitzpatrick (1995), 'Patriots and patriotisms: Richard Price and the early reception of the French Revolution in England', in M. O'Dea and K. Whelan (eds), *Ireland and the eighteenth-century context*. Oxford: Oxford University Press, pp. 211–30.
9. Mark Philip (2017), *Reforming Ideas in Britain: Politics and Language in the shadow of the French Revolution, 1789-1815*. Cambridge: Cambridge University Press, pp. 119–20.
10. Dawson (2019), p. 47.
11. Ibid.
12. Gregory Claeys (2007), *The French Revolution Debate in Britain*. London: Palgrave MacMillan, pp. 20–1.
13. Edmund Burke (1826), *Speech on the Petition of the Unitarians*. London: C. & J. Rivington.
14. Capel Lofft (1791), *Remarks on the letter of the Right Honourable Edmund Burke concerning the Revolution in France*. London: J. Johnson.
15. Joseph Priestley (1791), *Letters to the Right Honourable Edmund Burke: Occasioned by His Reflections on the Revolution in France*. Birmingham: Thomas Pearson, p. 3.

16. The National Archives (hereafter TNA) Home Office Papers (hereafter HO) 42/19/32 Folios 58-59. Letter to Priestley, 21 May 1791.
17. Dawson (2019), pp. 30–1. See also ibid., pp. 163–5.
18. William Turner (1792), p. 303.
19. TNA HO 42/19/256, Eyre to Dundas, 23 July 1791.
20. Ibid., HO 42/19/265, Wilkinson, Eyre, and Ward to Dundas, 23 July 1791.
21. Ibid., HO 41/191-140 296. Vincent Eyre to Portland 30 July 1791. See also ibid., HO 41/191-140 298. Vincent Eyre to Portland, 30 July 1791 12 o'clock at night.
22. *Evening Mail*, 29 July 1791.
23. Colin Haydon (1993), *Anti-Catholicism in eighteenth century England, 1714-1780*. Manchester: Manchester University Press.
24. *Leeds Intelligencer*, Monday, 11 May 1807.
25. TNA HO 42/19/294, Eyre to Dundas 29 July 1791. See also ibid., HO 42/91/ 296, Eyre to Dundas, 30 July 1791; Ibid., HO 42/91/354, Eyre to Dundas, 31 July 1791; ibid., HO 42/91/537, Eyre to Dundas, 25 August 1791.
26. Ibid., HO 42/19/296, Vincent Eyre to Portland, 30 July 1791.
27. West Yorkshire Archive Service [hereafter WYAS] ASSI 45/37/2/51-53, York assizes depositions, 30 July 1791.
28. TNA HO 42/19/294, Eyre to Dundas, 29 July 1791. See also ibid., HO 42/91/ 296, Eyre to Dundas, 30 July 1791; ibid., HO 42/91/354, Eyre to Dundas, 31 July 1791; ibid., HO 42/91/537, Eyre to Dundas, 25 August 1791.

## Chapter 3: Jacobin Clubs

1. TNA Treasurer Solicitors Papers [hereafter TS] 11/9523496ii.
2. Ibid., HO 42/30/64 Folios 152-153. Warrant issued by the Home Secretary, 20 May 1794.
3. SCA WWM F44/32. Address and Declaration, 20 September 1791.
4. Ibid., WWM F44/1, H. Hunter to Earl Fitzwilliam, 12 December 1791.
5. James Montgomery (4 November 1771–30 April 1854) was a Scottish-born hymn writer, poet and editor. His writings reflected concern for humanitarian causes such as the abolition of slavery and the exploitation of child chimney sweeps. He was raised in and theologically trained by the Moravian Church.
6. SCA WWM F44/45, handbill from Sheffield, Revolution Club.
7. Albert Goodwin (1979), *The Friends of Liberty. The English Democratic Movement in the Age of the French Revolution*. London and New York: Routledge, pp. 186–8.
8. Ibid.
9. Thomas Brand Hollis, Unitarian radical.
10. The Rev. Dr Jebb, Unitarian, abolitionist and radical, supporting the ideals of Thomas Paine and Marat.
11. Goodwin, pp. 186–8.
12. Ibid.
13. TNA HO 42/32-Folio 398, handwritten copy of a 'club book' containing the rules of the Constitutional Society of Leeds adopted on 14 April 1794 and contribution records for April and May maintained by the district delegate.
14. SCA WWM F44/2, Rev. H Zouch to Earl Fitzwilliam, 28 December 1791.
15. *Sheffield Register*, 24 February 1792
16. SCA WWM MD 251, 14 March 1792.
17. TNA TS 11/951/3495, John Horne Tooke to Sheffield Constitutional Society, 2 March 1792.
18. Anon (1792), *A Letter from His Grace the Duke of Richmond to Lieutenant Colonel Sharman, Chairman of the Committee of Correspondence appointed by the Delegates of*

45 *Corps of Volunteers assembled at Lisburn in Ireland, with Notes from a Member of the Society for Constitutional Information.* London: J. Johnson, p. 3.

19. Robert Birley (1924), *The English Jacobins from 1789 to 1802.* London, Oxford University Press, Appendix.
20. Emma Vincent Macleod (1998), *A War of Ideas: British Attitudes to the War Against Revolutionary France 1792-1802.* London: Routledge, pp. 26–7.
21. Claeys, p. 23.
22. SCA WWM F44/2, Rev. H Zouch to Earl Fitzwilliam, 28 December 1791.
23. Ibid.
24. Ibid., WWM F44/3, Rev. James Wilkinson to Rev. Henry Zouch, 6 January 1792.
25. Ibid., WWM F44/4, Rev. Henry Zouch to Earl Fitzwilliam, 6 January 1792.
26. Marianne Elliott (1982), *Partners in Revolution. The United Irishmen and France.* Yale University Press: New Haven and London. See also Roger A.E. Wells (1986), *Insurrection: The British Experience 1795-1803.* Stroud: Sutton Books; J. Ann Hone (1982), *For the Cause of Truth: Radicalism in London, 1796-1821.* Oxford: Oxford University Monographs.
27. SCA WWM F44/5, Rev. H. Zouch to Earl Fitzwilliam, 31 January 1792.
28. Ibid., WWM F44/7, Rev. H. Zouch, Sandal, to Earl Fitzwilliam, 3 March 1792.
29. TNA TS 951/3495.
30. SCA WWM F44/8, Sheffield Club account of proceedings dated 27 February 1792
31. Goodwin, p. 230.
32. *Derby Mercury,* Monday 29 September 1791, Address to Dr Priestley.
33. John Goodchild Collection. MSS notes Derby Friar Gate Unitarian Chapel.
34. Address of the Society for Political Information, Derby. London: Thomas Spence, 1793
35. Goodwin, p. 231.
36. SCA WWM F44/1, H. Hunter to Earl Fitzwilliam, 12 December 1791.
37. Ibid., WWM F44/19, James Wheat, Sheffield, to Rev. H. Zouch, 13 June 1792.
38. John Goodchild Collection. Shore MSS Notes.
39. SCA WWM F44/6, Abstract of Proceedings, 26 March 1792.
40. Dawson (2019), pp. 169–70.
41. https://shura.shu.ac.uk/4075/6/10694412.pdf

## Chapter 4: Sedition and Censorship

1. SCA WWM F44/9, Rev. H. Zouch to Earl Fitzwilliam, 5 April 1792.
2. Ibid., WWM F44/40, Charles Bowns to Earl Fitzwilliam, 13 December 1792.
3. Edmund Burke (1780), *Vindication of Natural Society.* London: J. Dodsley, p. 32.
4. Macleod, p. 17.
5. Ibid., pp. 26–7.
6. Claeys, p. 23.
7. Edmund Burke (1796), *Thoughts on the Prospect of a Regicide Peace, in a Series of Letters.* London: J. Owen, pp. 17–18.
8. *The Parliamentary History of England, From the Earliest Period to The Year 1803,* Vols 28–35. London, Longman et al., 1816–19, Col. 518–19.
9. Dawson (2019), pp. 161–2.
10. Thomas Christie (1791), *Letters on the Revolution in France,* Part 1. London: J. Johnson, pp. 47–8.
11. *Sheffield Register: Yorkshire, Derbyshire, & Nottinghamshire Universal Advertiser,* Friday 19 April 1793.
12. Stuart Andrews (2003), *Unitarian Radicalism. Political Rhetoric, 1770-1814.* New York: Pallgrave MacMillan, pp. 155–6.

13. NYRO Wyvill papers, 138 Letter to Rev. Dr Towers, 18 May 1793.
14. Live Free or Perish, referencing 'Liberty or Death', the motto of the Parisians Sans Culottes.
15. https://www.historyofparliamentonline.org/volume/1790-1820/member/erskine-hon-thomas-1750-1823
16. *A Complete Collection of State Trials*, various editors. London, 1809–26, vol. xxiii, col. 414-415.
17. *Leeds Intelligencer*, Monday 11 June 1792.
18. SCA WWM/F/44/29, resolutions of Wakefield meeting, 11 June 1792.
19. *Leeds Intelligencer*, Monday 25 June 1792.
20. SCA WWM/F44/30, handbill criticising resolutions of Wakefield meeting.
21. John Goodchild, pers comm, 2 October 2016.
22. SCA WWM/F44/30, handbill criticising resolutions of Wakefield meeting
23. James Milnes was elected a member of the Society for Constitutional Information on 30 January 1784 and his cousin Jack Milnes on 13 February the same year, Jack being sponsored by William Smith and Thomas Brand Hollis. James joined 'The Friends of the People' in 1792, along with his cousin Richard Slater Milnes, and both men were members of the Sheffield Society for Constitutional Information. In 1794 he entered into partnership with William Dawson, a wool stapler, who represented his interest as senior partner, who along with co-religionist Joseph Burrell, and London friend John Craven formed the company Dawson, Craven and Burrell to manage his land, banking and woollen trade interests. James withdrew from commerce and turned his attention full time to politics, backing Fox. At the general election of 1796, evidently at the instigation of Lord Lauderdale, Milnes was lured into a contest for Shaftesbury, in company with William Dawson, whose family had been business associates of his. Told that the outlay would probably be £4,000, he paid most of the estimated cost of failure (£17,000). Yet this did not stop him becoming a member of London society and Whig politics. He would become MP for Bletchingley from 1802 till his death in 1805. His wife, Mary Anne, was an 'A'-list celebrity of the day, hosting Georgiana Duchess of Devonshire, the Prince Regent and two future kings of France at her soirees.
24. SCA WWM F44/17, Rev. Henry Zouch to Earl Fitzwilliam, 13 June 1792.
25. SCA WWM F44/23, handbill, Wakefield.
26. Ibid., WWM F44/22, Rev. H. Zouch to Earl Fitzwilliam, 25 June 1792. Hurst was a recent convert to Unitarianism: his cousin Rowland had married the daughter of prominent Unitarian clock maker John Day. Rowlands son, also Rowland, would marry the daughter of his minister, the Rev. Thomas Johnstone.
27. Ibid., WWM/F/44/23, Rev. H. Zouch to Earl Fitzwilliam, 11 June 1792, citing letter from General Tottenham dated 10 AM 10 June 1792 enclosing handbill ridiculing the proposed Wakefield meeting.
28. Tottenham had joined the army on 10 June 1756, major of the 52nd Regiment of Foot in 1760, colonel of the 90th Foot in 1777, and general on 12 October 1793, holding the colonelcy of the 55th Foot. He and his family subscribed to the new Saint John's Church in Wakefield.
29. John Goodchild, pers comm, 2 September 2015.
30. SCA WWM F44/17, Rev. Henry Zouch to Earl Fitzwilliam, 13 June 1792.
31. West Yorkshire Archive Service [here after WYAS], Quarter Sessions 1/137/4.
32. TNA TS 11/1071/5061, Rex v Thomas JOHNSTONE and Robert BAKEWELL.
33. SCA WWM F44/10, Rev. H Zouch to Earl Fitzwilliam [illegible]. This is of course William Davies Shipley, dean of St Asaph, son of the Bishop of St Asaph, and a member and supporter of the Society for Constitutional Information who won a seditious libel case in 1784, represented by Thomas Erskine. The case

was instrumental in advancing the cause to return the decision of whether a publication is a libel to the jury, rather than being decided by the judge, finally enacted in Charles James Fox's Libel Act of 1792.

34. Francis Edmunds married Hannah Maria Offely, co-heir of Joseph Offely of Norton Hall. Her elder sister, Urith, married Samuel Shore of Sheffield. Shore had been a reformer, but became a staunch supporter of Pitt's measures. Edmunds, a nominal Unitarian, like his brother-in-law shied away from reform. He had been a member of the Yorkshire Association. The Edmunds family had been magistrate-landowners of Worsborough since the late seventeenth century, and became incredibly wealthy from the profits derived from their coal mines during the nineteenth century.

35. SCA WWM F44/12, letter from Francis Edmunds, Worsborough, to Rev. H. Zouch noting dispersal of the rioters at Sheffield and requesting help of other magistrates, 10 May 1792; Ibid., WWM F44/13 Letter from Mrs Edmunds (Hannah Maria, née Offely, wife of Francis) to Rev. H. Zouch sent by express from Sheffield asking other magistrates to join her husband, 10 May 1792.

36. Ibid., WWM F44/13, Rev. H. Zouch to Earl Fitzwilliam, 13 May 1792.

37. *Leeds Intelligencer*, Monday 2 July 1792.

38. SCA WWM F44/21, copy of enclosure found in Wakefield.

39. *Leeds Intelligencer*, Monday 25 June 1792.

40. SCA WWM F44/22, Rev. H. Zouch to Earl Fitzwilliam, 25 June 1792.

41. Ibid., WWM/F/44/24, Rev. H. Zouch, Sandal, to Earl Fitzwilliam, 3 July 1792.

42. *Leeds Intelligencer*, Monday 31 December 1792.

43. David Eastwood (1991), 'Patriotism and the English State in the 1790s' in Mark Philp (ed.), *The French Revolution and British Popular Politics*. Cambridge: 1991, p. 154.

44. Harry Dickinson (1990), 'Popular Loyalism in the 1790s' in Hellmuth Eckhart (ed.), *The Transformation of Political Culture: England and Germany in the Late Eighteenth Century*. Oxford: Oxford University Press, p. 511.

45. SCA WWM Y20. Armed associations.

46. Dawson (2019), p. 175.

## Chapter 5: Loyalism

1. BL Add MS 27814 Folios 45-6.

2. Archives Nationales de France [hereafter AN] Series C piece 242.

3. SCA WWM F45/a/72, Earl Fitzwilliam to Zouch, April 1792.

4. Kate Horgan (2016), *The Politics of Songs in Eighteenth Century Britain 1723-1795*. London: Routledge, p. 141.

5. *Sheffield Register*, Monday 30 November 1792.

6. Archives Diplomatique [hereafter AD] Correspondence Politiques Angleterre [hereafter CPA] 583 Folio 263.

7. AD CPA 584 Folio 58, Chauvelin to Lebrun, 5 Décembre 1792.

8. SCA WWM F44/38, Rev. James Wilkinson to Earl Fitzwilliam, no date; the next letter in sequence is 12 December 1792, so presumably this letter is from the last quarter of 1792.

9. Ibid., WWM F44/39, J.A. Athorpe to Earl Fitzwilliam, 12 December 1792.

10. Ibid., WWM F44/40, Charles Bowns to Earl Fitzwilliam, 13 December 1792.

11. TNA Foreign Office Papers [hereafter FO] 27/41 Folio 82, Monro to Grenville, 27 December 1792.

12. Dickinson, p. 517.

13. Dawson (2019), pp. 174–5.

14. Michael Duffy (1996), 'William Pitt and the Origins of the Loyalist Association Movement of 1792', *The Historical Journal*, No. 39, p. 943.
15. Claeys, pp. 69–70.
16. SCA WWM F44/40, Charles Bowns to Earl Fitzwilliam, 13 December 1792.
17. *Leeds Intelligencer*, Monday 7 January 1793.
18. Ibid.
19. *Sheffield Register: Yorkshire, Derbyshire, & Nottinghamshire Universal Advertiser*, Friday 1 February 1793.
20. John Goodchild Collection: Richard Munkhouse DD Discourse on the Revolution in France.
21. TNA HO 42/23/58 Folios 134-135, letter from Lieutenant Colonel W.P. Colyear Robertson, 5 December 1792.
22. Andrews, p. 124.
23. https://spartacus-educational.com/PRherald.htm
24. John Stevenson (1979), *Popular Disturbances in England 1700-1832*. London: Routledge, p. 177.
25. Robert Rae (1961), '"Liberty of the Press" as an Issue in English Politics, 1792–1793', *The Historian* No. 24, p. 35.
26. *Leeds Intelligencer*, Monday 31 December 1792.
27. *Leeds Intelligencer*, Monday 24 December 1792.
28. *Leeds Intelligencer*, Monday 17 December 1792.
29. *Leeds Intelligencer*, Monday 24 December 1792.
30. SCA WWM Y20/17/1, Henry Peterson to Earl Fitzwilliam, 24 May 1798.
31. Nicolas Rogers (1999), 'Burning Tom Paine: Loyalism and Counter-Revolution in Britain, 1791-1793', *Histoire Sociale* Novembre 1999, pp. 139–71.
32. *Leeds Intelligencer*, Monday 7 January 1793.
33. *Leeds Intelligencer*, Monday 31 December 1792.
34. *Leeds Intelligencer*, Monday 24 December 1792.
35. Rogers, pp. 156–9.
36. Philip, p. 79.
37. Linda Colley (2005), *Britons: Forging the Nation 1707-1837*. London: Yale University Press.
38. Dawson (2019), pp. 175–7.
39. *The Morning Chronicle*, 9 January 1795.

## Chapter 6: Henry Redhead Yorke

1. AN C11/278/40 piece 1-3.
2. TNA TS 11/959, George Monro, 6 December 1792.
3. Ibid., TS 11/960, George Monro, 21 December 1792.
4. *Sheffield Register: Yorkshire, Derbyshire, & Nottinghamshire Universal Advertiser*, Friday 19 April 1793.
5. TNA TS 24/3/35B, London Corresponding Society: Circular to Societies Concerning the Formation of a British Convention; Meeting of Delegates of Constitutional Society in Leeds, May 28, 1793.
6. Goodwin, pp. 279–81.
7. *Sheffield Register: Yorkshire, Derbyshire, & Nottinghamshire Universal Advertiser*, Friday 21 June 1793.
8. Derby Local Studies Centre. Address of the Society for Political Information, Derby. Thomas Spence, London 1793.
9. Ibid.
10. Stevenson, p. 66.

11. *A Complete Collection of State Trials*, Vol. 25.
12. TNA HO 102/9 Folio 303 Anonymous to W. Scott, 24 December 1793.
13. TNA TS 11/955/3499.
14. Henry Redhead Yorke (1794), *Thoughts on Civil Government: Addressed to the Disfranchised Citizens of Sheffield*. London: D.I. Eaton, pp. 3–4.
15. TNA TS 11/955/3499, Thelwall to Vellam, 23 January 1794.
16. Ibid., HO 42/30/44 Folio 100.
17. John Goodchild, pers com. Shore MSS.
18. Stevenson, p. 67.
19. Ibid., p. 25.
20. SCA WWM Y17/, James Wilkinson to Earl Fitzwilliam, 11 April 1794.
21. TNA HO 42/30/42 Folios 99-100. Two papers printed on the reverse of freehold register proformas.

## Chapter 7: The Net Closes In

1. TNA HO 42/32/269, Information of Pauncefort Cooke sworn before William Wickham, 30 June 1794.
2. Ibid., HO 42/19/4 Folio 7. Conclusion of letter to Joseph Priestley.
3. TNA TS 11/555/1793.
4. TNA HO 42/32/273 Folios 434A-434B, letter to William Wickham, 19 May 1794.
5. Ibid., HO 42/30/109 Folios 279-280, Samuel Marshall to John Mason, 25 May 1794.
6. Kenneth J. Logue (2002), *Popular disturbances in Scotland 1780-1815*. Edinburgh: Birlinn Ltd.
7. TNA HO 42/30/129 Folios 318-319, letter from the Reverend James Wilkinson, 29 May 1794.
8. Ibid., HO 42/31/1 Folios 1-3, Athorpe to Evan Nepean, 25 June 1794. Enclosure.
9. Ibid., HO 42/30/109 Folios 279-280, Samuel Marshall to John Mason, 25 May 1794.
10. Ibid., HO 42/32/273 Folios 434A-434B, letter to William Wickham, 19 May 1794.
11. Ibid HO 42/32 Folios 420-421, an account of the alleged fabrication of weapons by Josiah Webb of Pamber.
12. Logue, pp. 119–21.
13. *Sheffield Register*, Monday 22 June 1794.
14. TNA HO 42/30/64 Folios 152-153, warrant issued by the Home Secretary, 20 May 1794.
15. William Moult was a Unitarian and lived at Wickersley.
16. TNA HO 42/37/194 Folio(s) 356-358B, an account by Mr Ross of the arrest of seditious people in Sheffield [Yorkshire].
17. Ibid.
18. Ibid., HO 42/30/136 Folios 333-334, letter from Edward Miller, 31 May 1794.
19. Ibid., HO 42/30/129 Folios 318-319, letter from the Reverend James Wilkinson, 29 May 1794.
20. Ibid., HO 42/37/194 Folio(s) 356-358B, an account by Mr Ross of the arrest of seditious people in Sheffield [Yorkshire].
21. Ibid.
22. Ibid.
23. Ibid., HO 42/30/109 Folios 279-280, Samuel Marshall to John Mason, 25 May 1794.
24. Ibid., HO 42/30/117, invoice to H. D. Symonds.
25. Ibid., HO 42/32/196 Folios 280A-280B, an Order, signed by Stephen Cottrel, 8 July 1794.
26. Ibid., HO 42/31/140 Folios 303-304, warrant signed and sealed by Henry Dundas.

27. Ibid., HO 42/30/129 Folios 318-319, letter from the Reverend James Wilkinson, 29 May 1794.
28. Ibid.
29. Ibid., HO 42/31/95 Folios 215-216, letter from Robert Athorpe, 18 June 1794.
30. William Hague (2005), *William Pitt the Younger*. London: Harper Press.
31. TNA HO 42/31/117 Folios 259A-259B, memorandum to Evan Nepean.

## Chapter 8: I Arrest You for Treason!

1. TNA HO 42/31/1 Folios 1-3, Athorpe to Evan Nepean, 25 June 1794 with enclosure.
2. Ibid., HO 42/31 Folios 124-125, letter from Reverend John Griffith, magistrate of Manchester, 14 June 1794.
3. Amanda Goodrich (2019), *Henry Redhead Yorke, Colonial Radical: Politics and Identity in the Atlantic Word 1772-1813*. London: Routledge.
4. TNA PROB 11/1128/157, will of Samuel Readhead or Redhead of City of London, 6 April 1785.
5. TNA HO 42/31 117. Letter from John Brookfield, solicitor, of Sheffield, 9 June 1794
6. Ibid., HO 42/31 – HO 42, letters and papers. Folios 116-117. Letter from John Brookfield, solicitor, of Sheffield, 9 June 1794.
7. Ibid., HO 42/31/94I Folios 213-214, letter to Evan Nepean, Under-Secretary, Home Office, 14 June 1794. See also TNA HO 42/31/116 Folios 257-258, letter from John Wray, Mayor of Hull, 24 June 1794.
8. Ibid., HO 42/32/254 John Wray to Home Office, 16 July 1794.
9. Ibid., TS 11/892/3035, Rex v Henry REDHEAD alias Henry YORKE.
10. *Sheffield Iris*, 4 July 1794.
11. TNA HO 42/35/174, Mark Masterman Syke to Home Office, 16 August 1795.
12. Ibid., HO 42/31/99 Folios 222-223, John White to Evan Nepean, 23 June 1794.
13. SCA WWM F44/47, Rev. J Wilkinson to Earl Fitzwilliam, 6 October 1798.
14. TNA HO 42/36/102, letter from John Shaw, Mayor of Liverpool, 24 November 1794.
15. Ibid., HO 42/30/120 Folios 299-300, letter from John Brooke of Birmingham, 27 May 1794.
16. Ibid., HO 42/32/403, handwritten note to Cookson.
17. Ibid., HO 42/32-Folio 398 handwritten copy of a 'club book' containing the rules of the Constitutional Society of Leeds adopted on 14 April 1794 and contribution records for April and May maintained by the district delegate.
18. Ibid., HO 42/43/40, Cookson to Whickham, 15 April 1798.
19. Ibid., HO 42/33/155 Folios 310-311, letter from Alexander Turner to Home Office, 27 September 1794.
20. Ibid.
21. TNA, HO 42/43/40, Cookson to Whickham, 15 April 1798.
22. John Barrell and Jon Mee (eds) (2006–07), *Trials for Treason and Sedition, 1792–1794* 8 vols. London: Pickering and Chatto, 'Introduction', p. xiii.
23. TNA HO 42/19/245 Folios 649-650, instructions, signed by John King, 26 October 1794.
24. Arthur E. Sutherland Jr., *British Trials for Disloyal Association During the French Revolution*, 34 Cornell L. Rev. 303 (1949) Available at: http://scholarship.law.cornell.edu/clr/vol34/iss3/2
25. Edward Palmer Thompson (2013), *Making of the English Working Class*. London: Penguin Classics, pp. 137–8.

## Chapter 9: Pacte de Famine

1. *Sheffield Register: Yorkshire, Derbyshire, & Nottinghamshire Universal Advertiser*, Friday 2 May 1794.
2. Peter Spence (1995), *The Birth of Romantic Radicalism*. Taylor & Francis Ltd: London, p. 189.
3. Roger A.E. Wells (1977), *Dearth and Distress in Yorkshire 1793-1802*. York: Borthwick Institute, p. 4.
4. Paul Lindsay Dawson (2021), *A Potted History of Wakefield*. Stroud, Amberley Publishing.
5. *Leeds Intelligencer*, Monday 3 August 1795.
6. Hannah Barker (1999), *Newspapers, Politics and English Society 1695-1855*. Routledge: London, p. 180.
7. *The Times*, 25 June 1795. See also *The Times*, 8 August 1795
8. John Bohstedt (1983), *Riots and Community Politics in England and Wales, 1790-1810*. Cambridge: Cambridge University Press, pp. 1–3.
9. *London Sun*, 8 May 1795.
10. TNA HO 42/34, Pemberton Milnes to Portland, 7 June 1795 with enclosure.
11. Ibid., HO 42/35/164, Pemberton Milnes to William Windham, 15 June 1795.
12. Ibid., HO 42/35/171 Folio(s) 27-28, Letter from Pemberton Milnes, 22 June 1795 with enclosure.
13. *Leeds Intelligencer*, Monday 3 August 1795.
14. SCA WWM Y16/96/c, Reasons and Orders.
15. Ibid., WWM F 44/45, M.A. Taylor to Earl Fitzwilliam. See also *The Iris*, 26 June 1795.
16. TNA, HO 42/35/96 Folio(s) 227A-227B, an anonymous letter from Leeds, 20 July 1795
17. Thompson, pp. 143–6.
18. *Leeds Mercury*, Monday 15 August 1795.
19. TNA HO 42/35/149, letter from [John Smyth] of Heath near Wakefield [Yorkshire], [MP for Pontefract], 6 August 1795.
20. SCA WWM Y17/42, Spencer Stanhope to Earl Fitzwilliam, 6 August 1795.
21. TNA HO/42/35, John Smyth to General Scott, 6 August 1795.
22. Ibid., HO 42/35/377, Wilson to Portland, 9 August 1795.
23. *Leeds Intelligencer*, Monday 10 August 1795.
24. *Leeds Intelligencer*, Monday 17 August 1795.
25. *Leeds Intelligencer*, Monday 19 October 1795.
26. *Leeds Intelligencer*, Monday 17 August 1795.
27. *Hull Advertiser and Exchange Gazette*, Saturday 15 August 1795.
28. *Leeds Intelligencer*, Monday 17 August 1795.
29. *Leeds Intelligencer*, Monday 17 November 1795.
30. Roger A.E. Wells (1986), *Insurrection: The British Experience 1795-1803*. Stroud: Sutton Books, p. 44
31. Wells (1977), pp. 26–7.
32. *Leeds Intelligencer*, Monday 10 August 1795.
33. SCA WWN F45-a/102, Fitzwilliam to Burke, 9 August 1795.
34. TNA HO 42/35/161, letter from Rev. James Wilkinson, 13 August 1795.
35. Ibid.
36. *Sheffield Iris*, 7 August 1795.
37. Stevenson, p. 31.
38. SCA WWM/F/44/45, letter from [Michael Angelo] Taylor, Harrogate, to Earl Fitzwilliam, 5 August 1795.

39. Ibid., WWM/F/44/46/1, Rev. James Wilkinson and Samuel Tooker, 7 August 1795.
40. *Leeds Intelligencer*, Monday 24 August 1795.
41. TNA HO 42/34 Folios 277-279, John Lloyd to Portland, 1 April 1795. See also ibid., HO 42/34/302, Armitage to Portland, 6 April 1796.
42. Ibid., HO 42/37 Folios. 360-1, Anon., 'Address to the Soldiery of Great Britain', n.d. [July 1795].
43. *St James' Chronicle*, 11–14 July 1795.
44. SCA WWM Y17/47, Teesdale Cockell to Earl Fitzwilliam, 16 October 1795.
45. Ibid., WMM F45/103 Fitzwilliam to Burke, 17 December 1795.
46. Proceedings of a General Meeting of the London Corresponding Society, Held on Monday October the 26th, 1795, in a field adjacent to Copenhagen-House, in the County of Middlesex.
47. *Leeds Intelligencer*, Monday 30 November 1795.
48. *Hull Advertiser and Exchange Gazette*, Saturday 29 October 1795
49. Richard George Wilson (1971), *Gentlemen Merchants: The Merchant Community in Leeds 1700 – 1830*. Manchester: Manchester University Press, p. 168.
50. NYRO Wyvill papers 7/2/190/13.
51. Christopher Wyvill (1795), *The Address to the Worthy Freeholders of Yorkshire*.
52. Joseph Towers (1797), *Thoughts on National Insanity*. London: J. Johnson, p. 23.
53. Ibid., p. 24.
54. Dawson (2019), pp. 42–3.
55. Clive Emsley (1981), 'An Aspect of Pitt's "Terror": Prosecutions for Sedition during the 1790s', *Social History*, vol. 6, no. 2, pp. 155–184. JSTOR, www.jstor.org/stable/4285072. Accessed 22 August 2021.
56. Dawson (2019), p. 151.

## Chapter 10: The United Threat

1. J. Graham (2000), *The Nation, the Law and the King: Reform Politics in England, 1789–1799*, 2 vols. University Press of America, p. 754.
2. Ibid.
3. AD CPA Folio 47, Madgett à Delacroix, 11 Nivôse an V.
4. TNA O 42/43/7 Folio(s) 17-20, two voluntary examinations providing information about Charles Radcliffe.
5. Ibid., HO 42/36/134 Folio 282, Henry William Coulthurst to Home Office, 16 November 1795.
6. Ibid., HO 42/36/135 Folio 284, J.A. Busfield to Home Office, 9 November 1795.
7. Ibid.
8. TNA HO 42/36/135 Folio 175, J.A. Busfield to Home Office, 9 November 1795. See also TNA 42/36/1365 Folio 183, J.A. Busfield to Home Office, 5 November 1795.
9. Wells (1986), p. 75.
10. Service Historique du Armée de Terre [hereafter SHDDT] B11 1 Note pour général Clarke. See also Archives Diplomatique Correspondance Politique Angleterre [hereafter AD CPA] 589 Folios 288-289; CPA 590 Folio 287.
11. AN AF III Dossier 859 pièce 14 correspondance double écrite de Londres par l'agent Berthonneau.
12. National Records of Scotland [hereafter NRS]. JC 26/297–8, examination of Black, June 1798.
13. TNA HO 100/62/141, 21 July 1796.
14. Ibid., HO 100/62/144–5, July 1796.
15. NRS GD 26/15/55.

## Chapter 11: The Mission of Father O'Coigly

1. Wells (1986), p. 73.
2. TNA HO 42/45/137 Folio(s) 528-529, examination, before [Bow Street] magistrate Richard Ford, of James Dixon of Belfast, 5 May 1798.
3. Ibid HO 42/45/140 Folio(s) 535-538, notes made by Thomas Butterworth Bayley, 19 March 1798.
4. Ibid HO 42/45/137 Folio(s) 528-529, examination, before [Bow Street] magistrate Richard Ford, of James Dixon of Belfast, 5 May 1798.
5. TNA PC 1/41/A139, examination of Mary Perrins, 14 April 1798.
6. Graham, p. 753.
7. TNA PC 1/41/A139, examination of Mary Perrins, 14 April 1798.
8. Graham, p. 755.
9. Ibid, p. 816.
10. T.C. Hansard, (1818), *The Parliamentary History of England* Vol. XXXI. London: Longmans, pp. 642–5.
11. TNA TS 52/73.
12. Ibid.
13. SCA WWM F45/a/83, Fitzwilliam to Carlisle, 31 October 1792.
14. TNA HO 42/46/173 Folio 371, Joseph Beckett to Home Office, 27 January 1798.
15. Ibid.
16. TNA HO 42/42/145 Folio(s) 332-335, secret information from an unnamed informant taken by Richard Ford [Bow Street magistrate], 12 March 1798.
17. AD CPA Folio 161, Ashley au Talleyrand, 12 April 1798.
18. TNA HO 42/46/173 Folio 363, copy of Letter by John Waring, 15 February 1798.
19. Ibid.
20. TNA HO 42/46/173 Folio 369, extract of Information Respecting the United Irishmen.
21. Ibid., HO 42/43/12 Folios 33A-33B, letter from George Cartwright, 6 May 1797.
22. Claeys, p. 501.
23. John Gibney (2019), *The United Irishmen, Rebellion and the Act of Union, 1798-1803.* Barnsley: Pen & Sword.
24. TNA HO 42/42/145 Folios 332-335, secret information from an unnamed informant taken by Richard Ford [Bow Street magistrate], 12 March 1798.
25. TNA HO 42/43/40, Cookson to Whickham, 15 April 1798.
26. SCA WWM Y16/24, Teesdale Cockell to Earl Fitzwilliam, 21 April 1798.
27. Ibid., WWM Y17/47, Teesdale Cockell to Earl Fitzwilliam, 16 October 1795.
28. Graham, pp. 843–6.
29. Ibid., HO 42/45/138 Folios 531-532, letter dated Liverpool, 20 November 1798.
30. Ibid., HO 42/47 Folio 360.
31. Ibid., HO 42/47 Folio 364.

## Chapter 12: Annus Horribilis

1. Macleod, pp. 121–3.
2. TNA HO 42/47/19 Folios 51-54, James Green to Home Office, 17 April 1799.
3. Ibid., HO 42/47/155 Folio(s) 355-358, Thomas Bancroft to Home Office, 11 April 1799.
4. Ibid., HO 42/47/137 Folio(s) 311-312B, Thomas Bancroft to Home Office, 14 April 1799.
5. Ibid., HO 42/46/80 Folio(s) 195A-199, Thomas Bancroft to Home Office, 24 April 1799.

6. Iain McCalman (1988), *Radical Underworld: Prophets, Revolutionaries, and Pornographers in London, 1795-1840*. Cambridge: Cambridge University Press.
7. TNA PC 1/44/161, Barlow to Belgrave, 8 August 1799.
8. Ibid., PC 1/44/A161, Ford to Belgrave, 8 August 1799.
9. Ibid., PC 1/44/A161, Foxley to Belgrave, [illegible] August 1799.
10. Ibid.
11. TNA PC 1/44/A 161, Barlow to Richard Ford, 14 August 1799.
12. Ibid., PC 1/44/A 161, Barlow to Thomas Butterworth Bayley, 19 September 1799.
13. Ibid., PC 1/44/A 161, Barlow to Richard Ford, 19 October 1799.
14. Ibid., PC 1/44/A 161, Barlow to Richard Ford, 27 October 1799.
15. Ibid., PC 1/44/A 161, George Orr to John King undersecretary of state, 12 September 1799.
16. Ibid., PC 1/45/A 164, Thomas Butterworth Bayley to Duke to Portland, 4 December 1799.
17. Ibid., PC 1/45/A 165 T B Bayley to John King, 27 November 1799.
18. Wells (1977), p. 4.
19. Wells (1986), pp. 234–5.
20. *London Gazette*, May 1799, p. 507.
21. SCA WWM/F/45/83 Letter from William Cookson (mayor), Leeds, to Earl Fitzwilliam, 30 August 1802.
22. W.B. Crump and G. Ghorbal (1967), *History of the Huddersfield Woollen Industry*. East Ardsley: S R Publishers, p. 46.
23. A.L. Dawson pers comm.
24. WYAS Leeds. Radcliffe MSS1 Deposition of Mark Haigh, 24 August 1802.
25. *Leeds Intelligencer*, Monday 24 March 1800.
26. *Leeds Intelligencer*, Monday 27 January 1800.
27. Wells (1977), pp. 33–4.
28. *Leeds Intelligencer*, Monday 8 September 1800
29. TNA HO 43/11 Folios 365-366, Portland to Lord Viscount Kirkwall, 17 February 1800.
30. Roughly 200 tonnes.
31. Wells (1977), pp. 5–6.
32. WYAS, Wakefield, QS1/137/4.
33. SCA WWM F45/1, Michael Angelo Taylor to Earl Fitzwilliam, 21 October 1800.
34. Ibid., WWM F45/2, handbill posted at Tickhill ,17 October 1800.
35. Ibid., WWM F44/49, handbill posted in Sheffield, September 1800.
36. TNA HO 42/51/215 Fitzwilliam to Portland 3 September 1800
37. *Hull Advertiser and Exchange Gazette*, Saturday 20 September 1800
38. SCA WWM/F/44/215 Fitzwilliam to Portland 3 September 1800.
39. Ibid., WWM/F/44/52, Walker to Earl Fitzwilliam, 8 September 1800.
40. Ibid., WWM F/45/20, Dawson to Earl Fitzwilliam, 27 July 1800.
41. Wells (1977), p. 31.
42. Ibid., pp. 33–4.
43. TNA HO 50/91, Taylor to Dundas, 30 September 1800.
44. Ibid., HO 42/51/35 Folio(s) 80-83, letter from Earl Fitzwilliam, 8 September 1800.
45. Ibid., HO 42/51. Gott to Portland, 21 September 1800.
46. Ibid., HO 42/51/133 Folio(s) 321-322, Benjamin Gott to Home Office, 21 September 1800.
47. Ibid., HO 50/50, letter Lt Col Teesdale Cockell, dated Pontefract 25 May 1801.
48. Austin Gee (2003), *The British Volunteer Movement 1794-1814. Oxford: Oxford University Press*, p. 235.
49. TNA HO 42/55/60 Folios 163-176.

50. Charles Creighton (1894), *A History of Epidemics in Britain*. Cambridge: Cambridge University Press, Vol. 2, p. 160.
51. https://usir.salford.ac.uk/id/eprint/42567/1/Nevell per cent202017 per cent20 Excavating per cent20EngelsAcceptedText_MLPT_vol154.pdf accessed 28/02/2021
52. Creighton, pp. 162–4.
53. TNA HO 42/49/137 Folios 295A-295B, copy of an anonymous letter to Lord Eldon, 31 March 1800.
54. Ibid., HO 42/62/110 Folio(s) 310-311, letter to John Vivian, 30 July 1801.
55. SHDDT GR 1M 1420 Folio 97, Témoin sur l'Angelterre par Citoyen Thevenau.
56. AD Mémoires et Documents, 53. Folio 261-265, Watson au Reinhardt, 22 messidor an VII.
57. SHDDT GR 1M 1420, Journal de Voyage, Sept Ventôse An 7.
58. TNA HO 42/55/115 Folio(s) 393-406, observations relative to state prisoners.
59. Ibid., HO 42/51 Folios 168-9, Earl of Berkeley to Portland, 16 September 1800.
60. Ibid., HO 42/51/122 Folios 291-292, anonymous letter post marked Birmingham, October 1800.
61. Ibid., HO 42/52/91 Folios 229-230B.
62. Francis Russell, 5th Duke of Bedford, a Whig politician who opposed most of the measures brought forward by the ministry of William Pitt, and objected to the grant of a pension to Edmund Burke, an action which drew down upon him a scathing attack from Burke's pen. He was known as a 'Leveller' with regards to radical politics, so again his name being mentioned is understandable. Charles Stanhope, 3rd Earl of Stanhope, was a radical Whig politician. He was chairman of the Revolution Society (founded 1788), which urged the democratisation of Parliament. Calling himself Citizen Stanhope, he sympathised with the French republicans and opposed Great Britain's war with Revolutionary France. Later he attacked the suspension (1794) of the Habeas Corpus Act, Anglo-Irish parliamentary unification (1800), and the slave trade in British overseas possessions. Little wonder his name was attached to the radical plot.
63. TNA HO 42/52/84 Folios 209-214, letter from George Simcox and William Hicks, magistrates of the Public Office, Birmingham, 28 October 1800.
64. Ibid., HO 42/53/20 Folios 54-55, Thomas Bancroft to Home Office, 3 November 1800.
65. Ibid., HO 42/53/130 Folio(s) 355-356, Thomas Bancroft to Home Office, 18 November 1800.
66. Ibid., HO 42/53/134 Folio(s) 365-366, Thomas Bancroft to Home Office, 19 November 1800.
67. Ibid., HO 42/55/35 Folio(s) 89-90, Thomas Bancroft to Home Office, 15 December 1800.
68. SCA WWM F44/63, John Lowe to Earl Fitzwilliam, 8 December 1800.
69. Ibid., WWM F44/57, John Lowe to Earl Fitzwilliam, 8 December 1800.
70. Ibid., WWM F44/59, John Lowe to Earl Fitzwilliam, 8 December 1800.
71. Ibid., WWM F44/62, Captain Warris to John Lowe, 9 December 1800.
72. Ibid., WWM F44/63 Anonymous to Earl Fitzwilliam.
73. TNA HO 43/12 Folios 318-24, Portland to Earl Gower, 29 November 1800.
74. Ibid., HO 42/55/12 Folio 25, Rev. J. Lower to Lord Pelham, 5 December 1800.
75. Ibid., HO 42/55/47 Folios 116-120, letter from Henry Perrin Bailiff of Kidderminster, 17 December 1800.
76. Ibid., HO 42/55/32 Folio(s) 81-82. Letter from William Dawson of Wakefield [Yorkshire, West Riding] enclosing a copy of an advertisement which has been issued offering a reward for information regarding the writers or senders of seditious letters. Annotated: Enclosure sent to the Gazette, 15 December 1800.

77. Ibid., HO 42/55/18 Folio(s) 40-43, deposition of Thomas Amsden, 9 December 1800.
78. Wells (1986), p. 189.
79. Ibid., pp. 192–4.

## Chapter 13: Anti-War Liberalism

1. Wells (1986), p. 197.
2. NYRO Wyvill papers Folio 168.
3. William Wood (1801), *A Sermon preached at Mill-Hill Chapel, in Leeds, on the commencement of the Nineteenth Century*. Leeds: Edward Baines, p. 13
4. Oates (1752–1811) was the grandson of Joseph Oates (1675–1729); his uncle was George Oates who married Mary Hibbert, the daughter of a slave trader. His father Samuel Oates (died 1789) had married Mary Hamer, the granddaughter of James Ibbetson, builder of Call Lane Unitarian Chapel in 1691. Samuel Hamer Oates married Mary Sarah Coape: her sister married General Sir John Sherbroke.
5. John Goodchild pers comm 17 June 2017.
6. Wilson, pp. 188–90.
7. J.E. Cookson (1982), *The Friends of Peace. Anti-war liberalism in England 1793-1815*. Cambridge: Cambridge University Press, p. 200.
8. *York Herald*, Saturday 31 January 1801.
9. *Leeds Intelligencer*, Monday 26 January 1801.
10. *Leeds Mercury*, Monday 28 February 1801.
11. SCA WWM F45/e/29, John Dixon to Earl Fitzwilliam, 1 February 1801.
12. NYRO Wyvill papers Folio 148-150, Wood to Wyvill, 13 February 1801.
13. SCA WWM F45/e/33, Leeds, 21 February 1801.
14. Ibid., WWM/F/45/29, letter from Col. John Dixon, Gledhow, to Earl Fitzwilliam, 1 February 1801.
15. *York Herald*, Saturday 7 February 1801.
16. SCA WWM F45/e/37, Petition to the King for Peace, Bradford, 29 January 1801.
17. *Leeds Mercury*, Monday 31 January 1801.
18. *Leeds Intelligencer*, Monday 23 February 1801.
19. SCA WWM F45/e/30, William Dawson to Earl Fitzwilliam, 1 February 1801.
20. *York Herald, Saturday 21 February 1801. See also Leeds Intelligencer*, Monday 16 February 1801.
21. SCA WWM F45/e/29 John Dixon to Earl Fitzwilliam, 1 February 1801.
22. *Leeds Intelligencer*, Monday 9 March 1801.
23. *York Herald*, Saturday 14 February 1801.
24. *Leeds Mercury*, Monday 7 February 1801.
25. *York Herald*, Saturday 21 February 1801.
26. *Hull Advertiser and Exchange Gazette*, Saturday 21 February 1801.
27. *York Herald*, Saturday 14 February 1801.
28. SCA WWM F45/13/b, J.A. Busfield to Earl Fitzwilliam, 14 April 1801.

## Chapter 14: Planning Revolution

1. TNA HO 42/61/109 Folios 301-303, letter from William Ayshford Sanford, 23 March 1801.
2. Ibid., HO 42/54/35 Folios 455-456, letter from S.R. Grier, November 1800.
3. McCalman, p. 15.
4. TNA HO 42/65/114 Folio 300, 4 June 1802.
5. Ibid., HO 42/61/194 Folio(s) 570-573, letter from Earl Fortescue, 14 April 1801.

6. Ibid., HO 42/61/40 Folios 122-123, Thomas Bancroft to Home Office, 9 February 1801.

7. Ibid., HO 42/61/116 Folios 319-341, Thomas Butterworth Bayley to Lord Pelham, 11 April 1801.

8. Ibid.

9. TNA HO 42/61/79 Folios 222-223, Thomas Bancroft to Home Office, 14 March 1801.

10. Ibid., HO 42/61/106 Folio(s) 292-295, Thomas Bancroft to Home Office, 22 March 1801.

11. Ibid., HO 42/61/112 Folio(s) 308-310, John Singleton to Home Office, 24 March 1801

12. Ibid., HO 42/61/156 Folio(s) 459-465, Thomas Bancroft to Home Office, 6 April 1801.

13. Ibid., HO 42/62/30 Folio(s) 72-73, Thomas Bancroft to Home Office, 17 May 1801.

14. Ibid., HO 42/62/6 Folio(s) 11-14, William Robert Hay to Home Office, 4 May 1801.

15. Ibid., HO 42/62/34 Folio(s) 87-88, Ralph Fletcher to Home Office, 20 May 1801.

16. Ibid., HO 42/62/7 Folio(s) 15-16, John Entwistle to Home Office, 4 May 1801.

17. Ibid., HO 42/62/32 Folio(s) 76-79, letter from the Reverend William Robert Hay, magistrate, of Dukinfield, 18 May 1801.

18. Ibid., HO 42/62/42 Folio(s) 112-113, John Singleton to Home Office, 27 May 1801.

19. Ibid., HO 42/62/41 Folio(s) 109-111, Thomas Bancroft to Home Office, 27 May 1801.

20. Ibid., HO 42/62/55 Folio(s) 149-152, William Robert Hay to Home Office, 7 June 1801.

21. Ibid., HO 42/62/18 Folio(s) 41-42, memorandum from Charles Bragge, 31 May 1801. Emphasis in the original.

22. Wells (1986), pp. 217–18.

23. TNA HO 42/62/54 Folio(s) 145-148, Ralph Fletcher to Home Office, 6 June 1801.

24. Alan Brooke and Lesley Kipling (1993), *Liberty or Death: Radicals, Republicans and Luddites 1793-1823*. Huddersfield: Gairn Press, p. 8.

25. TNA HO 42/62/304, handbill of Black Lamp.

26. Ibid., HO 42/61/100 Folio 271, J.A. Busfield to Earl Fitzwilliam, 21 March 1801.

27. SCA WWM F45/9, John Gowder to Earl Fitzwilliam, Tuesday 31 March 1801.

28. TNA HO 42/61/89 Folio 245, Rev. Thomas Bancroft to Home Office, 18 March 1801.

29. Ibid., HO 42/61/78 220, Rev. Dr Thomas Coke to Home Office, 14 March 1801.

30. Ibid., HO 42/61/217 Folio 637, Rev. Dr Thomas Coke to Home Office, 18 April 1801.

31. Rev. Jonathan Bish MA, pers comm, 22 March 2021.

32. Sarah Hollingsdale, pers comm, 11 August 2021.

33. *Leeds Intelligencer*, Monday 07 December 1807. See also *Leeds Intelligencer*, Monday 14 December 1807.

34. Sarah Hollingsdale pers comm, 11 August 2021.

35. Gareth Lloyd, *From Earth to Heaven and Hell – and back: The strange and wonderful journey of Elizabeth Dickinson*. Unpublished MS.

36. SCA WWM F45/11, Bacon Frank to Earl Fitzwilliam, 9 April 1801.

37. Ibid., WWM F45/13/b, Bacon Frank to Earl Fitzwilliam, 16 April 1801.

38. Ibid., WWM F45/13/b, J.A. Busfield to Earl Fitzwilliam, 14 April 1801.

39. Ibid., WWM F45/13/a, J.A. Busfield to Earl Fitzwilliam, 17 April 1801.

40. TNA HO 42/61/616, Fitzwilliam to Portland, 18 April 1801.

41. Ibid., HO 42/61/678, Garforth to Home Office, 20 April 1802.

42. Ibid., HO 42/62/40 Folio (s) 106-108, Rev. William Robert Hay to Home Office, 24 May 1801.
43. Ibid., HO 42/62/1 Folio(s) 1, Thomas Bancroft to Home Office, 2 May 1801.
44. SCA WWM F45/18, Radcliffe to Earl Fitzwilliam, 23 May 1801.
45. Wells (1986), pp. 214–16.

## Chapter 15: Preventing Revolution: The Loyalist Response

1. TNA HO 42/62, Hay to Portland, 24 May 1801.
2. Ibid., HO 42/62, Radcliffe to Portland, 23 May 1801.
3. Ibid., HO 42/62/3 Folio 76, Hay to Portland, 18 May 1801.
4. SCA WWM F45/e/39, William Robert Hay to Home Office.
5. Ibid., WWM F45/e/40, Lord Pelham to William Robert Hey, 17 June 1801.
6. TNA HO 42/62/71 Folio(s) 195-196, Major Gore to Home Office, 23 June 1801.
7. This is likely to be Richard Garnett and his wife Susannah, who was a member of the Rev. Thomas Johnstone's congregation at Westgate Chapel Wakefield, where he had seven children baptised between 1793 and 1803.
8. TNA HO 42/62/73 Folio(s) 199-200, Thomas Bancroft to Home Office, 23 June 1801.
9. Ibid., HO 42/62/78 Folio(s) 211-215, Thomas Bancroft to Home Office, 29 June 1801.
10. Ibid., HO 42/62/59 Folio 164-167, letter from Bertie Markland, magistrate, Blackburn, 10 June 1801.
11. Ibid., HO 42/62/85 Folio 232-237, letter from Ralph Fletcher, magistrate of Bolton le Moors, 6 July 1801.
12. Ibid., HO 42/62/165 Folio 441-444, letter from Ralph Fletcher, Bolton le Moors, 31 August 1801.
13. Ibid.
14. SCA WWM/F/45/20, William Dawson to Earl Fitzwilliam, 27 July 1801.
15. TNA HO 42-62/335, William Dawson to Earl Fitzwilliam, 27 July 1801.
16. SCA WWM/F/45/22, William Dawson to Earl Fitzwilliam, 31 July 1801.
17. TNA HO 42/62/312, Fitzwilliam to Portland, 30 July 1801.
18. Ibid., HO 42-62/Folio 363, Fitzwilliam to Portland, 31 July 1801.
19. SCA WWM/F/45/27, William Dawson to Earl Fitzwilliam, 22 August 1801.
20. Ibid., WWM/F/45/28, William Dawson to Earl Fitzwilliam, 7 September 1801.
21. TNA HO 42/62/117, Fitzwilliam to Portland, 1 August 1801.
22. Ibid., HO 42/62/331, Brooke to Earl Fitzwilliam, 31 July 1801.
23. Ibid., HO 42/62/134 Folio(s) 373-376, John Brooke to Home Office, 1 August 1801.
24. Ibid., HO 42/62/149 Folio 409, Rev. Dr Thomas Coke to Home Office, 19 August 1801.
25. Ibid., WWM F45/26, John Beckett to Earl Fitzwilliam, 22 August 1801.
26. AN AFIII 572, Humbert au Bernadotte, 27 Prairial an IX.
27. BL Additional MS 33107 Folio 48.
28. *Leeds Mercury*, 1 August 1801. See also *Leeds Mercury*,15 August 1801; *Sheffield Iris*, 18 July 1801.
29. TNA HO 43/13 Folios 130-1, Pelham to Mayor of Leeds, 8 August 1801.

## Chapter 16: The Despard Coup

1. AD CPA 592 Folio 411, report 13 7bre 1799.
2. TNA HO 42/62/196 Folio(s) 535-536, letter to Major-General Isaac Gascoyne, 31 October 1801.
3. Ibid., HO 42/62/110 Folios 310-311, letter to John Vivian, 30 July 1801.

4. Wells (1986), pp. 220–2.
5. TNA TS 11/121/332. See also ibid., TS 11/121/332 report of John Connell.
6. Ibid., HO 42/62/197 Folios 537-538, Ralph Fletcher to Home Office, 1 November 1801.
7. John Pollitt is the author's direct ancestor.
8. TNA HO 42/62/142 Folios 391-392, letter to Lord Hobart, 8 August 1801.
9. Ibid., PC 1/3535 report by 'F.J'. dated 28 December 1801.
10. *Cowdroy's Manchester Gazette*, 20 February 1802.
11. TNA TS 11/122/333. See also ibid., HO 100/100/132 for Despard in Ireland.
12. TNA HO 42/65/198 Folios 442-443, Ralph Fletcher to Home Office, 3 April 1802.
13. TNA TS 11/127/333.
14. Ibid., declaration of Daniel Krantz, August 1803.
15. Clifford D. Conner, (2000), *Colonel Despard. The life and times of an Anglo-Irish rebel.* Pennsylvania: Combined Publishing, pp. 208–10.
16. Wells (1986), p. 226.
17. Ibid., pp. 226–7.
18. Ibid., p. 231.
19. SCA WWM F45/d/53, Richard Walker to Earl Fitzwilliam, 13 June 1802.
20. TNA HO 42/65/224 Folios 491-492, Ralph Fletcher to John King, 7 July 1802.
21. Ibid., HO 42/65/212 Folio 468, J.A. Busfield to Home Office, 17 July 1802.
22. Ibid., HO 42/64/2 Folio 2, Earl Fitzwilliam to Lord Pelham, 1 July 1802.
23. Ibid., HO 42/64/2 Folio 6, See also ibid., Folio 10.
24. Ibid., HO 42/64/2 Folio 4, Richard Walker to Earl Fitzwilliam, 28 June 1802.
25. Ibid., HO 42/65/347, Fitzwilliam to Home Office, 20 July 1802.
26. SCA WWM F45/d/57, John Dixon to Earl Fitzwilliam, 17 July 1802.
27. Ibid., WMM F45/d/65, anonymous to Earl Fitzwilliam, 24 July 1802.
28. TNA HO 42/65/351, Earl Fitzwilliam to Home Office, 21 July 1802.
29. Ibid., HO 42/65/356, Lord Pelham to Earl Fitzwilliam, 26 July 1802.
30. Ibid., HO 42/65/362, troops in Yorkshire.
31. SCA WWM F45/d/63, Joseph Radcliffe to Earl Fitzwilliam, 24 July 1802.
32. Ibid., WWM F45/d/63, handbill posted to Earl Fitzwilliam, 27 July 1802.
33. Ibid., WWM F45/d/71-1. See also WWM F45/d/71-2, F45/d/71-3.
34. Ibid., WWM/F/45/60, letter from Lord Pelham to Earl Fitzwilliam, 23 July 1802.
35. Ibid., WWM/F/45/62, letter from William Cookson (Mayor), Leeds, to Earl Fitzwilliam, 24 July 1802.
36. TNA HO 42/65/343, Fitzwilliam to Home Office, 20 July 1802.
37. Marianne Elliott, 'The 'Despard Plot' Reconsidered', *Past & Present* 75 (1) May 1977, pp. 46–61.
38. TNA HO 42/65/219 Folios 481-482, Ralph Fletcher to John King, 31 July 1802.
39. Ibid., HO 42/66/2 Folio 4. Earl Fitzwilliam to Lord Pelham, 9 August 1802.
40. Ibid.
41. Ibid.
42. SCA WWM F45/d/80-1, William Cookson to Earl Fitzwilliam, 19 August 1802.
43. Ibid., WWM F45/d/81, John Dixon to Earl Fitzwilliam, 19 August 1802.
44. Ibid., WWM F45/d/82, John Dixon to Earl Fitzwilliam, 19 August 1802.
45. Ibid., WWM F45/d/82a, enclosure to Earl Fitzwilliam, 24 August 1802
46. Ibid., WWM F45/d/88, General Bernard to Earl Fitzwilliam 6 September 1802.
47. Ibid., WWM F45/d/89, Fitzwilliam to Bernard, 7 September 1802.
48. TNA HO 42/66/29 Folio 130, Joseph Radcliffe to Home Office, 24 August 1802.
49. SCA WWM F45/83, Cookson to Earl Fitzwilliam, 30 August 1802.
50. Ibid., WWM F45/d/91, John Beckett to Earl Fitzwilliam, 13 September 1802.
51. Ibid., WWM F45/d/92, John Beckett to Earl Fitzwilliam, 15 September 1802.

52. Ibid., WWM F45/d/94b, Henry Legge to Pelham, 20 September 1802.
53. Ibid., WWM F45/d/95, Fitzwilliam to Pelham, 20 September 1802.
54. Ibid., WWM F45/d/95b, Pelham to Earl Fitzwilliam, [illegible] September 1802.
55. TNA HO 42/66/29 Folio 130, Joseph Radcliffe to Home Office, 24 August 1802.
56. Ibid., PC 1/3117, Ford to Notary, November 1802.
57. BL Add MSS 33112 Rumbold to Hervery, 18 March 1803.
58. Lewis Goldsmith (1811), *The Secret History of the Cabinet of Bonaparte*. London, p. 253.
59. AN AFIV 1672 piece 26 Folios 63-66, 1re note de Fiévée.
60. Ibid., pièce 27 Folios 67-70, 2e note de Fiévée.
61. Ibid., pièce 28 Folio 71-72, note de Fiévée, 17 juin 1802.
62. AD CPA 601. Folio 80, Talleyrand to Poterat, 30 7bre 1802.
63. Ibid., Folio 84, deuxième mémoire sur l'Irlande, 17 Fevrier 1803.
64. Ibid., pièce 30 Folios 74-75, lettre du chef d'escadron Beauvoisin, 23 vendémiaire an XI.
65. Olivier Blanc (1995), *Les espions de la Révolution et de l'Empire*. Paris: Perrin, pp. 219–24.
66. AN AFIV 1672 pièce 31 Folios 76-77, lettre Beauvoisin, 29 vendémiaire an XI.
67. Ibid., pièce 36 Folios 91-96, mémoire on daté, après le 29 novembre 1802.
68. AD CPA 600, Andréossy au Talleyrand, 4 Frimaire an XI.
69. SCA WWM F45/d/94-13, Deposition of Thomas Hirst.

## Chapter 17: The Revolution That Never Was

1. TNA HO 42/66/85 Folios 248-253, letters from John Jones junior, 1 August 1802.
2. Ibid., HO 42/66/62 Folios 201-203, Henry Legge to Home Office, 20 September 1802.
3. Wells (1986), p. 229.
4. TNA HO 42/66/24 Folios 70-72, report of information received by Lord Pelham, 25 September 1802.
5. SCA WWM F45/d/97, deposition of Thomas Hirst.
6. East Sussex and Brighton and Hove Record Office, AMS5440/296, Thomas Pelham to Lord Sheffield, 22 May 1797.
7. Anonymous (1804), *A Full Account of the Proceedings at the Middlesex Election, etc.* London: M.C. Springworth, p. 11.
8. TNA PC 1/42/143, Corresponding Societies, May 1798.
9. Wells (1986), p. 246.

## Chapter 18: A Show Trial?

1. Conner, pp. 220–1.
2. SCA WWM F45/d/104, deposition of Hirst to Earl Fitzwilliam, 22 November 1802.
3. SHDDT GR 1M 1420 Folio 63, Aperçu d'une expédition sur l'Irlande.
4. Wells (1986), p. 246.
5. SCA WWM F45/106, indictment, 2 December 1802.
6. Ibid., WWM F45/107, John Low to Earl Fitzwilliam, 3 December 1802.
7. *Newcastle Courrant*, Monday, 26 March 1803.
8. TNA HO 42/62, Fletcher to Pelham, 3 April 1802. See also TNA 42/174, HO 42/176, HO 40/9.
9. Ibid., HO 42/70/33 Folios 87-91, copy of the minutes relative to the trial of Edward Marcus Despard and twelve others for High Treason, 20 February 1803.
10. Ibid., HO 42/66/24 Folios 76-90, report of information received by Lord Pelham.

11. Ibid., HO 42/66/24 Folios 91-93, report of information received by Lord Pelham.
12. Ibid., HO 42/66/10Folios 27-41, report and draft notes of evidence taken in relation to the Despard conspiracy.
13. Ibid., HO 42/70 Folios 67-70, Ralph Fletcher to Home Office, 3 February 1803.
14. Joseph Gurney and William Brodie Gurney (1803), *The Trial of Edward Marcus Despard Esquire*. London: M. Gurney, pp. 109–10.
15. TNA HO 42/70 Folios 67-70, Ralph Fletcher to Home Office, 3 February 1803.
16. Gurney, p. 79.
17. TNA HO 42/70 Folios 81-97, to the King's Most Excellent Majesty, 15 February 1803.
18. Gurney, pp. 121–2.
19. Mike Jay (2004), *The Unfortunate Colonel Despard*. London: Bantam Press. p. 147. See also ibid., pp. 232, 276, 268 and 297–304.
20. TNA HO 42/70/22 Folios 60-65, Spencer Percival to Lord Pelham, 16 February 1803.
21. *The Morning Chronicle*, 22 February 1803.
22. 'Execution of Colonel Despard &c.', *Salisbury and Winchester Journal*, 28 February 1803, p. 2.
23. Ibid.
24. National Library Scotland APS.3.82.27 Broadside entitled 'The last Speech confession and dying words of Colonel Despard and his associates'.
25. Ibid.
26. 'Execution of Colonel Despard &c.', *Salisbury and Winchester Journal*, 28 February 1803, p. 2.
27. *The Morning Chronicle*, 22 February 1803.
28. Ibid.
29. TNA HO 42/70/26 Folios 74-75, John Gifford to Home Secretary, 20 February 1803.
30. Conner, pp. 259–60.

## Chapter 19: After Despard

1. TNA HO 42/70/10 Folios 41-43, Earl Fitzwilliam to Lord Pelham, 30 January 1803.
2. Ibid., HO 42/70 Folios 67-70, Ralph Fletcher to Home Office, 3 February 1803.
3. SCA WWM F45/11,3 Lord Pelham to Earl Fitzwilliam, 24 January 1803.
4. AN AFIV 1672 plaquette 2, Folio 268-273, Rapport sur le voyage de M. Middleton en Angleterre, 1803.
5. Thompson, p. 553.
6. SCA WWM F45/e/118a, Joseph Radcliffe to Earl Fitzwilliam, 9 April 1803.
7. Ibid., WWM F45/e/118b sworn statement.
8. Ibid.
9. TNA HO 42/70/43 Folios 119-122, William Hay to Home Office, 10 March 1803.
10. Leslie Mitchell (2004), 'Fox, Charles James (1749–1806)', *Oxford Dictionary of National Biography*.
11. SCA WWM Y16/141, Francis Foljambe to Earl Fitzwilliam, 28 June 1803.
12. TNA HO 42/70/66 Folios 207-208, John King to John Lead, 24 May 1803.
13. Ibid., HO 42/71/1 Folio 67, handbill posted Teignmouth.
14. Ibid., HO 42/70/2 Folios 223-226, letter William Goldson, 23 March 1803.
15. Ibid., HO 42/70/30 Folios 249-251, Ralph Fletcher to Home Office, 8 April 1803.
16. https://www.napoleon-series.org/research/government/diplomatic/letters/c_letters57.html.
17. SCA WWM Y16/154/b, Busfield to Earl Fitzwilliam, 13 August 1803.

18. Ibid., WWM Y16/155/a, Busfield to Earl Fitzwilliam, 12 August 1803.
19. TNA HO 42/72/86 Folios 277-278, letter from Thomas Robarts, Vicar of Tottenham, 9 August 1803.
20. Ibid., HO 42/72/1 Folios 548-550, a letter from R. Fletcher, Bolton, 4 August 1803.
21. Brooke and Kipling, p. 4.
22. TNA HO 42/72/1 Folios 548-550, a letter from R. Fletcher, Bolton, 4 August 1803.
23. SCA WWM F45/e/120, Earl Fitzwilliam to Pelham, 29 August 1803
24. TNA HO 42/74/2 Folio 172-173, evidence of James Wood, 6 December 1803.
25. Ibid., HO 42/74/2 Folio 161, C. Alston to John King, 19 December 1803.
26. Ibid., HO 42/73/4 Folios 479-480, evidence of John Pope, 32 Chapel Street, Shoreditch, 20 October 1803.
27. Ibid., HO 42/73/4 Folios 464-465, memorandum, 22 September 1803.
28. Ibid., HO 42/73/95 Folios 303-304, letter from Ralph Fletcher, 10 September 1803. Joseph Kavanagh, a shoemaker, though a native of Lille, was evidently of Irish extraction. He participated in the revolution of 1789, and was incriminated in the September massacres.
29. Ibid., HO 42/73/4 Folios 452-453, Johnathan Williams to Lord Hobart, 15 September 1803.
30. Ibid., HO 42/73/4 Folios 473-475, report 22 September 1803.
31. Ibid., HO 42/73/85 Folios 259-260., letter from Major General Whitelock, 23 October 1803.
32. Ibid., HO 42/79/139 Folios 443-445, Fletcher to Home Office, 23 November 1804.
33. Ibid., HO 42/73/82 Folios 251-252, letter from H Clark, Mayor of Leicester, 21 October 1803.
34. AN AF IV 1961 pièce 85. Folio 203-208, Rapport présenté par Thomas Addie Emmet au ministre de la Guerre.
35. Ibid., Piece 78 Folio 180-185, Mémoire de Duverne, chargé de mission en Angleterre 6 vendémiaire an XII.
36. *Leeds Intelligencer*, Monday 25 July 1803.
37. AN 215AP/1, Fonds Talleyrand Dossier 3.
38. John E. Cookson (1997), *The British Armed Nation*. Oxford: Clarendon Press, pp. 209–20.
39. Anthony L. Dawson, pers comm, 7 March 2021.
40. TNA HO 42/83/121 Folios 329-331, Ralph Fletcher to John King, 24 December 1805.

## Chapter 20: Conclusions

1. MacLeod, pp. 204–05.
2. Ibid., p. 96.
3. SCA WWM F45/a/97, Fitzwilliam draft letter, 17 February 1794.
4. Ibid., WWM F45/a/87, Fitzwilliam to William Adams, 15 November 1793.
5. MacLeod, p. 163.

# BIBLIOGRAPHY

## Archive Sources

### United Kingdom
### British Library
Additional Manuscripts MSS 27814 folios 45-6.
Add MS 27814, Add MS 59363, Add MS 64814.

### Cumbria Archive Centre
D SEN 5/5/1/8/36 Threats to Humphrey Senhouse, 1797.

### East Sussex and Brighton and Hove Record Office
AMS5440/296.

### Kent History Centre
U840 Pratt Papers.

### North Yorkshire Record Office
Wyvill MSS.

### National Records of Scotland
JC26/276 A. examination David Black.

### National Library Scotland
APS.3.82.27 Broadside entitled 'The last Speech confession and dying words of Colonel Despard and his associates'.

### The National Archives, Kew
Home Office Correspondence series 68, 40, 42, 100.
Foreign Office Papers.
Pricy Council Papers.
Treasury Solicitor Papers.
War Office Papers.

## Sheffield City Archives
Wentworth Woodhouse Muniments, Rockingham papers.
Wentworth Woodhouse Muniments, Fitzwilliam papers.

## West Yorkshire Archive Service
John Goodchild Collection.
Quarter Session Records, 1637–1914.
Radcliffe MSS1.

## York City Library
Yorkshire Association Papers.

## France
## Archives Nationales de France
AF III 186.
AFIV 1961.
Serie C.
AN 215AP/1, Fonds Talleyrand.

## Archives Diplomatique de France
Correspondance Politiques Angleterre boxes 585, 586, 587.

## Service Historique du Armée de Terre
GR 1M 1420.

## Digital Sources
https://www.british-history.ac.uk
https://founders.archives.gov
https://www.historyofparliamentonline.org/
www.jstor.org/
https://spartacus-educational.com
Napoleon Series

## Printed Sources
*A Complete Collection of State Trials*, various editors, London, 1809–1826, vol. xxiii.
Andrews, Stuart (2003), *Unitarian Radicalism. Political Rhetoric, 1770-1814*. New York: Pallgrave MacMillan.
Barker, Hannah (1999), *Newspapers, Politics and English Society 1695-1855*. London: Routledge.
Barrell, John, and Jon Mee (eds) (2006–07), *'Introduction'. Trials for Treason and Sedition, 1792–1794*. 8 vols. London: Pickering and Chatto.
Bohstedt, John (1983), *Riots and Community Politics in England and Wales, 1790-1810*. Cambridge: Cambridge University Press.
Bradley, James E. (1990), *Religion, Revolution and English Radicalism: Nonconformity in Eighteenth-Century Politics and Society*. Cambridge: Cambridge University Press.

Brooke, Alan, and Lesley Kipling (1993), *Liberty or Death: Radicals, Republicans and Luddites 1793-1823*. Huddersfield: Gairn Press.

Blanc, Olivier (1995), *Les espions de la Révolution et de l'Empire*. Perrin: Paris.

Bruce, Archibald (1799), *A Brief Statement and declaration of the genuine principles of seceders*. Edinburgh.

Burke, Edmund (1796), *Thoughts on the Prospect of a Regicide Peace, in a Series of Letters*. London: J. Owen.

_____ (1826), *Speech on the Petition of the Unitarians* London: C. & J. Rivington.

Christie, Thomas (1791), *Letters on the Revolution in France*, Part 1. London: J. Johnson.

Claeys, Gregory (2007), *The French Revolution Debate in Britain*. London: Palgrave MacMillan.

Colley, Linda (2005), *Britons: Forging the Nation 1707-1837*. London: Yale University Press.

Conner, Clifford D. (2000), *Colonel Despard. The life and times of an Anglo-Irish rebel*. Pennsylvania: Combined Publishing.

Cookson, John E. (1982), *The Friends of Peace. Anti-war liberalism in England 1793-1815*. Cambridge: Cambridge University Press.

_____ (1997), *The British Armed Nation*. Oxford: Clarendon Press.

Cooper, Thomas (1792), *A Reply to Mr. Burke's Invective Against Mr. Cooper, and Mr Watt*. London: J. Johnson.

Creighton, Charles (1894), *A History of Epidemics in Britain*. Cambridge: Cambridge University Press.

Crump, W.B. (1931), *The Leeds Woollen Industry 1780-1820*. Leeds: Thoresby Society.

Dart, Gregory (1999), *Rousseau, Robespierre, and English Romanticism*. Cambridge and New York: Cambridge University Press.

Dawson, Paul L. (2019), *Lexington to Waterloo: Yorkshire Unitarianism and National Politics*. Wakefield: Westgate Chapel.

_____ (2020), *Wakefield at Work*. Stroud: Amberley Publishing.

Dickinson, Harry (1990), 'Popular Loyalism in the 1790s' in Hellmuth Eckhart (ed.), *The Transformation of Political Culture: England and Germany in the Late Eighteenth Century*. Oxford: Oxford University Press.

Ditchfield, G.M. (2007), *The Letters of Theophilus Lindsey (1723-1808)*. Woodbridge: Church of England Record Society.

Duffy, Michael (1996), 'William Pitt and the Origins of the Loyalist Association Movement of 1792', *The Historical Journal*, No. 39.

Eastwood, David (1991), 'Patriotism and the English State in the 1790s' in Mark Philip (ed.),*The French Revolution and British Popular Politics*. Cambridge: Cambridge University Press.

Eaton, Daniel Isaac (1793), *Extermination, or an Appeal to the People of England on the Present War with France*. London: D.I. Eaton.

Elliott, Marianne (1977), 'The "Despard Plot" Reconsidered', *Past & Present* 75 (1). pp. 46–61.

_____ (1982), *Partners in Revolution. The United Irishmen and France*. New Haven and London: Yale University Press.

Emsley, Clive (1981), 'An Aspect of Pitt's "Terror": Prosecutions for Sedition during the 1790s', *Social History*, vol. 6, no. 2, pp. 155–84. JSTOR, www.jstor.org/stable/4285072. Accessed 22 August 2021.

Frykmann, Niklas (2020), *The Bloody Flag: Mutiny in the Age of Atlantic Revolution*. Oakland: University of California Press.

Gibney, John (2019), *The United Irishmen, Rebellion and the Act of Union, 1798-1803*. Barnsley: Pen & Sword.

Graham, Jenny (2000), *The Nation, the Law and the King: Reform Politics in England, 1789–1799*, 2 vols. University Press of America.

Gregory, Derek (1982), *Regional Transformation and Industrial Revolution: A geography of the Yorkshire Woollen Industry*. London: The Macmillan Press.

Goldsmith, Lewis (1811), *The Secret History of the Cabinet of Bonaparte*. London: Richardson.

Goodrich, Amanda (2019), *Henry Redhead Yorke, Colonial Radical: Politics and Identity in the Atlantic Word 1772-1813*. London: Routledge.

Goodwin, Albert (1979), *The Friends of Liberty: The English Democratic Movement in the Age of the French Revolution*. London: Routledge.

Gurney, Joseph, and William Brodie Gurney (1803), *The Trial of Edward Marcus Despard Esquire*. London: M. Gurney.

Hague, William (2005), *William Pitt the Younger*. London: Harper Press.

Hanson, Joseph (1808), *A Defence of the Petitions for Peace*. Manchester: J Ridgway.

Haydon, Colin (1993), *Anti-Catholicism in eighteenth-century England, 1714-1780*. Manchester: Manchester University Press.

Hone, J. Ann (1982), *For the Cause of Truth: Radicalism in London, 1796-1821*. Oxford: Oxford University Monographs.

Horgan, Kate (2016), *The Politics of Songs in Eighteenth Century Britain 1723-1795*. London: Routledge.

Jay, Mike (2004), *The Unfortunate Colonel Despard*. London: Bantam Press.

Lofft, Capel (1791), *Remarks on the letter of the Right Honourable Edmund Burke concerning the Revolution in France*. London: J. Johnson.

Logue, Kenneth J. (2002), *Popular Disturbances in Scotland 1780-1815*. Edinburgh: Birlinn Ltd.

Macleod, Emma Vincent (1998), *A War of Ideas: British Attitudes to the War Against Revolutionary France 1792-1802*. London: Routledge.

Mansfield, Nick (2019), *Soldiers as Citizens*. Liverpool: Liverpool University Press.

McBride, Ian (2009), *Eighteenth-Century Ireland: The Isle of Slaves*. Dublin: Gill and Macmillan.

McCalman, Iain (1988), *Radical Underworld: Prophets, Revolutionaries, and Pornographers in London, 1795-1840*. Cambridge: Cambridge University Press.

Morris, Robert John (2008), *Men, Women and Property in England, 1780-1870*. Cambridge: Cambridge University Press.

Pakenham, Thomas (1997), *The Year of Liberty: The Great Irish Rebellion of 1798*. London: Weidenfeld & Nicolson.

Philip, Mark (2017), *Reforming Ideas in Britain: Politics and Language in the shadow of the French Revolution, 1789-1815*. Cambridge: Cambridge University Press.

Price, Richard (1789), *Discourse delivered on the love of our country*. London: J. Johnson.
_____ (1992), *Political Writings*. Cambridge: Cambridge University Press.

Priestley, Joseph (1791), *Letters to the Right Honourable Edmund Burke: Occasioned by His Reflections on the Revolution in France*. Birmingham: Thomas Pearson.

Rae, Robert. (1961), '"Liberty of the Press" as an Issue in English Politics, 1792–1793', *The Historian* No. 24.

Reid, William Hamilton (1800), *The rise and dissolution of the infidel societies in this metropolis: including, the origin of modern Deism and Atheism . . . .* London: J. Hatchard.

Rogers, Nicolas (1999), 'Burning Tom Paine: Loyalism and Counter-Revolution in Britain, 1791-1793', *Histoire Sociale* Novembre 1999.

Roscoe, William (1808), *Considerations on the Causes, Objects and Consequences of the Present War.* Philadelphia: Birch and Small.

Seed, John (1985), 'Gentlemen Dissenters: The Social and Political Meanings of Rational Dissent in the 1770s and 1780s', *The Historical Journal*, 28(2).

Simms, Samuel (1937), *The Rev. James Coigley, United Irishmen.* Belfast: Quinn.

Smith, Harry (2010), '"The blessedness of those who are persecuted for righteousness's sake": The Role of "Candour" and the Priestley Riots in Birmingham Unitarian Identity, 1791–1815', *Midland History* Vol. 35, No. 2.

Society for the Friends of the People (1793), *Authentic copy of a Petition praying for a Reform in Parliament.* London: J. Ridgeway.

Spence, Peter (1995), *The Birth of Romantic Radicalism.* London: Taylor & Francis Ltd.

John Stevenson (1979), *Popular Disturbances in England 1700-1832.* London: Routledge.

*The Parliamentary History of England, From the Earliest Period to The Year 1803*, Vols 28–35. London: Longman.

Thelwall, John (1795), *The Tribune, A Periodical Publication, consisting chiefly of the Political Lectures of J. Thelwall. Taken in Short-hand by W. Ramsey and revised by the Lecturer.* London: Printed for the Author.

Thompson, Edward Palmer (2013), *Making of the English Working-Class.* London: Penguin Classics.

Tone, William Theobald Wolfe (1831), *The Life of Theobald Wolfe Tone.* London: Whittaker, Treacher and Arnot.

Towers, Joseph (1797), *Thoughts on National Insanity.* London: J. Johnson.

Turner, William (1777), *The whole service as performed in the congregation of Protestant dissenters, at Wakefield, on Friday, December 13, 1776: Being the day appointed for a general fast. Printed at the request of the congregation. By William Turner.* Wakefield: Thomas Waller.

_____ (1792), *Sermons on various subjects published at the request of the congregation of Protestant Dissenters in Wakefield.* London: J Johnson.

Walker, Thomas (1788), *Two Sermons preached in Mill-Hill Chapel, in Leeds.* Leeds: Thomas Wright.

Wells, Roger A.E. (1977), *Dearth and Distress in Yorkshire 1793-1802.* York: Borthwick Institute.

_____ (1986), *Insurrection: The British Experience 1795-1803.* Stroud: Sutton Books.

_____ (1991), 'English Society and revolutionary politics in the 1790s: the case of insurrection' in Mark Phillip, *The French Revolution and British Popular Politics.* Cambridge: Cambridge University Press, pp. 288–96.

Williams, John (1833), *Memoirs of the Late Reverend Thomas Belsham.* London: John Williams.

Wilson, Richard George (1971), *Gentlemen Merchants: The Merchant Community in Leeds 1700 – 1830.* Manchester: Manchester University Press.

Wood, William (1801), *A Sermon preached at Mill-Hill Chapel, in Leeds, on the commencement of the Nineteenth Century*. Leeds: Edward Baines.

Wyvill, Christopher (1795), *The Address to the Worthy Freeholders of Yorkshire*.

Yorke, Henry Redhead (1794), *Thoughts on Civil Government: Addressed to the Disfranchised Citizens of Sheffield*. London: D.I. Eaton.

# INDEX